A History of Antisemitism in Canada

A History
of Antisemitism
in Canada

IRA ROBINSON

WLU PRESS

**WILFRID LAURIER
UNIVERSITY PRESS**

Wilfrid Laurier University Press acknowledges the support of the Canada Council for the Arts for our publishing program. We acknowledge the financial support of the Government of Canada through the Canada Book Fund for our publishing activities. This work was supported by the Research Support Fund.

LAURIER
Inspiring Lives.

ONTARIO ARTS COUNCIL
CONSEIL DES ARTS DE L'ONTARIO
an Ontario government agency
un organisme du gouvernement de l'Ontario

Library and Archives Canada Cataloguing in Publication

Robinson, Ira, 1951–, author
    A history of antisemitism in Canada / Ira Robinson.

Includes bibliographical references and index.
Issued in print and electronic formats.
ISBN 978-1-77112-166-8 (paperback).—ISBN 978-1-77112-168-2 (epub).—
ISBN 978-1-77112-167-5 (pdf)

    1. Antisemitism—Canada—History. 2. Canada—Ethnic relations. I. Title.

DS146.C2R62 2015   305.892'4071   C2015-903244-X
                                                    C2015-903245-8

Cover design by Angela Booth Malleau. Front-cover photo: "Christians Only" restrictive signage, ca. 1938, taken probably in Quebec; Federal Photos image / Canadian Jewish Congress Charities Committee National Archives. Text design by James Leahy.

© 2015 Wilfrid Laurier University Press
Waterloo, Ontario, Canada
www.wlupress.wlu.ca

To my grandson, Aaron Mark Epstein:

May you grow up to see a world in which the phenomenon described in this book is of only historical interest.

Contents

Preface

How odd of God / To choose the Jews.
                              —Attributed to William Norman Ewer[1]

In 1932, A.M. Klein had this to say about the phenomenon of antisemitism in Canada: "Anti-Semitism in this country is a mild affair compared with the persistent and malignant forms which it assumes in some countries."[2] Over eighty years later, the situation of antisemitism in Canada could well be summarized in a similar way. Thus the index of Robert Wistrich's exhaustive 2010 publication *A Lethal Obsession: Anti-Semitism from Antiquity to the Global Jihad* indicates a mere thirteen pages referring to "Canada" as opposed to well over one hundred for a country like France, not including an entirely separate series of references to "French anti-Semitism."[3] Why, then, devote an entire volume to the subject of antisemitism in Canada, especially given the fact that Jews were never the sole targets of national, racial, and religious vilification in Canada? For the moment, let us begin by saying that antisemitism has become and remains an important component of the historical memory and contemporary consciousness of Canadian Jews as well as of the cultural and political discourse of Canada. Despite that reality there is, as yet, no comprehensive study of the phenomenon of antisemitism in Canada.[4]

What This Book Hopes to Do

This book on antisemitism in Canada seeks to present a comprehensive, up-to-date account of the phenomenon. It builds on the foundation of numerous previous studies on antisemitism in general, and on

antisemitism in Canada in particular. It is especially beholden to the
pioneering collaborative work *Antisemitism in Canada: History and
Interpretation*, edited by Alan Davies, and published some twenty years
ago by Wilfrid Laurier University Press.[5] It builds as well on the large and
growing body of interdisciplinary scholarship on the Jewish community
of Canada.[6] While this book uses some archival sources, for the most
part it relies on published sources, including journalistic and Internet,
as well as published scholarly analysis. In this connection, I draw inspiration from the words of German historian Jürgen Osterhamel:

> To know all there is to know is not the key qualification ... No one has
> sufficient knowledge to verify the correctness of each detail ... or to
> draw fully adequate conclusions from the existing body of research in
> countless different areas. Two other qualities are the really important
> ones: first, to have a feel for proportions, contradictions, and connec-
> tions, as well as a sense of what may be typical and representative, and
> second, to maintain a humble attitude of deference toward professional
> research.[7]

This book will attempt to understand the many ways in which
antisemitism has impacted Canada as a whole, and will examine most
especially its influence on the development of Canada's Jewish community. It will give readers interested in the phenomenon of antisemitism
in Canada the tools to understand why antisemitism in general is such
a controversial subject. It will acquaint them with the deep ambiguities
inherent in the historical relationship between Jews and Christians and
will then show them these ambiguities at play in the unfolding historical
relationship between Jews and their fellow Canadians of other religions
and ethnicities. It will examine present relationships in light of history and, most particularly, will consider the influence of antisemitism
on the social, religious, and political history of the Canadian Jewish
community.

This book presents the reader with the first full-length study of the
phenomenon of antisemitism in Canada. While there are numerous
books and articles devoted to various aspects of the subject, this is the
first one that seeks to present a comprehensive account of antisemitism

and its effect on the Jewish community of Canada. This will make it valuable to students and scholars of Canadian history, Canadian Jewish studies, Canadian ethnic studies, and antisemitism.

The Book's Organization

The book is divided into four sections. The first is an introduction designed to accomplish several things. The first chapter discusses the complexities involved in any careful and nuanced definition of the term "antisemitism." It then looks at the broad historical sweep of relations between Jews and non-Jews in premodern times. The second chapter examines more specifically the presence of Jews in the cultures, stories, and imaginations of the French and the English in the medieval and early modern periods. These ideas about Jews were what the first European settlers in what would become Canada brought with them from their homelands. It is these ideas that informed early reactions to the presence of Jews and Judaism in British North America.

The second section examines the interaction between Jews and other Canadians from the mid-eighteenth century to the First World War. Chapter 3 thus details the ways in which Jews and non-Jews interacted in the territories that would become the Dominion of Canada in the eighteenth and nineteenth centuries. The chapter brings the account of antisemitism up to the beginnings of the mass eastern European Jewish immigration at the turn of the twentieth century. The fourth chapter speaks of the fundamental changes that occurred in Canadian society with the simultaneous arrival in Canada of a major Jewish immigrant population and a societal discourse, imported from Europe, which brought the "Jewish problem" in Canada to wide public notice.

Section three speaks of antisemitism in the period between the onset of the First World War and the end of the Second World War, in which Canada greatly developed its sense of itself as a culture and polity. Chapter 5 discusses the Canadian social and institutional policies that affected relationships between Jews and non-Jews in this period. Chapter 6 examines the two major twentieth-century ideologies, communism and fascism, that greatly influenced the ways in which Canadian Jews and non-Jews related to each other in that era.

The fourth section deals with post–Second World War Canada. The discerning reader will notice a difference in the presentation because, in this relatively contemporary period, there really is much less scholarly work to go on; much of the more contemporary material is necessarily journalistic in nature. Chapter 7 discusses the postwar development of Canadian society with specific reference to changing attitudes toward Jews and alternate models for understanding who is a Canadian. These alternative models tended to be more inclusive of Jews and others. It further examines the ways in which the Canadian Jewish community was affected by these trends as well as how these trends influenced the Canadian discourse on antisemitism. Chapter 8 looks at the implications of the Holocaust for Canadian Jews, and the influence of both ongoing antisemitic manifestations and Holocaust denial on relations between Jews and non-Jews in Canada. Chapter 9 discusses the implications of the State of Israel and the Israel–Arab conflict for the phenomenon of antisemitism in Canada. Finally, chapter 10 attempts to evaluate the phenomenon of antisemitism in twenty-first-century Canada.

Entering into this subject is asking for trouble. For, as C.P. Snow stated, "If you want to keep out of trouble, there are about five subjects you should never mention in a speech or in print, either in praise or dispraise or even natural curiosity." One of them is anything having to do with Jewish culture or Jewish people.[8] With respect to antisemitism in Canada as a whole, what Phyllis Senese wrote in the 1980s about Quebec remains largely correct: "the history of antisemitism in Quebec remains to be written" and, further, "a great deal of superficial and shallow writing on antisemitism in Quebec is in print."[9] I also agree with André Elbaz when he states that antisemitism in Quebec, while similar to manifestations in Europe and the United States, "reveals here specific lines of the historical and ideological evolution of Quebec."[10] I therefore fully expect that my interpretations in this book can and will be challenged. Nonetheless it is my responsibility to present my interpretation of antisemitism in Canada as best I can and to let those who think they have a better idea bring that idea to the attention of the public. It is with this clash of ideas that our understanding will increase.

Portions of this book were previously published by me in the following articles: "The Bouchard-Taylor Commission and the Jewish Community of Québec In Historical Perspective," in Howard Adelman and

Pierre Anctil, eds., *Religion, Culture and the State: Reflections on the Bouchard-Taylor Report* (Toronto: University of Toronto Press, 2011), 58–68, 125–29; "David Ahenakew and His Antisemitism" in Zionism, An Indigenous Struggle: Aboriginal Americans and the Jewish State, *Israzine* 48, no. 4 (November 21, 2014), http://www.isranet.org/israzine/zionism-indigenous-struggle-aboriginal-americans-and-jewish-state/editorial/#ira; "Reflections on Antisemitism in French Canada," *Canadian Jewish Studies* 21 (2013): 90–122.

I am pleased to acknowledge the financial assistance of Concordia University's Institute for Canadian Jewish Studies in the publication of this book. I would also like to express my appreciation for the efforts and encouragement of Ryan Chynces, former acquisitions editor of Wilfrid Laurier University Press, and Blaire Comacchio, the developmental editor of Wilfrid Laurier University Press, without whom this volume would not have seen the light in this particular form. My colleague and friend Pierre Anctil shared with me both his great knowledge and some of his significant archival discoveries. I am pleased to have this opportunity to thank Dr. Maxine Jacobson, who has done extensive research work for this volume. I save the best for last: my wife, Sandra Moskovitz Robinson has provided me with the help and encouragement that allowed me to undertake and complete this book. She read and commented on the manuscript of this book and has materially contributed to the final product you see before you.

Montreal, December 29, 2014

PART ONE

INTRODUCTION

CHAPTER ONE

Defining Antisemitism:
Jews and Non-Jews in Historical Perspective

Si Christianum est odisse Iudeos, hic abunde Christiani sumus omnes.
[If it is Christian to hate the Jews, here we are all abundantly Christian.]
—Desiderius Erasmus[1]

Defining Antisemitism

As Anthony Julius puts it, antisemitism "is the background noise against which we [Jews] make our lives."[2] It has been that way for far longer than the word "antisemitism" has been in existence. Indeed Jews in ancient and medieval times often expressed their sense that gentile hatred, gratuitous from their perspective, was their lot. This feeling was expressed pithily in an aggadic (non-legal) opinion found in the Babylonian Talmud in the names of Rav Ḥisda and Rabba son of Rav Huna: "What is the meaning of "Sinai" [the mountain upon which Israel received the Torah]? It is the mountain upon which hatred [*sin'a*] came to the gentiles."[3] The eleventh-century commentator on the Talmud, Rabbi Solomon ben Isaac (Rashi), concurred, commenting on that Talmudic statement that hatred ensued "because they [the gentiles] didn't receive Torah on it."

The word "antisemitism" itself was coined in the latter part of the nineteenth century in Germany, under conditions that will be described later in this book. Once it entered the vocabularies of Jews and non-Jews alike, however, it was found to be useful in describing much more than the specific nineteenth-century political movement it was named for. A short period after the term was launched, American Jewish historian Gotthard Deutsch, writing in the entry "anti-Semitism" in *The*

Jewish Encyclopedia (1901), thus stated: "While the term 'anti-Semitism' should be restricted in its use to the modern movements against the Jews, in its wider sense it may be said to include the persecution of the Jews at all times and among all nations as professors of a separate religion or as a people having a distinct nationality."[4] As Julius has further observed: "This 'wider sense' [depicted by Deutsch] has indeed been adopted, with the consequence that hatred of Jews tends to be viewed as a continually present, integral aspect of a single "mentality" summarily identified as "Western civilization." Julius concludes:

> This has been very unfortunate, not least because it is false … I regard anti-Semitism as a discontinuous, contingent aspect of a number of different mentalités and milieus, none of which has so dominated the West as to make dissenting perspectives impossible. It is a heterogeneous phenomenon, the site of collective hatreds, and of cultural anxieties and resentments. The search for a single, unified theory of anti-Semitism is an idle one. There is no essence of anti-Semitism. It is instead in the irreducible plurality of its forms of existence that anti-Semitism is to be understood and studied.[5]

Julius here partially echoes Hannah Arendt's well-known warning against understanding modern antisemitism as "yet another manifestation of 'eternal hatred' prevalent in the Christian world against Jews from time immemorial."[6] Another important caveat to bear in mind at the commencement of a book on the subject of antisemitism was well expressed by German historian of antisemitism Reinhard Rürup and deserves to be cited at length:

> Studies into antisemitism are always in danger of isolating its object of study. As a rule, whoever is on the lookout for antisemitism and antisemites will make a find, but at the same time may easily lose any sense of proportion. This already begins with the sources: because they disturb public order, antisemitic actions have a far greater chance of being recorded and passed on than the peaceful cooperation or even coexistence between Jews and Christians. Whoever goes out on the street and screams or breaks laws attracts attention; whoever goes about their business without creating such a spectacle remains unnoticed. A rumor of

ritual murder with all its turmoil and fears, the gathering of a riotous mob and outbreak of excesses, will produce, even when things calm down after a few days, far more official documents than thirty years of conflict-free coexistence … It is therefore with good reason that calls for more contextualization are becoming louder within antisemitism research in recent times. It is still the case that too little is known about the "silent majority." … Moreover, too seldom distinctions are drawn between anti-Jewish prejudices and antisemitic attitudes. Negative "images of Jews," religious and social prejudices towards Jews, were widespread in Europe, including the camps of the bourgeois liberals and the socialist labor movement. The situation could not be expected to be any different given the centuries-old anti-Jewish traditions deeply rooted in folk culture. Such prejudices are not without consequences in a modern or a modernizing society, but they are not the same as modern antisemitism, which is programmatic and focused on taking action, not only cultivating a social distance to Jews but committed to changing the world by combating the Jews. There are many examples of liberals and democrats who actively supported the emancipation of Jews and campaigned against antisemitism, but also confessed that they themselves were not free of prejudice against Jews. The situation was similar for many socialists who not only fought resolutely against antisemitism in theory but also in practice, while in a surprising and often appalling manner they took advantage of private correspondence or "off-the-record" statements to use anti-Jewish clichés.[7]

As well, it is worth noting that, as Dutch journalist Fritz Bernstein pointed out in the 1920s,

there has not been a single antisemitic occurrence whose antisemitic character has not been simultaneously denied with absolute conviction. And such denial does not always come from the antisemites, who often regard the term as an accusation against them, and thus reject it. Jews, too, and often Jews who are injured [by the incident], often stubbornly and vehemently reject its antisemitic character although every bystander regards it as a clearly antisemitic episode.[8]

It will be readily seen, therefore, that the very term that denotes antisemitism is both equivocal and controversial. Even the spelling of the word has evoked debate. Thus Emil Fackenheim, the twentieth-century

Canadian Jewish philosopher, insisted on spelling it "antisemitism" instead of "anti-Semitism," explaining: "the spelling ought to be antisemitism without the hyphen, dispelling the notion that there is an entity 'Semitism' which 'anti-Semitism' opposes."[9]

To further complicate our understanding of the problems inherent in understanding antisemitism historically, as this book attempts to do, we would do well to consider medieval historian Gavin Langmuir's conundrum: "We cannot discuss antisemitism without referring to … 'Jews' and 'Christians' who practiced 'religions' that proclaimed the existence of 'God.' But Jews cannot agree as to who is a Jew; Christians cannot agree as to what is true Christianity; historians or social scientists when acting professionally can say nothing about the existence of God; and social scientists cannot even agree on a definition of 'religion.'"[10] We will nonetheless persevere in this investigation, understanding its difficulties, accepting its ambiguities, and attempting to overcome the numerous hurdles inherent in any approach to the subject. This perseverance is necessary because, as David Nirenberg, in explaining the prevalence of antisemitism over the centuries, states, anti-Judaism was a central defining feature of Western civilization. As Nirenberg has amply demonstrated, there are many "important ways in which 'Jewish questions' have shaped the history of thought" in the Western tradition.[11]

One of the most acute of the difficulties we face is the question whether all historical manifestations of hostility to Jews and Judaism in premodern times should be termed "antisemitism." This issue has been much debated in the scholarly literature.[12] In this book, for the most part, I will try to follow Langmuir's practical conclusion: "Certainly, many pagans in the Roman Empire were strongly, even violently anti-Judaic … But … I do not think their attitudes significantly influenced the formation of antisemitism in Western Europe, whereas a connection between Christianity and antisemitism is undeniable."[13]

Christianity and Judaism

The remainder of this introductory chapter will, therefore, concentrate on illuminating the ways in which Christians and Jews interacted with one another from late antiquity through the Middle Ages. The next chapter will take the story further, examining the place of Jews in the religions and literatures of the French and the English, the two peoples who together would form the primary European population of the territory that would become known as Canada.

The story of Christianity and its relationship with Jews and Judaism necessarily begins with the fact that its central focus, Jesus of Nazareth, was born a Jew, extensively interacted with Jews during his lifetime, and had Jews as his first followers. Possibly before, but certainly after Jesus's death by crucifixion at the hand of the Romans, his disciples proclaimed that he was the messianic saviour promised by the prophets of the Hebrew Bible. These first Jesus believers made this proclamation, at least initially, as Jews. They also engaged in extensive debates as to whether those who believed in Jesus's salvific mission were required as well to observe the commandments of the Torah, like circumcision for males, or not. They also debated whether and how belief in Jesus could be preached to gentiles as well as Jews. While, ultimately, the position expressed in the Epistles of Paul of Tarsus that belief in Jesus as the Christ superseded the observance of the commandments of the Torah prevailed among Christians, many if not most of the first generation of the followers of Jesus felt themselves to be faithful Jews in every way. [14]

Ultimately, however, the movement of believers in Jesus became Christianity, and Christianity very rapidly became an almost entirely gentile movement. Under these conditions, Christianity and the Judaism characterized by the observance of the commandments of the Torah began to separate, and it became increasingly possible to distinguish between communities of Jews and Christians. These communities, in the throes of divorce, often expressed hostility to one another because each group—Jewish and Christian—claimed to be the sole legitimate heir to the Hebrew Bible (the Old Testament for Christians) and its promises. As historian of early Christianity, John Gager states: "The point has been made repeatedly ... that the origins of Christianity within first century Judaism and its painful separation from Judaism meant that its sense of identity and legitimacy took shape within the framework of opposition to Judaism. Or, as Rosemary Ruether has put it, 'for Christianity, anti-Judaism was not merely a defense against attack, but an intrinsic need of self-affirmation.'" [15] Under these conditions, and in order to assert the distinctiveness and superiority of their own identity, Christians began to think of Jews as their opponents and to express in the New Testament gospels "a self-conscious Christian tradition that deliberately distanced itself from the historical Jewish context in which Jesus had lived and died."[16] Thus Christians asserted among themselves and in their discussions with Jews that Christians and their beliefs were in the right and that the Jews were plainly wrong in their beliefs and expectations. A clear example of this tendency is to be found in the words of the fourth-century Church Father John Chrysostom, who stated of his own faith and that of the Jews: "If our way is true, as it is, theirs is fraudulent."[17] Thus, as Gavin Langmuir argues, "for Christians, the ability of Jews to maintain their own identity was not only hateful in the way ethnic differences so often are; it was an intimate and enduring threat to their sense of identity, a challenge built into their own religion."[18]

The historical attitude of Christians to what they came to call "Judaism" was thus necessarily deeply ambivalent, to say the least. Judaism was understood by many Christians over the centuries as "a sort of dark mirror image of Christianity."[19] On the one hand, "the Jews," who were so often condemned in the collection of early Christian documents known as the New Testament, were understood to be not merely those Jews alive at the time of the crucifixion, but all their descendants, forever.[20] All Jews therefore were considered "guilty" of having "killed Christ." It has indeed been cogently argued by Elaine Pagels that the portrayal of Jews in the Gospels "involved a demonization of those opponents, a projection of Jewish ... opposition onto a cosmic canvas ... assuring for future Christian readers a sense of Jewish hostility that knew no bounds of time and place."[21] For that cosmic hostility, Jews appeared to Christians to deserve the worst possible punishment. And indeed, as John Connelly states, "From the third century at the latest, church authorities taught that the Jews' destiny was to wander the earth suffering retribution from God for rejecting Christ, serving in their destitution as the most direct evidence that the church's claims to God's favor were correct."[22]

There was, however, another aspect of Christian attitudes toward Jews, one which held that "the Jews" were not to be destroyed or eliminated, as they might otherwise have deserved, but rather preserved. The first reason why "the Jews" needed to be preserved is that they were understood to be the people who bear witness to the truth, validity, and antiquity of the Hebrew Bible (Old Testament), the veritable basis of the Christian message.[23] Especially because they were hostile witnesses, who did not share the Christian belief that the prophecies of the Hebrew Bible foretold the birth, death, and resurrection of Christ, Jews guaranteed the antiquity of Christian belief in a world in which that which was "ancient" was deemed true and valid and that which was "modern" was suspect. The second reason for preserving "the Jews" was the Christian hope that they would ultimately convert and be reconciled to the church before the Second Coming of Christ. This was a widespread Christian interpretation of Paul's words in Romans (11:25–27): "For I would not, brethren, that ye should be ignorant of this mystery, lest ye should be wise in your own conceits; that blindness in part is happened to Israel, until the fullness of the Gentiles be come in. And so all Israel shall be saved: as it is written, There shall come out of Sion the Deliverer, and shall turn away ungodliness from Jacob: For this is my covenant unto them, when I shall take away their sins." Thus the Jews, however blameworthy they might be for their disbelief in the Christian message, had to be spared destruction and persuaded of their own free will, and not through coercion, to convert to Christianity.

In the Middle Ages, during which Jews lived as practically the only non-Christian religious minority tolerated within Christendom, the ambivalence with which Jews were treated by Christians continued. The Church and its hierarchy were committed to protect Jews' lives and their right to live as Jews within Christian society.[24] On the other hand, especially in the later Middle Ages, Jews found themselves targets of accusations on the part of Christians that they required Christian blood (preferably the blood of innocent Christian children) for their own ritual purposes.[25] The Jews' post-biblical literature, particularly the Talmud, was deemed blasphemous to Christianity and repeatedly condemned, destroyed, and censored by Church authorities.[26] Their practice of lending money at interest, condemned by the Church as "usury," became nonetheless their characteristic occupation in high- and late-medieval Christendom.[27]

All of these accusations against the Jews, but most particularly the blood libel, meant that Jews came to be commonly understood as existentially hating Christians and their religion, and seeking to express this hatred and harm Christians in both symbolic and concrete ways. Above all, as Jewish historian Elisheva Carlebach has written, "the perception that Jews were inherently deceitful was an all encompassing component of the medieval perception of Jews and the Jewish religion."[28] This perception created an atmosphere in which both individual Jews and entire Jewish communities were imprisoned, brought to trial, tortured, and condemned to death.

Another anti-Jewish accusation that was particularly widespread held that Jews sought to desecrate the host, that element of the Christian mass that represented for believing Christians the body of Christ. Such accusations had a particularly significant subtext: that the Jews, in their perversity, actually *knew* the truth that the host was Christ's body and therefore wished to avenge themselves on it. Indeed, as Langmuir points out: "[Christians] did not accuse and punish Jews for not believing in Christ and the Eucharist. Just the reverse. In a contorted way, their fantasies made Jews believers in Christ! The fantasy that Jews were still trying to harm and torture Christ made it seem that even Jews believed, however antagonistically, in Christ's continuing supernatural existence and presence in the Eucharist."[29]

That these anti-Jewish accusations did not necessarily diminish with the coming of the Protestant Reformation can be seen in the works of Martin Luther, whose theology, David Nirenberg argues, "was achieved by thinking with, about, and against Jews and Judaism."[30] As historian Jonathan Israel states, Luther "treated the Jews to the full blast of his invective, assailing them as 'disgusting vermin,' and their synagogues as 'devils' nests of insolence and lies.'"[31] On the contrary, it has been asserted by Carey Newman that "many of Christianity's anti-Jewish assumptions originated in a line of interpretation stemming from the Christian Reformation."[32]

It is fair to say, therefore, that European Christian society, by the end of the medieval period, was suffused with ideas about "the Jews," who they were and what they stood for. While these ideas were never completely negative, they nonetheless materially contributed to a general perception of Jews as a group that was actively inimical to Christians and Christianity. This in turn also tended to foster the idea that "the Jews" constituted a threat to the well-being of Christian society, and that

Christians therefore needed to be protected from them.[33] The late medieval period as well as the early modern period thus witnessed numerous attempts in many European countries to severely limit where Jews could live by the institution of formally decreed areas (often called "ghettos" after the most famous of them, established in Venice in 1517) where Jews were required to live separately from non-Jews. Other countries, among which France, England, Spain, and Portugal were to be counted, took the more radical step of expelling all Jews living in their domains.[34] The absence of professing Jews in these countries, however, did not affect the menace "the Jews" represented. Indeed, as David Nirenberg points out, the invisibility of "Judaism" only made it more of a threat.[35]

Thus by the beginning of the seventeenth century, when both the French and the English competitively began to explore and colonize the North American continent, there were, practically speaking, no openly professing Jews legally residing in the kingdoms of France and England. Both countries nonetheless shared in full the heritage of a millennium and a half of largely negative Christian perceptions of Jews and Judaism. Both countries would, as Nirenberg states, harbour anti-Jewish attitudes that did not "draw their strength from the interaction of individuals and groups within a society, but from collective beliefs ... formed in the Middle Ages and transmitted to the present day."[36] Both countries would, in the course of the seventeenth and eighteenth centuries, acquire new Jewish communities and have to deal with these communities both at home and in their colonial outposts. The encounter of Jews with Canada, therefore, must be understood in the context of Jews in the societies and the cultures of early modern France and England. That is the subject of the next chapter.

CHAPTER TWO

Jews in Medieval and Early Modern France and England

Let me say "amen" betimes, lest the devil cross my prayer, for here he comes in the likeness of a Jew[1]

—William Shakespeare

As the previous chapter indicates, it is impossible to understand the ways in which Jews have been perceived in Canadian society without properly comprehending the ambivalence with which Christianity in its historical and intellectual development had dealt with them. In the same way, it is impossible to complete the contextualization of the picture of "the Jews" in the minds of early non-Jewish Canadians without first examining the ways in which Jews figured in the cultures, folklores, and politics of the two European peoples, the French and the English, who set their mark upon the territories that would become Canada.

Mythologies of "the Jews"

By the beginning of the seventeenth century, when the process of colonization of these territories had begun in earnest, the French and their English rivals shared in common the heritage of ancient and medieval Christian mythologies concerning Jews. As will be seen, however, their respective histories with respect to actual professing Jews differed, and their cultures generated somewhat different emphases when it came to the "imaginary" Jews they constructed in literature and legend.

In the Middle Ages, both France[2] and England[3] possessed vibrant Jewish communities, and both countries ultimately resorted to the radical expedient of expelling from their lands all Jews who would not agree to become Christians. England was the first to do so, in 1290. Royal

France followed in 1306, readmitted Jews for a brief time in the course of the fourteenth century, and finally decreed their permanent expulsion in 1394. Both countries, therefore, existed with but minor exceptions for several centuries without a legally recognized Jewish population.[4]

That did not mean, however, that Jews were absent from either the consciousness or the imaginations of the English and the French peoples. On the contrary, "the Jews" remained important elements in both French and English folklore in the medieval and early modern periods.[5] As well, the fact that the Jews figured so prominently in the teachings of Christianity, whether in its elite or popular form, meant that, while actual professing Jews may have been physically absent, "the Jews" as a concept was nevertheless constantly in front of them because of the pervasive nature of the religious message of the Church to its faithful. Thus denunciations of the Jews who had long since been expelled continued to appear. In the seventeenth century, the French theologian Jacques Bossuet characterized the Jews as "a monstrous people, animated by Satan, who are universally mocked and hated."[6] In this period as well, traditional charges of Jewish host desecration and ritual murder remained credible in the kingdom of France.[7] Similarly, the story of Ahasuerus, the Jew condemned to endlessly wander the world, was well established among the French and became symbolic of the fate that befell the Jewish people because of their rejection of Christ.[8] As well, at least with respect to the English, it could be said that "the Jews" remained as a noticeable theme not merely for theology and folk tales, but also for literature. As Julius has noted: "Absent from England itself, the Jews soon became a constant in the English cultural imagination. They figured, and to a diminished extent still figure in England's oral literature of ballad and song, in its quotidian drama and fiction and poetry, and, last, in some major works in its literary canon—works that adversely characterize Jews, Jewish history, and Judaism."[9] Geoffrey Chaucer, the fourteenth-century English poet, whose "Prioress' Tale" features Jews murdering a young Christian boy, is but the most prominent of many English literary works in the later Middle Ages to use Jews for various purposes.[10] William Shakespeare's prominent Jewish character Shylock in his play *The Merchant of Venice* has likewise captured the literary imagination of readers and literary critics from the late sixteenth century to the present.[11]

Renewal of Jewish Communities in
Early Modern France and England

While both France and England in 1600 were, with rare exceptions, bereft of professing Jews, they acquired new communities of Jews in the course of the seventeenth and eighteenth centuries, even though neither country formally rescinded its edict of expulsion. This happened partly as a result of French conquests of Germanic territories to its east, when France incorporated the provinces of Alsace and Lorraine, which contained a significant Jewish population. More importantly, for both France and England, resettlement of Jews came about as a result of a major demographic movement of Jews in the early modern period. This significant demographic shift originated with the expulsion of the Jews from the Iberian Peninsula at the end of the fifteenth century. In 1492, the newly united Spanish Christian kingdoms of Castile and Aragon conquered the last Muslim bastion in the Iberian Peninsula, Granada. Shortly thereafter, the Spanish monarchy moved to expel the Jews from Spain. The Spanish expulsion of 1492, and the action of the Portuguese crown in 1497 to forcibly convert en masse all Jews residing in its territory, brought to an abrupt end the public presence of what was arguably one of the largest and most culturally creative Jewish communities in medieval times, Sephardic Jewry. During the 1490s, therefore, tens of thousands of Iberian Jews went into exile, while as many or more converted to Christianity under duress, joining other Jewish converts to Christianity in Spain from earlier anti-Jewish violence and concerted attempts to convert Jews.[12]

The major initial result of the Expulsion of 1492 was the creation of communities of Spanish Jewish exiles in North Africa, Italy, and the Ottoman Empire. A further result of the forced conversion of those Jews who remained in Spain and Portugal was the creation of a class of former Jews within Iberian society whose adherence to Christianity was openly questioned, and whose basic security of life and property was threatened by the Inquisition. The Inquisition had been established in order to extirpate "heresy" and had the power to imprison those suspected of opposing the teachings of the Church, confiscate their property, and even to condemn them to death. These people of Jewish origins, called variously New Christians, Conversos, and Marranos,[13] constituted one of the Inquisition's major targets. It is no wonder, therefore, that they began leaving the Iberian Peninsula in significant numbers when it was possible, starting in the late sixteenth century.

Some of these Spanish and Portuguese New Christians fled to places like the Ottoman Empire to join the established Jewish communities there. Others, however, emigrated to countries like France, England, and the Low Countries, where professing Jews were not officially allowed to live. They were able to settle in these countries, however, because whatever their actual state of personal identification as Jews,[14] they were validly baptized Roman Catholics, and thus were able to officially enter these places as Christians. Thus, for example, the French King Henri II issued in 1550 *lettres patentes* allowing New Christians from the Iberian Peninsula to settle in France.[15] Many of those New Christians who settled in countries where the open practice of Judaism was not allowed were evidently content to live as New Christians without any public Judaic practice, happy simply to be free of the threat of the Inquisition to their lives and property. In the course of the seventeenth and eighteenth centuries, however, many others manifested an increasingly public expression of their Jewish faith. As a result, open and more or less formally recognized Jewish communities began to emerge in places like Amsterdam,[16] Bordeaux,[17] and London.[18] The new Western European Jewish communities founded by Spanish and Portuguese New Christians that emerged in the early modern period shared in the prosperity of the Atlantic world in an era of burgeoning and increasingly globalized commerce and colonization. These communities also intensively networked with each other and with other Jewish communities worldwide to form a global Sephardic diaspora that created extraordinary prosperity for its leading merchants.

Did the immigration of the "New Christian" merchants who gradually emerged as openly professing Jews in France and England in the seventeenth and eighteenth centuries affect the ways in which "Jews" were thought of in England and France? On the level of popular perceptions, there was probably not all that much effect. The medieval images of Jews as enemies of Christ and the Church were deeply engrained and persistent. Thus Jewish historian Todd Endelman finds that, in eighteenth-century England, "it was believed by many persons that the Jews continually blasphemed Jesus in their prayers and writings; that they considered it meritorious to plunder Christians; that they murdered Christian children in order to obtain their blood."[19] The anti-Jewish stereotypes of the medieval period had quite obviously not been put to rest by the presence of actual Jews on British soil. Milder attitudes of contempt toward Jews as individuals, similar to the contempt meted out to the Irish and other "foreigners," are to be found in abundance in English literature of the eighteenth and nineteenth centuries.[20]

Tolerance, Enlightenment, and Jews

On the other hand, across Europe in the seventeenth and eighteenth centuries new ideas that had arisen from the destructive religious strife of the sixteenth century were maturing. During that bloody century, large numbers of both Catholics and Protestants had been victimized and killed because of sincerely held religious beliefs that were not to the liking of the dominant Christian church in their country. In reaction to this massive slaughter of religious opponents in the religious wars of the sixteenth century, many European intellectuals began asking whether there was not a better way to live, one in which people's differing religious beliefs could be tolerated, provided that these individuals obeyed the law and contributed to the prosperity of the nation. The intellectuals' response to this issue coalesced as a concept called "toleration," in which religious "error" would be enforced and punished by God alone, and not by human hands. Thinkers like Jean Bodin thus wrote in favour of the rule of law and against religious coercion. Toleration was at first a concept designed to include only Christians of different beliefs and practices, i.e., Catholics and Protestants. Many advocates of toleration were loath to have it extended to Jews, Muslims, and others.[21] Ultimately, however, western European intellectuals in the seventeenth and eighteenth centuries created a climate of thought, often called the "Enlightenment," in which it was conceivable that toleration, at least theoretically, could and should be extended to Jews as well.

Thus, starting in the late seventeenth century, the rights of the Jews to toleration and their potential as citizens of the state became a subject of animated discussion among European intellectuals and political leaders alike. Should the Jews be tolerated in Christian countries like England, France, Holland, Prussia, and Austria, and under what conditions? For some of these intellectuals, like the eighteenth-century Englishman John Toland, it was apparent that "Tis manifest almost at first sight that the common reasons for a GENERAL NATURALIZATION are as strong in behalf of the *Jews* as of any other people whatsoever. They encrease [*sic*] the number of hands for labor and defence, of bellies and backs for consumption of food and raiment, and of brains for invention and contrivance no less than any other nation."[22] The issue was not as apparent to other contemporary observers, however. For them, the Jews remained essentially what they had been, a present danger to Christians and to Christian society. To allow Jews access to the rights and privileges associated with membership in Christian polities on anything approaching a basis of equality seemed to them to be the height of folly.

Many of these critics of the Jews approached the subject on the basis of a strong and unwavering adherence to the historical teachings of Christianity on the Jews. Some, like the German Johann Andreas Eisenmenger, purported to have discovered the nefarious intentions of the Jews from their own writings. As Julius wrote: "[Eisenmenger's] *Judaism Exposed* (1711) was an immense work of misrepresentation, mistranslation and (on occasion) fabrication ... Its essential argument was that the Jews are permitted by their religion to commit any excess against non-Jews, whom they are taught to hate."[23]

Others, however, came to their opposition to extending the principle of tolerance to the Jews on the precise basis of their opposition to the Church and its teachings. These European intellectuals, of whom Voltaire is a good example, proclaimed their liberation from what they considered the antiquated and false basis of Christianity. However, while generally rejecting the teachings of the Church, they did not seem to dispute historical Christianity's verdict on the inferiority of the Jews and their beliefs. As early modern historian Jonathan Israel wrote: "It is not simply that one or two leading *philosophes*, notably Voltaire, were themselves anti-Semitic and identified Jewish 'superstition' as being of the root and essence of the priestly obscurantism they so passionately wanted to sweep away. With very few exceptions, the dismissing of Jewish erudition and observance as archaic, obscurantist, and barbaric was part and parcel of the Enlightenment itself."[24] Ronald Schechter basically concurs, writing that "Voltaire's obsession with the Jews was frequently inseparable from his obsession with *l'infâme*, the fanaticism that the philosophe saw above all in the Catholic Church. As victims of that fanaticism, the Jews were living (or dead) indictments of the church ... He was equally capable of portraying the Jews as fanatics themselves."[25] Voltaire denounced Jews as the embodiment of an array of vices of which he himself was frequently accused—a classic case of projection.[26] While it is true that Voltaire was also occasionally capable of more nuanced presentations of Jews and Judaism, it remains nonetheless valid as a generalization that, as Israel has written, "the European Enlightenment and its later offshoot, the ideology of the French Revolution, proclaimed that Jewish tradition and Jewish separateness were obstacles to human progress having neither dignity nor value."[27]

Though Jews in the seventeenth and eighteenth centuries found themselves subject to a debate on their theoretical relationship to European Christian society, the new Jewish communities that arose in England, France, and Holland in this period enjoyed substantially more rights than Jewish communities that had had an uninterrupted existence elsewhere in Europe. Most of these older Jewish communities lived with significant restrictions on the number of Jews allowed to live in a given location, where Jews were allowed to reside, and how they were allowed to make a living. However, because Jewish communities in Amsterdam, London, and Bordeaux arose out of settlements of Portuguese New Christians who had never been formally "admitted" as "Jews" by their governments, they were practically unrestricted by statute with respect to their residence and economic rights.

This development is most remarkable because of both the persistence of anti-Jewish sentiment among ordinary Christians and the reification of these ideas on the part of many contemporary intellectuals. Indeed, whenever the issue of granting Jews specific rights was publicly debated, there was evidence of strong public sentiment against the granting of such rights. In the mid-seventeenth century, for instance, Menasseh ben Israel came to London from Amsterdam in order to petition the English government to formally admit Jews to England and thereby rescind the expulsion edict of 1290. While Oliver Cromwell was himself favourably disposed toward this petition, the Whitehall conference at which this issue was debated aroused such extensive debate and criticism that the petition was not acted upon, though this ultimately did little or nothing to discourage Jews from settling in London and elsewhere in England. [28]

By the eighteenth century, Jews born in England were considered to be British subjects by birth. As Gertrude Himmelfarb states, "Whatever disabilities they had were those of all non-Anglicans who could not take the required religious oath to hold municipal office, vote, sit in Parliament, or get a university degree."[29] Until the mid-nineteenth century, however, there remained some legal restrictions concerning the public promotion of Judaism.[30]

In 1753, the British parliament passed a piece of legislation popularly called the "Jew Bill." This legislation applied not to Jews in general, whose basic equality of economic and residential rights was never in question, but only to Jewish immigrants to England. The bill made provision for the possibility that "persons professing the Jewish religion may, upon application for that purpose, be naturalized by Parliament without receiving the sacrament of the Lord's Supper." Though the legislation itself seems to have passed the houses of Parliament without significant dissent, the public furor that followed its passage was such that the "Jew Bill" was speedily revoked. Opponents of the bill argued that "the particular rites of the Jews were formidable obstacles to their incorporation within other nations; and that if they were admitted to rank of citizens, they would engross the whole kingdom, gain possession of the landed estates, and dispossess the Christian owners."[31] The revocation of the "Jew Bill," however, was done without putting the rights already held by British Jews into jeopardy.[32] Indeed, agitation to also revoke the Plantation Act of 1740, which gave Jews the right to be naturalized in British colonies, was attempted, but this initiative was soundly defeated in the House of Commons.[33]

In France, the emergence of open communities of professing Jews occurred much more gradually than in England. Indeed, it is not until the early eighteenth century that the Jewish community of Bordeaux entirely abandoned its "New Christian" guise and emerged fully and openly as a Jewish community, though one whose presence had been for some decades an increasingly open secret.

For both France and England, then, Jewish communities emerged at the point at which both countries looked to the New World for economic expansion as well as national prestige and fulfillment. The two countries' national and colonial ambitions clashed all over the world in the eighteenth century and came to blows in North America, as a result of which the French crown ceded its North American territories, with the exception of a couple of small islands off Newfoundland, Saint-Pierre and Miquelon, to the British. These territories, which evolved into the Canada of today, were marked indelibly by the religious ideas, cultures, and politics of both the French and the British. When it comes time to speak of Jews and Judaism in the early history of Canada, therefore, attitudes that had developed in the mother countries in the early modern period certainly set the stage for what was to come.

PART TWO

CANADA AND THE JEWS:
EARLY ENCOUNTERS (1759–1914)

CHAPTER THREE

Jews in the Consciousness of Canadians in the Eighteenth and Nineteenth Centuries

> You will be opposed as a Jew. You may go to law, but be assured; you will never find a jury to favour you or a party in the House to stand up for you.
>
> —Aaron Hart[1]

The beginning of Jewish settlement in the territories that would become the Dominion of Canada in 1867 occurred in the mid-eighteenth century under British rule. However, prior to the settlement of openly professing Jews in these territories, there had been no tabula rasa with respect to "the Jews." Stories about them and attitudes toward them had come to Canada with the first European settlers and were propagated along with the teachings of Christianity and the folkways of both the French and the English.

French Colonial Policy and Jews

There was, however, a basic difference between French and English colonization with respect to Jews, for the French specifically forbade all non-Catholics (including Protestants and Jews) from coming to settle in New France, whereas their settlement in British North American colonies was openly allowed. The exclusionary policy adopted by France in 1627 had the consequence that Jews in France, even if they wished to settle in the remote and struggling French North American colonies, would not have been allowed to stay.[2] While it is entirely possible that some people conscious of their Jewish ancestry were among the settlers in French Canada, there was no question of overt Judaic practice in the colony. As historian Pierre Anctil points out, "With very few exceptions, ignorance and indifference were the local responses to the official absence of Jews in New France."[3]

British Colonial Policy and Jews in Quebec

With the British takeover, the situation became completely different. Jews had not been excluded from the British overseas colonies. On the contrary, significant Jewish communities had been established in the seventeenth and eighteenth centuries in British Caribbean colonies such as Jamaica and Barbados, and in the British North American colonies of New York, Pennsylvania, Rhode Island, South Carolina, and Georgia. It is little wonder, therefore, that among the original British civilians coming to the newly won British North American territory of Quebec were a small number of Jews. Like their Christian counterparts, these Jews were for the most part both merchants and British subjects. This was an important consideration because, as Lord Brougham, the British Lord Chancellor, stated in the early nineteenth century, "His Majesty's subjects professing the Jewish religion were born to all the rights, immunities and privileges of His Majesty's other subjects, excepting so far as positive enactments of the law deprived them of those rights, immunities and privileges."[4] What this meant in essence was that there was no legal basis for discriminating against these merchants as Jews with respect to their pursuit of a livelihood. It meant as well that the Jewish immigrants were English speaking and relatively accustomed to British ways. They were therefore a generally good "fit" insofar as the new British rulers of Quebec were concerned. Furthermore, Jews constituted a significant proportion of Quebec's small English mercantile community in the eighteenth century, perhaps 10 percent,[5] and therefore were accepted reasonably well within that community simply because they were needed. Even if the Jewish merchants were resented by others, it is most likely that they were not primarily resented as Jews but as part of a British mercantile class that had aggressively displaced French Canadian merchants in the late eighteenth century through their superior political and trade connections.[6] They would thus have been largely assimilated by French Canadians into their resentment of the British "other."[7] It is not unlikely that the ambivalent Christian attitude toward Jews that was the heritage of both British Protestants and French Catholics in Quebec may have occasionally come to the surface, but historian Gerald Tulchinsky, in his history of the Jews in Canada, finds "little evidence" of this.[8] Denis Vaugeois goes further than this. In his recent work on the Hart family of Trois-Rivières, Vaugeois takes issue with a statement of Jacob Rader Marcus that Aaron Hart had encountered "a great deal of anti-Jewish sentiment." "Where did he find this 'anti-Jewish sentiment'?" Vaugeois writes, "I searched long and hard for it, in vain. And that, in fact, was the reality of 'Canadian' Jews: there was not an ounce of anti-Jewish sentiment around them ... Rather than 'anti-Jewish sentiment', all doors were open to Jews."[9]

The Issue of Jewish Political Rights in Quebec

There was, however, one area of life where Jews in Quebec were subject to prejudice. This was in the arena of political life. For centuries, western European nations like France and England had self-consciously referred to themselves as "Christian," in opposition to "heathen" or "Muslim" countries. Thus British law, as classically presented by William Blackstone, clearly stated: "Blasphemy against the Almighty ... or uttering contumelious reproaches on our Saviour Christ ... is punished at common law by fine and imprisonment, for Christianity is part of the laws of the land."[10] In Pennsylvania in 1824, a state court judgment similarly stated that "Christianity is and always has been part of the common law of Pennsylvania."[11]

In early modern times, some of these Christian countries tolerated Jews and gave them a greater or lesser degree of social, religious, and economic freedom. In none of them, however, was it understood that this toleration gave Jews any rights at all in the political arena. On the contrary, it was assumed as a given by Jews and Christians alike that Jews constituted a different and separate "nation" that had no inherent political rights in the country in which they actually lived. Jews living in France, for instance, were thus considered to be Jews, not French.

One of the most radical and revolutionary changes in the position of the Jews in the late eighteenth and nineteenth centuries would be the attainment by Jews of political rights on a basis of equality with

Christians. This issue arose most prominently in the course of the French Revolution, in the aftermath of the Déclaration des droits de l'homme (1789), which stated in its tenth article: "No one shall be disquieted on account of his opinions, including his religious views, provided their manifestation does not disturb the public order established by law." Originally, the provisions of the Déclaration were to be applied in full only to "active citizens." In the course of giving legal meaning to the concept of "active" citizenship in France, a debate ensued in the French National Assembly on whether Jews should be given active citizenship rights. The debate lasted sporadically from 1789 until 1791, at which time French Jews were granted active citizenship, and, as a quid pro quo, Jewish communal autonomy in France was abolished. In this significant debate, opponents of giving Jews equality of political rights utilized many of the widely held Christian anti-Jewish theological and folkloric arguments and held that Jews were loyal only to themselves and that they were bound by their religion and character to be hostile and inimical to Christians and Christianity. We will see these arguments echoed later on in our story.

In England, as was already said, native-born Jews were British subjects possessing all the rights and privileges of any native-born English person "excepting so far as positive enactments of the law deprived them of those rights, immunities and privileges." These "positive enactments of the law" in the eighteenth and early nineteenth centuries included nearly all of what we would consider to be the "political arena," which was reserved for members of the Church of England. Dissenting Protestants, Catholics, and Jews were therefore included in the economic and social life of England and excluded from its political life.

In many of the British North American and Caribbean colonies in this era, these rules excluding non-Anglican Christians and Jews from political participation were more or less upheld. In others, however, changes were instituted reflecting the makeup of the white population. The colony of Maryland, for instance, was founded by Lord Baltimore as a refuge for Catholics and hence did not disenfranchise Catholics.[12] In the case of Jews, however, only the colony of New York consistently allowed them the right to vote, though even there not without challenge.[13]

What was the case with the newly British colony of Quebec? It was governed by the Quebec Act of 1774, legislation passed by the British Parliament which gave Catholics along with Protestants equality of political rights but was essentially silent with respect to Jews. Despite this silence, it is noteworthy that a number of the colony's Jews were signatories of petitions to the Crown asking for a legislative assembly and other reforms.[14] These Jews were in effect acting as though they had the same political rights as their Christian counterparts. Their assumption was to be the subject of a significant challenge in the early nineteenth century.

The Hart Affair

This key moment in the history of Jewish political rights in Canada came when Ezekiel Hart, a Jewish resident of Trois-Rivières, submitted his name as a candidate for election to the Legislative Assembly of Lower Canada in 1807. His brother, Moses, who likewise seems to have had political ambitions, had previously been warned by his father, Aaron Hart, that "I should be glad if you were elected a Member of the House … But what I do not like is that you will be opposed as a Jew. You may go to law, but be assured; you will never find a jury to favour you or a party in the House to stand up for you."[15] In the 1807 election, the electoral officer, who favoured one of Hart's two rivals, Thomas Coffin, reportedly "adverted to the religion of Mr. Hart" such that "no Spanish monk, in the height of ascetic zeal, could have poured on this subject more bitter invective or intolerant warmth."[16] Despite these anti-Jewish opinions injected into the electoral process, Hart was duly elected. When, in 1808, Hart came to take his seat in the Assembly, his Jewishness was taken to be an important public issue, that of the legality and propriety of the election of a Jew to the Assembly. The contemporary political debate in the colony on this issue, which was of a distinctly virulent and partisan nature, included the following comment relative to Hart's ability, as a Jew, to represent his constituency: "The Jews are everywhere a people apart from the body of the nation in which they live … a Jew never joins any other nation. He makes it a religious duty, a consistent rule of conduct, to keep separate from other people … By what right can a Jew be entrusted with the care of the interests of an entire people when he thinks only of himself and of his sect?"[17]

This and other anti-Jewish statements expressed during the Hart affair mostly seem to be echoes of contemporary European discussions of the appropriateness of Jewish participation in the political life of Christian nations. They also doubtlessly expressed ambient anti-Jewish stereotypes prevalent among both French and English Canadians. The result of the Hart affair was that he was definitively judged, as a professing Jew, to be barred from the legislative seat to which he had been elected. This precedent meant, as Tulchinsky states, that in Lower Canada, in principle, "Jews were now second class citizens. They were ineligible for membership in the Assembly and legally unfit to hold other office, civil, judicial, or military." On the other hand, as Tulchinsky also points out, "except for the Assembly, the ban does not seem to have been enforced."[18] Meanwhile, in Cornwall, John Elmsley, the chief justice of Upper Canada, reported to the governor an opinion that "Jews cannot hold land in this province," a ruling that was not overturned until 1803.[19] Benjamin Hart, applying in 1812 for a militia commission, was told that "Christian soldiers would not tolerate a Jew in their midst," though other Jews did obtain such commissions.[20]

The 1832 Law Concerning Jewish Political Rights

The legal assumption that Jews were to be barred from holding public office was changed in 1832 through the adoption by the Legislative Assembly of Lower Canada of "An Act to declare persons professing the Jewish religion entitled to all the rights and privileges of the other subjects of His Majesty in this Province." This bill ultimately stemmed from an 1830 attempt to appoint Samuel Becancour Hart, a son of Ezekiel, as magistrate. The attorney general's legal opinion that Hart as a Jew could not take the requisite oath led to a petition to the government that resulted in the Act of 1832.[21] Significantly, this act was adopted with apparently little of the virulence of the 1807–9 debate.[22] A similar question that arose over the election of Selim Franklin as a member of the British Columbia Assembly on the grounds of his Jewishness was relatively quickly settled by the passage of legislation with almost no publicly broadcast anti-Jewish opinion.[23]

Anti-Jewish Opinion in the Mid-Nineteenth Century

Anti-Jewish opinion had not completely disappeared from Canada, however. In the aftermath of the failure of the failed rebellions of 1837, a manifesto of the "Hunters' Lodges" (*Frères Chasseurs*) called for "the strangling of all Jews and the confiscation of their property."[24] Dr. Aaron Hart David confided to his diary that his move in 1840 from Montreal to Trois-Rivières was occasioned by the "aversion to our religion" in Montreal, which made it impossible for him to establish a medical practice.[25] Nevertheless, while Jews and Judaism may have been an issue in the minds of some, it failed to become an overt political issue in an ongoing way in early and mid-nineteenth-century Canada.

This situation may be explained at least partially by the Jews' small numbers. In 1831 the first official Canadian census found a mere 107 Jews to be resident of Upper and Lower Canada (Ontario and Quebec). This number rises only moderately to 154 in 1841, 451 in 1851, and 1186 in 1861.[26] As a rule, the relatively few Jews who did live in British North America in these decades were well acculturated into the Anglo-Canadian community and did not particularly predominate in any neighbourhoods or fields of endeavour.

This does not mean, however, that anti-Jewish prejudice was absent from the Canadas. Stories about Jews and vague references to them were present in early French Canadian literature.[27] Historian Richard Menkis has further observed that many Roman Catholic publications distributed in Canada in this era contained fairly standard anti-Jewish remarks consistent with the historical development of Catholic thought on the Jews, and that Protestant merchants, in letters preserved in the papers of the R.G. Dun credit-rating company sometimes privately expressed their belief that Jewish businessmen "are secretive and deceptive, practicing a dubious morality in their dealings with non-Jews."[28] Nonetheless, as Gerald Tulchinsky remarks, "non-Jews did business with Jews despite the existence—possibly even the prevalence—of attitudes that held Jews in contempt, fear, and mistrust.[29]

To the extent that Jews were prominently involved in the political life of their community, they opened themselves up to their political opponents' using the term "Jew" in denigrating them. Thus George Benjamin, editor of the Belleville, Ontario, *Intelligencer* was lampooned by Dr. John

Edward Barker, editor of the rival Kingston *British Whig*, in February 1834 as "the Belleville Jew" who was killed by eating pork.[30] That same newspaper, four years later, objected to Benjamin's militia captaincy on the same grounds.[31] Clearly, however, this did not impede Benjamin's election to the Legislative Assembly of Upper Canada in 1857.[32]

The first prime minister of Canada, John A. Macdonald, on being told of the possibility of Russian Jews coming to Canada, responded with these words: "The Old Clo move is a good one. A sprinkling of Jews in the North-West would be good. They would at once go in for peddling and politicking, and be of as much use in the new country as cheap jacks and chapmen [peddlers]."[33] This is stereotypical language, but no worse, and demonstrates as well a certain readiness to accept these "old clo" people for the sake of the development of Canada's Northwest Territories as well as for the sake of possibly ingratiating the Canadian government with Jewish financiers in London who might then invest in the Canadian Pacific Railway.[34] The reality of Jews as peddlers in the Canadian west that would bring out much more vituperative attacks on the honesty and morality of the Jews will be dealt with in the following chapter.[35]

In sum, by the middle of the nineteenth century the small Canadian Jewish community was situated in a fairly enviable position, most certainly in comparison with many other groups.[36] It had achieved legal and civil rights on the basis of equality with those of Christian Canadians. It had done so, however, not without effort, and even experienced temporary setbacks. Nonetheless, in comparison with contemporary efforts to achieve political equality for Jews in certain states of the United States, such as Maryland,[37] the Jewish issue in the Canadas seemed not to have caused any sustained, vociferous, and divisive public debate. Public pronouncements against "the Jews" in Canada were few and far between, even if privately held anti-Jewish prejudices were still apparently widely held.

In retrospect, historians of the Jewish community in Canada have tended to agree with historian Irving Abella that "if there was a golden age of Canadian Jewry, one could make a strong case for the period before Confederation, particularly the 1830s and 1840s."[38] Even so, there were harbingers of trouble to come. When, in 1858, an Italian Jewish child, Edgar Mortara, was taken from his parents on the grounds of his alleged baptism by his Catholic nanny, there was great protest in many Jewish communities worldwide. Significantly, a leader of the Jewish community in Montreal was reported as having stated publicly at a protest in New York that Montreal Jews hesitated at speaking out in their hometown because "those with whom we are in daily intercourse ... are subject to the Church of Rome."[39]

It would take two major historical trends in the later nineteenth century to alter this fairly enviable situation: the phenomenon of mass immigration to Canada and the emergence of racist antisemitism in Europe. These phenomena and the momentous changes they wrought in the relationship of Jews and non-Jews in Canada will be discussed in the next chapter.

CHAPTER FOUR

The Jewish Problem Comes to Canada

I know the Jewish Question is the axis around which the wheel of world history revolves.

—Wilhelm Marr[1]

When the Dominion of Canada came into existence in 1867, it had a number of serious issues to confront, including most prominently the position of French Canadians within Confederation and the development of the Canadian west.[2] It did not, however, possess a "Jewish problem"—yet. That by the end of the nineteenth century it would have one was the result of two powerful forces that decisively impacted Canada in the last years of the nineteenth century: mass immigration to Canada by people of non-British origins, and the emergence of racist antisemitism in Europe. As historian Irving Abella stated, "As the numbers of Jews in the country increased, so did the opposition to their presence."[3]

Canadian Immigration Policy

It was clear to the Fathers of Confederation that the Dominion of Canada, and particularly the Canadian west, was underpopulated and needed settlers. Hitherto, the population of Canada had been made up overwhelmingly of people of either British or French Canadian origins. Indeed, up to the very end of the nineteenth century, fully 90 percent of immigrants to Canada came from the British Isles.[4] The Canadian political leadership certainly would have liked that to remain the case and they vigorously recruited immigrants from the British Isles as well as the United States.[5] Canada in the late nineteenth century, nevertheless, was becoming open to the immigration of large numbers of people from other areas of Europe, and experiencing as well some pressure for immigration from Asia, particularly China and Japan. The government of Canada did not want to accept just anyone, however. The Canadian political leaders of that era had a distinct vision of the type of immigration they desired. First of all, they wanted Europeans and not Asians. Secondly, they wholeheartedly embraced an immigration of farmers and agricultural workers and decidedly distanced themselves from welcoming immigrants who wished to settle in cities.[6] Their preference for farmers as immigrants was demonstrated practically by the fact that, at the beginning of Confederation, the responsibility for immigration to Canada was placed in the Ministry of Agriculture before being transferred to the Ministry of Interior in 1892. This preference was most clearly stated by Clifford Sifton, who is widely credited for establishing the broad outlines of Canada's immigration policy in the late nineteenth century. He stated on one occasion: "I think a stalwart peasant in a sheep-skin coat, born on the soil, whose forefathers had been farmers for ten generations, with a stout wife and six children, is good quality. A Trades Union artisan, who will not work more than eight hours a day and will not work that long if he can help it, will not work on a farm at all and has to be fed by the public when his work is slack is, in my judgment, quantity and very bad quality."[7] This vision would have important implications for Jewish immigrants to Canada, who did not really fit into this vision with respect to two important factors. They were, first of all, overwhelmingly not farmers.[8] Moreover, when they immigrated to Canada, Jews tended to settle in large urban communities and formed a proletariat that strongly supported trade unionism, among other causes.

Jewish Immigration to Canada

In the first census of the Dominion of Canada, in 1871, people declaring their religion to be Jewish numbered but 1,333, or 0.03 percent of the total population. This number increased to 2,443 in the census of 1881, 6,501 in 1891, and 16,401 in 1901 (0.31 percent of the total population).[9] In other words, Canada's Jewish population increased fifteen-fold in a mere thirty years, and ten-fold as a percentage of total population.

Where did this increase come from? Where did the new Jewish immigrants to Canada settle at the end of the nineteenth century? In answering these questions, we will uncover some of the important factors that went into the increasingly negative profile of Jews in Canada.

In the first place, the major source of the great increase in the Jewish population of Canada was immigration. Moreover, most of the Jewish immigrants entering Canada in the first decades after Confederation were not English speaking, nor did they originate in the British Isles. These facts are of great importance, because Canada in the late nineteenth century was predominantly populated by people who traced their European origins to the British Isles or to France, and the small Jewish community that had been established in Canada was likewise made up of people who were of British and/or American origin and were therefore thoroughly acculturated to the English language and civilization. Overwhelmingly, however, the new Jewish immigrants at the turn of the twentieth century tended to be Yiddish speaking and came from the various countries of eastern Europe. Their aim, like nearly all of the tens of millions of immigrants coming from southern and eastern Europe to North America at the turn of the twentieth century, was to leave their homes, where they could most often see no viable way of improving their economic situation, and to go to a place where they hoped they would be able to create better lives for themselves and their families. For numerous historical reasons, Jews in Europe had generally not been allowed to own land and engage in agriculture. This meant that, practically speaking, the Jewish immigrants to Canada were overwhelmingly neither farmers nor trained as farm workers. Their vocational experience, such as it was, tended to be mostly as artisans or shopkeepers. Despite notable attempts by various Jewish organizations to settle Jews on farms in Canada, the great majority of Jewish immigrants naturally headed to large cities, where the most appropriate social, economic, and religious opportunities beckoned to them. In these urban centres, they rapidly formed an urban proletariat and began to fill crowded, poverty-stricken inner-city neighborhoods in Montreal, Toronto, and Winnipeg that quickly became identified as "Jewish," often to the acute dismay of the acculturated, middle-class Jewish communities that had been established in Montreal and Toronto. The well-established Jews in those communities understood that, justly or unjustly, they too would be judged by the conduct and mores of these new immigrants.

All of these factors taken into consideration, the new Jewish migration at the end of the nineteenth and the beginning of the twentieth centuries would have been looked upon as less than desirable when compared to the Canadian elite's overall vision of the ideal immigrant. There were three strikes against them. They did not come from the British Isles; they were not English speaking; they were not farmers. The ambivalence of the situation is well captured in a 1935 *Canadian Encyclopedia* article on the Jewish immigrants in Canada: "Possessing keen business instincts, the Jews have displayed a marvelous power of acquiring wealth since their arrival in the country: many have come, wretchedly poor, and yet have, in some way, managed to exist and make money. The majority are disinclined to hard manual labour: yet they are most industrious and make a living where others would starve. Despite several prosperous farm colonies in Saskatchewan, the Jews are, in general, economically, non-producers."[10]

Jews in the Eyes of Other Canadians

For many Canadian observers at the turn of the twentieth century, therefore, Jews constituted one among several less-than-desirable groups of immigrants, including "the Oriental and Negro races ... and the Slavs [which] not only failed to assimilate but [were] relatively inassimilable."[11] It was apparent to observers in western Canada that anti-Jewish prejudice was "widespread and deep-rooted."[12] Even those Jews who tried to settle on the land as farmers confronted these stereotypes. Thus in 1887, a meeting in the Wapella region of Saskatchewan objected to the settlement of Jews in their district because "Not only are Jews a most undesirable class of settlers but they are keeping a number of desirable settlers out."[13]

Jews who came to Canada in this era, moreover, had more than their origins, language, and occupation going against them. They also faced the rapidly rising tide of an ideological movement that had begun in Europe in the late nineteenth century and quickly spread to the New World—antisemitism. Antisemitism was an ideology that successfully assimilated the powerful anti-Jewish legends and stereotypes of previous centuries, and added to them the powerful modern ideology of scientific racism.

"Scientific" Racism and Antisemitism

It is of great significance to our story that antisemitism claimed to be "scientific." That is because the modernity celebrated by the nineteenth century was characterized by significant advances in science and technology in practically every field. Transportation had been revolutionized by railways and steamships; communications had been revolutionized by the telegraph and the telephone; medicine had seen great advances such as anaesthesia, germ theory, and vaccination; biology had witnessed the impact of Darwin's revolutionary theory of evolution. In this milieu, other areas of study, like history and linguistics, also strove for a "scientific" perspective, and many people in the nineteenth century confidently expected that the scientific perspective in all fields of knowledge would ultimately yield a truer understanding of nature and humanity, many useful inventions, and an ever greater improvement of life in general.

One of the most important intellectual phenomena in the increasingly globalized world of the late nineteenth century was racism. Racism presented itself as a "science" and laid claim to "objectivity" in its assertion of the superiority of one group of human beings over others. Its ultimate "scientifically objective" message was that the domination of the white European race over great expanses of the globe was no accident; it was essentially the result of that race's natural superiority over others. This "scientific" racism was, among other factors, one of the major arguments of slave owners in the pre–Civil War United States and of segregationists in both the post–Civil War United States and South Africa. As historian of science Elazar Barkan states, "During the nineteenth century, scientists reified the concept of race and endowed it with explanatory powers beyond its initial taxonomic purpose."[14]

One of the most significant offshoots of nineteenth-century "scientific" racism was antisemitism.[15] Its very name showcases its scientific pretensions. It claimed to build upon differences perceived by linguists between "Aryan" [Indo-European] languages and "Semitic" languages, of which Hebrew and Arabic are prime examples. Differences in linguistic structure between these two linguistic groups, discovered and analyzed by renowned nineteenth-century scholars like Max Müller and Ernest Renan, were deemed by them to serve as indications of basic mental and moral qualities inhering in members of the "Semitic" and "Aryan" races.[16] As Jewish historian Susannah Heschel states: "Müller invoked a distinction between Semites as rootless wanderers and Aryans as rooted cultivators of nature that subsequently served to reinforce anti-Jewish stereotypes in insidious ways."[17]

In nineteenth-century Europe and North America, speakers of Arabic, that other major modern language belonging to the Semitic linguistic family, were negligible in number. Even were they present, as "orientals" they would have been widely considered to be politically and culturally insignificant.[18] Thus, when antisemitism was promulgated in the nineteenth century Western world, Jews were in effect the sole actual "representatives" of the "Semitic race" in Europe and the Americas and hence became the sole centre of attention of the antisemitic movement, while, as historian Shulamit Volkov points out, "scientific knowledge of Semitic qualities was meager enough to allow the term a full measure of ambiguity."[19]

Antisemitism as a political movement was born out of a conviction that, as Anthony Julius stated, "the Jews were somehow in charge of modern affairs. Secretly, sinisterly, beyond the reach of the law and even of governments, they were plotting, or already enjoying global power. This anti-Semitism was thus no longer confined to descriptions of the Jews' unregenerate condition; it also offered an account of the allegedly determinative part they played in the modern world."[20]

The term "antisemitism" was coined by a German, Wilhelm Marr, who expressed his opposition to Jews in the following way: "We have among us a flexible, tenacious, intelligent, foreign tribe that knows how to bring abstract reality into play in many ways. Not individual Jews, but the Jewish spirit and Jewish consciousness have overpowered the world."[21] The ideas expressed by Marr resonated deeply among many Europeans, who saw in the Jews a symbol of all that they felt was wrong with the morality and values of the modern Western world. The following are the sort of pointed questions antisemites asked as they assessed the "Jewish problem" that confronted them. Prior to the French Revolution, they reasoned, had it not been the case that Jews were almost universally the objects of Christian hatred and fear, such that they were ghettoized and expelled in order to protect Christian society from them and their influence? Had the godless French Revolution not emancipated them, giving them an equality of rights and privileges while at the same time removing the time-honoured privileges of the Church? Had the emancipation of the Jews not demanded of the Jews, as a quid pro quo, the renunciation of their separate nationality? And did the Jews not now seem to have retained their entire national solidarity, that they were supposed to have renounced, expressing it in the creation of Jewish organizations of an international scope such as l'Alliance Israëlite Universelle? Were the Jews not, therefore, in a much better position to threaten Christian society and civilization than they had been a century before? Should the world not be informed about the new Jewish threat to Christian civilization? Should the world, once informed, not organize to eliminate the Jewish menace?

Antisemitism in Canada

The term "antisemitism," once coined, spread rapidly from Germany to England[22] and France, and soon enough found its way into all Western countries, including Canada. All over the world, it rapidly became a common term for expressing negative feelings toward Jews that ranged from ambivalence about accepting Jews as societal equals to absolute fear and loathing. As early as 1884, Yosef Bernstein, an eastern European Jewish immigrant living in Montreal, wrote an article on the Jews of Canada for a Russian Hebrew-language newspaper, *ha-Melitz*. In this article, Bernstein reported to his readers that Canada was certainly not immune from antisemitism. Bernstein's conclusions bear citation at length:

> Here, also, we are considered to be strangers and foreigners [in] a land that is not our own. Here also we will meet Haman-like[23] people such as Stöcker[24] and Istóczy[25] and others who impatiently await the day when they can demonstrate their anger against the children of Shem, for their

anger against the Jews is great. Has not Dr. Goldwin[26] Smith, the great-
est of the antisemites, come out in the journal, *The Nineteenth Century*,
to criticize and mock the hosts of the children of Israel in this country,
to discredit us in people's eyes, and to turn backward the hearts of the
inhabitants of the land [so that they] hate the Jews who live in their
midst?[27] Praise be to the Most High God, this enemy quickly realized that
his words did not penetrate the hearts of the inhabitants of [this] country
and he had none who heeded him because the number of Jews in this
land is quite small, and they can find no excuse to attack them as [occurs]
in other lands. Because of this, the hope of this antisemite was dashed,
and just as it came, so it went away. Who among us, however, can guarantee that [the antisemite's] dashed hope will remain so even after the
number of Jews in the land multiplies? We, the inhabitants of the lands
of America cannot lie to ourselves and assert that we have established a
covenant with the gentiles; that the rod of punishment will not reach us
when it passes. For who would have believed ten years ago that in Russia and Germany the demon of antisemitism would rise from the earth
to renew the Crusade in the lands of Europe, and to revive the Inquisition in the nineteenth century, a time when civilization has achieved
great heights? Who could have told us that the infectious leprosy[28] of
antisemitism, which had [apparently] already passed from the earth,
should once again move the hearts of the nations to attack us? What is
its strength now in this country as we begin [to settle]? Is the New World
not similar to Russia? Is not the rest of the world like Germany? Both
here and there we dwell among scorpions. Both here and there [we find]
religious bigotry, hatred of the [Jewish] nation, and ancient ideas which
oppose us to our destruction.[29]

Goldwin Smith

In his comments, Bernstein makes special reference to Goldwin Smith,
and rightly so. Smith was one of the most outspoken and influential
purveyors of hatred of Jews in English Canada in the late nineteenth
century. Smith was a well-connected and prominent public intellectual
who had enjoyed a successful academic career in England, the United
States, and Canada. His writings against the Jews centred on his opposition to what he considered the essential Jewish characteristic of "tribalism," the Jews' supposed inability to care about anyone other than a

fellow Jew. For Smith, Jews were thus enemies of the "Gospel of Human-ity."[30] For him, it was the Jews' "tribalism" that made it impossible for any modern society to accept Jews on a basis of equality with its other citizens. As Smith stated:

> Judaism is not, like Unitarianism or Methodism, merely a religious belief in no way affecting the secular relations of the citizen; it is a distinction of race, the religion being identified with the race, as is the case in the whole group of primaeval and tribal religions, of which Judaism is a survival. A Jew is not an Englishman or Frenchman holding particular tenets: He is a Jew with a special deity for his own race. The rest of mankind are to him not merely people holding a different creed, but aliens in blood.[31]

In a letter to the *Manitoba Free Press* Smith wrote of Jewish attempts at farming the Canadian West: "These people, besides their want of agri-cultural aptitude, are as a rule, not producers of native labour. It is on this account and from hatred of their financial practices, not on account of their religion, that the people of Europe, and especially the peasantry, began rising against them."[32]

Smith maintained firmly that the term "antisemite" was indeed appli-cable to him, "if [antisemitism] means simply fear of political, social, and financial influence, without the slightest shadow of religious antipa-thy, from which I can truly say that I am absolutely free."[33] In this analy-sis, Smith seems to be following the trend of antisemitic thought in Eng-land in this period. As Susan Terwey has written of British antisemitic discourse, "the most prominent element was the Jews' wholesale and categorical exclusion from the nation, their denial of being English and British."[34]

For Smith, the only possible solution that would make Jewish indi-viduals acceptable in contemporary Canadian society was their com-plete de-Judaization. Only thus could they hope to become acceptable in modern society. All other Jews, who did not wish to choose this radical de-Judaization, should go to Palestine, or, in any case, leave Canada.

Goldwin Smith despaired of Canadian society when he witnessed what to him appeared to be a veritable flood of Jews, whom he thought of as "the least desirable of all elements of population" coming to his hometown, Toronto, and elsewhere in Canada.[35] As Canadian Jewish historian Gerald Tulchinsky explains, Goldwin Smith was thus a confirmed and principled antisemite who created a voluminous and sustained body of writing on this subject over a period of several decades.

Smith's Influence

Smith may have stopped short of attempting to put his antisemitic views into action in terms of a political movement;[36] however his views had great influence both through his personal social and intellectual prominence and through the pages of the *Toronto Evening Telegram*, which Smith founded with an investment of $10,000, and whose editor, John Ross Robertson, was a disciple.[37] It is likely that Smith founded this newspaper to combat what he felt was the Jewish domination of the press, for, in his view, "they [the Jews] seem to be behind the press everywhere, or at least be able to muzzle it."[38] It need hardly be said that the pages of the *Telegram* were decidedly unsympathetic to the Jews in general and to the Canadian Jewish community in particular. While in the 1880s and 1890s this lack of sympathy with Jews was apparently unique to the *Telegram*, by the early twentieth century it had spread to other Toronto newspapers.[39] Future prime minister of Canada William Lyon Mackenzie King recalled his interchanges with Smith on the subject of the Jews. As he reported, Smith understood the Jews to be "the poison in the veins of the community [and] that in a large percentage of the race there are tendencies and trends which are dangerous indeed."[40] To Smith may be attributed at least in part the social character of upper-middle-class Toronto in his era, which has been described as "thoroughly anti-Semitic"[41] and which initiated social ostracization of Jews from clubs, resorts, neighbourhoods, and professional associations.[42] This way of thinking also influenced progressive Canadians, like Winnipeg minister James S. Woodsworth, who would become one of the key founders of the Co-operative Commonweath Federation. Woodsworth would have been horrified had his thought been characterized as antisemitic. Nonetheless in his 1909 book on immigrants in Canada, *Strangers within Our Gates*, he showed that he had absorbed the then-widespread idea that "the Jews" controlled world finance when he stated: "It is a far cry from the Jewish pedlars or sweatshop tailors to the money-barons who control the world's finances."[43]

Going one important step beyond Smith in turn-of-the-century Toronto was a pioneer woman lawyer, Clara Brett Martin, whose social circle was close to Smith's. In a 1915 letter to the Attorney General of Ontario, Martin accused "Jews" of perpetrating fraud in property transactions on a broad scale. Whereas Smith merely fulminated against the menace of the Jews, Martin was, in effect, as Canadian feminist historians Brenda Cossman and Marlee Kline state, "lobbying the state to take legislative action on anti-Semitic grounds."[44]

Smith was a genteel antisemite, conscious that strongly expressed antisemitism was not entirely acceptable in polite British discourse.[45] Thus, though Smith expressed an understanding of events like the anti-Jewish pogroms in Russia for which he felt that the Jewish victims themselves were to blame because of their wrongs against the Russian peasantry, he himself did not call for violence against Jews in Canada. There were others in Canada, however, who did not hesitate to utilize violence as a weapon against Jews. Once Russian Jewish immigrants began establishing communities in Montreal, Toronto, and Winnipeg, they began experiencing frequent harassment and physical violence.[46] Some of this simply expressed religious and racial prejudice. Other violent acts against Jews, however, were apparently perpetrated by people who were angered that the Jews were taking jobs they considered theirs.[47]

While Goldwin Smith marked an extreme of publicly expressed anti-Jewish feeling in English Canada at the turn of the twentieth century, there nonetheless remained clearly demarcated limits within the society of the Dominion as a whole beyond which Jews, as Jews, could not advance. These limits, not surprisingly, were similar to those prevalent in England which have been described by Anthony Julius in the following way:

English toleration exercised a limiting, and in certain respects repressive influence on Anglo-Jewish freedom ... English society was monolithic and exclusive: Jews could either join it on given terms, or live outside it, free of undue hardship. Jews who wished to embrace received English values were permitted to do so, and reap the rewards; other Jews, who wished to stand apart, were permitted to do so, but paid a small price in social exclusion. What Jews were *not* able to do was to play a full, participating part in English society on their *own* terms.[48]

The social exclusion referred to included membership in gentile social clubs and golf clubs. While in 1907 it was reported in the *Jewish Times* of Montreal that Jews were not being excluded from resort hotels in Canada as they were in the United States, Jews at Canadian resorts did begin to experience such exclusion in the years prior to the First World War,[49] and Canadian Jews were thus forced to create their own resort areas.[50]

The Jewish Issue in Quebec

Since Montreal was Canada's largest city in this era, and housed its largest Jewish community, it naturally constituted the major place to which the new eastern European immigrant Jews were attracted. In Montreal, beyond the challenges they faced elsewhere in Canada, the Jewish community faced additional factors that increased tensions, particularly with French Canadians. Some of these factors were cultural, and others were purely political and not at all specific to Jews but applied to all immigrant newcomers to Quebec.

First of all, Jews coming to the province of Quebec had to contend with the idea that prevailed among French Canadian political leaders that mass immigration to Canada would only serve to diminish the percentage of French Canadians in the population of Canada and hence reduce the political power of French Canada in Ottawa.[51] For this reason alone, immigrants as such would be resented by many French Canadians. A second factor was likely connected with the general French Canadian resentment of English social and economic domination of the province of Quebec and of Canada as a whole. Whereas in the early part of the twentieth century, the economic and social position of the English in Quebec seemed all too powerful, the Jews, who quickly adopted the English language and sent their children to English Protestant schools, were perceived as constituting a weak point that could be attacked with little fear of the consequences.[52] A third factor in French Canadian attitudes toward the Jews was the predominantly urban character of the Jewish immigration. For many French Canadian intellectuals, like Lionel Groulx, the ideal French Canadian life was rural, and cities were considered a threat to the purity and integrity of this life.[53] Jews thus became a symbol of all that was wrong with the big city.

The fourth factor also had clear political implications, but was essentially more religious and cultural in nature. It had much to do with the fact that Roman Catholicism, in Quebec and Canada as a whole, had taken on a decidedly ultramontane character by the end of the nineteenth century. Ultramontane Catholicism was, as historian Bernard Vigod put it, "an arch-conservative, authoritarian reaction to liberal influences and revolutionary events."[54] It emphasized strict obedience to the papacy and its doctrines, and it contributed significantly to the ways in which Roman Catholics in Canada, and particularly in Quebec, understood their relationship with the Jews. As Canadian Catholic historian Terence Fay states: "At the beginning of the nineteenth century, after the destruction wrought on Catholicism by the French Revolution, neo-ultramontanes encouraged loyalty to the spiritual and political leadership of the Holy See as the best way to reconstruct Catholic life, worship, and culture. Catholics in France and in other European countries sought a new spirituality beyond the rationalism of the French Enlightenment."[55] Though there were significant opponents of ultramontanism within the Church, one of the most significant outcomes of the ultramontanism embraced by most Catholics in Canada stemmed from the fact that the papacy in the nineteenth century was vehemently opposed to the very aspects of the modern world that had revolutionized the civil and political status of Jews and enabled their equality.

In 1864, Pope Pius IX promulgated a *Syllabus of Errors* that condemned, among dozens of other "errors," the fallacy that "the Roman Pontiff can, and ought to, reconcile himself, and come to terms with progress, liberalism and modern civilization."[56] This *Syllabus of Errors* was accepted by the Roman Catholic hierarchy in Quebec, and its ideas gained considerable influence among the Catholic laity, given the firm control the Church maintained over the education of French Canadians at the turn of the twentieth century. Since ultramontane Catholics in Quebec tended to oppose many of the movements characteristic of the modern era, they naturally took exception to the modernist, liberal, and leftist perspectives that "enjoyed a fairly warm reception among lower-class immigrants in Montreal, especially in the Jewish community."[57]

With respect to the Jews specifically, French Canada's ultramontanism also led to a sympathetic hearing for traditional Catholic condemnations of Judaism. This certainly included traditional deprecations of Jews as killers of Christ, but it went far beyond this. It also included revivals of medieval and early modern condemnations of the Talmud and reiterations of Jewish hatred of Christians and Christianity, as well as accusations that Jews were commanded to kill Christians and to use Christian blood in their rituals. Many Catholics embraced the work of nineteenth-century Catholic writers such as Father August Röhling, a professor of theology at the German University of Prague. In his book *Der Talmudjude* [Talmud Jew, 1871], Röhling accused the Talmud, and the rabbinic Judaism on which it was based, of being motivated by hatred of non-Jews and of giving Jews licence to cheat gentiles in business and to do them bodily harm where possible. The goal of Judaism, according to the author, was the destruction of Christianity by any and all means.[58] The book also embraced the theory of a secret cabal between the Jews and the Freemasons to control the world.[59] On the basis of these traditions and writings, which had been widely circulated in French translation,[60] the Jews of Quebec would find themselves accused of tremendously heinous crimes.

Among many French Canadians in this era, there also existed close intellectual ties with reactionary Catholic France.[61] After 1905, when church and state were separated in France, many conservative French clerics immigrated to Quebec and exerted a reactionary influence in person.[62] This as well as the strongly ultramontane nature of French Canadian Catholicism engendered a respectful hearing for antisemitic writings coming from France. As historian of antisemitism Robert Wistrich notes, "anti-Semitism in France tended to be reactionary, antimodernist, and Catholic."[63] Historian of France Pierre Birnbaum likewise states, "The Catholic world and the populist movements combined with them was the force behind that [French] anti-Semitic movement, which was part of its plan to reject the secular state."[64] Thus there should be little surprise that the arguments of antisemitic French intellectuals, like Maurice Barrès, that "a true national ethics ... *obligated* an anti-Semitic posture toward the Jews"[65] resonated deeply in many clerical circles in Quebec. They tended to heed French seminary professor Canon Emmanuel Chabauty's teaching that the Jews, in league with Freemasonry, were the forces behind modernization and revolution, and that Jews were more under the power of Satan than other peoples.[66] These cultural influences tended to differentiate French Canadian antisemites from their English Canadian brethren. As Susanne Terwey has written, contrasting Continental (including French) and British antisemitism: "Unlike their continental counterparts, British anti-Semites did not question Jewish emancipation and even distanced themselves from 'antisemitism' at a time when elsewhere in Europe, being an 'antisemite' was a positive social and political stance."[67]

In the 1880s and 1890s antisemitism in France had demonstrated such strength that some French politicians won elections on the sole platform of hating Jews. Édouard Drumont's virulently antisemitic book *La France juive* (1886), which purported to show the dangers of Jewish control of France, became a runaway bestseller.[68] Drumont's perspective may be summarized in one of his sentences: "All comes from the Jew, all returns to the Jew."[69]

The ideas of Drumont's book were absorbed and propagated by Jules-Paul Tardivel in Quebec, and he himself published articles in this vein in the Montreal daily *Le Devoir*.[70] When, in 1894, a French army officer of Jewish ancestry named Alfred Dreyfus was condemned for treason to France, the resultant furor exposed deep divisions between a pro-Dreyfus liberal, leftist, anticlerical, republican France, and an anti-Dreyfus conservative, Catholic, monarchical France.[71] It is evident that many French Canadian clerics and those who looked to them as spiritual and intellectual leaders had great sympathies for the political and intellectual positions of the anti-Dreyfusards that they would retain through the era of Vichy France.[72]

Another point made by French antisemites that spoke politically to many French Canadians was French clerical antisemitism's denial that Jews could truly form an integral part of the general polity. Whereas nineteenth-century liberal nationalism, exemplified by that of republican France, sought to regard all those living within the borders of the nation as equal citizens of the state, integral nationalists insisted that only those who had shared a common religious, cultural, and biological past could truly constitute part of the nation.[73] This struggle between liberal inclusionist and integral exclusivist nationalism in Quebec was an issue of profound importance for the political history of Quebec as a whole, and in the heated debates stemming from this struggle, the Jewish issue played a prominent part.

Moreover French Canadian traditionalist nationalism, as reflected in the works of well-known public intellectuals like journalist and politician Henri Bourassa and historian Lionel Groulx, viewed French Canadians as a "race" whose sacred life, divine mission,[74] and integrity were threatened by urbanization and new cultural models.[75] Thus they looked upon Jews, who symbolized all the various threats to the integral French Canadian way of life, as a foreign people,[76] whose influence on Quebec society, like that of the English, had to be resisted.[77] Indeed, as Michael Oliver states, "it was difficult to see that nationalists of the Groulx school could be anything but suspicious in their relations with other 'races.'"[78] Of both the English and the Jews Groulx had this to say: "We do not prevent anyone from living, but we want to live too ... I am, if I may say, neither anti-English nor anti-Jewish. But I see that the English are pro-English and the Jews are pro-Jewish. And insofar as such an attitude contradicts neither charity nor justice, I am careful not to blame them for so doing. But then I wonder why the French Canadians are everything except pro-French Canadian."[79] For his part, Bourassa wondered why English Canadians preferred "Sicilians, with their knives, Polish Jews, and Syrians" to French Canadians.[80] But Bourassa also chastised French Canadians for "That childish revenge of empty words spent on denouncing the Jews, swearing against the Irish and depicting the whole of the English-speaking people as coalesced against the French instead of winning the respect of all races by struggling for our rights and showing respect for ourselves.[81]

While Groulx was not really comfortable self-identifying as an antisemite, his way of explaining himself is most revealing. In 1954 he wrote:

It is clear that Christian charity forbids us any form of antisemitism. On the other hand, with respect to the Jew, should we behave with carelessness and recklessness? History and daily observation have all too well demonstrated to us [the Jew's] most revolutionary tendency. Lacking roots wherever he is, refusing any assimilation, he is quite indifferent to the political and social order around him. That is the reason, therefore, that he is mixed into all revolutions [even] when he is not one of its main agents. We must also equally contend with his innate passion for money, an often monstrous passion which lacks all scruples.[82]

Unlike the case of Goldwin Smith, whose antisemitic views generally remained personal positions, principled opposition to Jews and Judaism at the turn of the twentieth century in French Canada expressed itself clearly in the public square. This tendency led some organizations, like the Union of Franco-Canadians, and L'Association catholique de la jeunesse canadien[83] to adopt openly antisemitic resolutions, and led others to consider the foundation of political groups similar to the powerful Ligue Antisémitique de France.[84]

As antisemitic sentiment in both English and French Canada was coalescing in the last years of the nineteenth century the Canadian Jewish community, led by its longer-settled and more acculturated elements, saw fit to react by creating a newspaper in Montreal, the *Jewish Times*, that was founded at least in part to combat antisemitism.[85] The columns of the *Jewish Times* at the beginning of the twentieth century were filled with numerous stories in which the social, religious, and political position of Canadian Jews had been brought into question. In 1909 Montreal Jewish community leader Maxwell Goldstein wrote in the *Jewish Times* that one of the major issues "facing Canadian Jewry was the difficulty posed by the influx of foreign Jews who formed ghettos and fostered prejudice among French Canadians."[86] The newspaper's response was, first of all, to instruct Jews on how to avoid giving offence. Thus in the *Jewish Times*, Jewish readers were instructed to learn proper manners, the alleged lack of which had led resort hotels to bar Jews as patrons.[87]

The Jewish School Issue

One of the most prominent problems stemming directly from mass Jewish immigration was the Jewish school issue in Montreal. The British North America Act of 1867 that had established the Dominion of Canada had guaranteed educational rights in Quebec specifically to

Catholics and Protestants. Jews, who were neither Protestant nor Catholic, attended Protestant schools. This situation was to a certain extent uncomfortable for Jews insofar as there was overtly Christian content at school, such as prayer, Bible reading, and celebrations of Christian holidays such as Christmas. However the presence of so many Jewish children also caused discomfort for the Protestant School Board of Montreal. In the first place, the Protestant Board faced the necessity of educating numerous immigrant Jewish children whose parents, because they were mostly not property owners, did not contribute financially to the system based as it was on property taxes. Secondly, it faced the prospect of the adulteration of the Christian character of some of the schools within the system, and indeed of the system itself, due to the increasing numbers of Jewish students. The situation came to a head in 1901 when a Jewish student, Jacob Pinsler, was denied a high school scholarship for which he was otherwise qualified on the grounds that his parents did not pay taxes to the Protestant School Board. The board argued at the time that Jews had been accepted into the Protestant schools not by right but rather by the goodwill of the board, which could impose any conditions it wished.

The litigation stemming from the Pinsler case resulted in a 1903 law in Quebec that regularized the admission of Jewish students in the Protestant school system. That system, however, remained all but closed to Jewish teachers, who found it nearly impossible to find employment in Quebec. Moreover, although Jews were, through their property taxes, helping to fund the Protestant School Board, they were specifically forbidden to play any role in the governance of the Protestant schools.[88] Evidently many Montreal Protestants were concerned about the possibility that Jewish teachers might teach Protestant children or that Jews might be elected to positions of leadership on the school board. Thus, the underlying issue, as in the nineteenth-century case of Ezekiel Hart, was the fear that Jews might have authority over Christians.[89] These sentiments were summed up by Anglican Bishop of Montreal John Farthing, who stated: "Weakening of the Christian influence in the schools by the appointment of non-Christians to the school board or the teaching staff ... would inevitably undermine the civilization based on Christian religion."[90] In a 1913 letter to the editor, a Protestant parent in Montreal

protested a school commission replacement of the Easter Monday holiday with a school holiday coinciding with the Jewish Passover holiday in
this way: "Is the Montreal High School a Hebrew or a Christian school?
Are our children to be taught to observe Christian or Jewish holidays?"[91]

Continuing tensions over these issues would lead, among other
things, to a strike by Jewish students over antisemitic remarks regarding
Jewish lack of cleanliness by a teacher at Montreal's Aberdeen School,
heavily populated by Jewish immigrant children, in March 1913.[92] In
Toronto in 1914, similar tensions surrounded the issue of the compulsory singing of Christmas carols by Jewish schoolchildren.[93]

Canada as a Christian Country

While the Jewish school question of Montreal had highlighted the
Christian nature of the Quebec school system, there were other attempts
to assert the Christian nature of Canada through national legislation. In
1906, the Canadian Parliament considered a piece of legislation called
the Lord's Day Act. This legislation was designed to enforce the establishment of the Lord's Day (Sunday) as a legislated day of rest. The law
thus forbade nearly all businesses to open on Sundays. In the House
of Commons debate on this bill, the minister of justice, Charles Fitz-
patrick, addressed the position of Jews in Canada with these words: "It
is not desirable for us to be too considerate of the wishes of alien immigrants who ... while they are obtaining the benefits which this country is affording them, will not be subject to undue hardship if they are
obliged ... to obey any rules which we, as a Christian community, find it
necessary to lay down for the observance of the Sunday."[94] Parliamentary
debate on the issue elicited numerous opinions on the Jews and their
relation to Canada. Quebec's Henri Bourassa, who at that time believed,
as did Goldwin Smith, that the pogroms against the Jews in Russia were
essentially the Jews' fault,[95] stated: "They [the Jews] do not adapt themselves to the customs of the people among whom they live, but on the
contrary they conduct themselves in such a way that they are vampires
on the community instead of being contributors to the general welfare
of the people."[96] Jewish attempts to obtain an exemption from the law
whereby "whoever conscientiously and habitually observes the seventh

day of the week as the Sabbath ... shall not be subject to prosecution for performing work ... on the first day of the week" were unavailing.[97]

The Lord's Day Act was hardly the only piece of Canadian legislation in those years asserting Canada's overtly Christian character. Queen's University in Kingston, Ontario, sought legislative approval for a charter that declared Queen's to be "distinctively Christian" and stipulated that "the trustees shall satisfy themselves of the Christian character of those appointed to the teaching staff."[98] The question was publicly raised whether the charter thus worded would allow Queen's to go so far as to bar Jews.[99]

Polemical Opposition to Jews and Judaism

An incident in 1913 put into question the ability of Jews in Canada to have access to kosher meat. The Halifax Society for the Prevention of Cruelty to Animals charged the local kosher slaughterer with cruelty to animals, specifying that the traditional Jewish method of slaughtering animals was cruel and in contravention of the Nova Scotia Cruelty to Animals Act. It took the expert testimony of Rabbi Simon Glazer of Montreal and a local professor of physiology to convince the court that kosher slaughter was humane and should be tolerated.[100]

In early twentieth-century Quebec, anti-Jewish feeling expressed itself in several well-publicized incidents. In 1910, a Jewish man, Ernesto Nathan, had been elected mayor of Rome. Accusations that he had insulted the pope led not merely to the adoption of anti-Nathan resolutions, but also to large and vociferous anti-Nathan rallies in Montreal and Quebec City that included denunciations of the Jews by Catholic clergy and French Canadian students, journalists, and politicians.[101]

In that same year, notary and journalist Joseph-Édouard Plamondon addressed the Association canadienne de la jeunesse catholique in the parish of Saint-Roch, Quebec City. This same association had sponsored in 1908 a lecture by L.C. Farly, who had urged driving Jews out of Canada and Quebec, boycotting Jewish merchants, and creating an antisemitic league.[102] Plamondon's talk argued that the Jews were ritual murderers, usurers, and enemies of the Church, and utilized to the full the Catholic Church's historical and contemporary accusations against the Talmud. He further called for revocation of equal rights for Jews and recommended that they be excluded from the country.[103] As a result of his speech and its subsequent publication in *La Libre Parole*, of which he was a founder and collaborator,[104] Jewish businesses, homes, and the synagogue in Quebec City were vandalized and individual Jews were assaulted.[105] The Plamondon affair that followed was the result of a civil action brought against Plamondon by Benjamin Ortenberg and Louis Lazarowitz, Jews who resided in Quebec City. During his trial, Plamondon's arguments against the Talmud were aired in court and sustained by three expert witnesses, all of whom were Catholic priests. The anti-Jewish charges were refuted by expert witnesses from the Jewish side, including a Montreal rabbi, Herman Abramowitz, and a Quebec City Anglican priest, Rev. F.G. Scott.[106] It is of some significance that the case was tried in 1913, simultaneously with the ritual murder trial of Mendel Beilis in Russia,[107] as well as the murder trial of Leo Frank in the United States,[108] which also brought to public attention sensational accusations against Jews and their supposed murderous proclivities against gentiles.

At the end of the trial, Plamondon was acquitted by the court on the grounds that though he had indeed defamed "the Jews" in his speech and writings, no single individual had been libelled.[109] He was, however, ultimately found guilty of defamatory libel by the Quebec Court of Appeal.[110] The Plamondon case represented for Canada the beginnings of an attempt to protect the Canadian Jewish community and its members from defamation through the utilization of the Canadian system of justice. The ambiguous results of the Plamondon case presaged the difficulty Jews would find in gaining redress for the harm done by antisemites in the Canadian court system.

By 1914, with the onset of the First World War, the Dominion of Canada found itself the home of a burgeoning Jewish community. It had also witnessed the beginnings of fairly widespread antisemitic expressions in nearly all parts of the country. These beginnings would become socially and institutionally endemic in large parts of Canadian society in the following decades, as will be seen in the next section of the book.

PART THREE

JEWS AND CANADIAN SOCIETY
(1914–1945)

CHAPTER FIVE

Social and Institutional Antisemitism

Et, pour vrai dire, what more political is there to say after you have said:
À bas les maudits Juifs!

—A.M. Klein[1]

In this chapter, we will survey the social and institutional antisemitism
that prevailed in Canada from the beginning of the First World War to
the end of the Second World War. This brings the story of antisemitism
in Canada to approximately the middle of the twentieth century. The
Canada of that era has been described by Canadian Jewish historian Irving Abella as "a benighted, xenophobic, anti-Semitic country" in which
"Jews were excluded from almost every sector of Canadian society and
some were even excluded from the country itself by a government and
a people who felt there were already too many Jews here."[2] In that era,
the one issue that united an otherwise deeply divided Jewish community was opposition to an antisemitism that seemed both pervasive and
personal.[3]

Harassment of Jews

As Allan Levine, speaking of the Winnipeg Jewish community of the
interwar era, states, "Few Jewish children ... were not at one time or
another accosted merely for being Jewish.[4] In nearby Minnedosa, Manitoba, the Asper children, in a community with two Jewish families,
recalled "frequent anti-Semitic taunts but only the occasional beating."[5]

French Canadians and Jews in this era had an ambiguous and complex relationship that began with their proximity in the same or adjoining Montreal neighbourhoods. As Gerald Tulchinsky points out, this

residential pattern might have been due to "the historical accident of where settlement first occurred ... and where institutions ... were first established. But it is equally plausible to interpret the definite persistence of Jewish settlement by the overwhelming majority of Montreal's Jews from 1900 to 1950 amongst French Canadians as an indication that Jews felt more comfortable with them as neighbors."[6]

Proximity, however, meant conflict as well as comfort. Montreal Jewish funeral cortèges were occasionally stoned.[7] Poet Irving Layton remembered growing up Jewish in Montreal in the 1920s in this way: "The strongest memory I have is of clashes. Around Easter ... something seemed to happen to the gentiles. They took it as a cue to come and beat up on the Jews. So, without fail, every Easter, they would descend on the embattled Jews with bottles and bricks, and we'd be waiting for them on the roofs, like an army, with sticks, and stones, with anything."[8]

In Toronto, it was not uncommon for Jewish peddlers to be attacked physically, and Jewish parents instructed their children to make themselves inconspicuous in order to avoid assault.[9] The antisemitism of the first decades of the twentieth century thus seemed to be both physical and ubiquitous. Even when it did not involve physical bullying, taunts of "Christ-killer" remained with many Jewish children growing up in this era.[10] Antisemitism was something that deeply affected Canadian Jews' psyches not merely at the time, but for generations after, as we shall see.[11]

The Position of Jews in a "Christian" Canada

The first important thing that we have to understand about the Canada of that era is that most Canadians consistently thought of Canada as a "Christian" country. For them, this meant first and foremost that their country was part of the "civilized" world.[12] For many Canadians, though, it also meant that Canada as a whole should overtly espouse the values of Christianity.[13] The idea came with a usually unexpressed conclusion that becoming Canadian in the fullest sense would necessitate conversion to Christianity.[14]

This attitude was well expressed by M. Ceslas Forest in a 1935 article, "La question juive au Canada," which stated that, by becoming Canadian citizens, Jews had accepted to live in a Christian country. This fact implied a limit to the Jews' freedom in Canada. Jewish demands, however legitimate they may be, "must never interfere with the character of our [Christian] institutions and our laws."[15] Jews, along with Americans, were seen by the Quebec Catholic hierarchy as threatening Quebec culture and morality, not least with the films that were coming to dominate public entertainment in the 1920s. Archbishop Georges Gauthier of Montreal thus wrote in 1926: "I deny Americans and Jews the right to speculate on our morals."[16]

Thus those who stood outside the Christian community in Canada became targets for exclusion. This certainly included Jews as the largest non-Christian minority in the Dominion as a whole. It included as well other groups, including Canada's Chinese and Japanese communities, then significantly concentrated in British Columbia, who also faced virulent racism.[17]

Jews and Public Education

There were numerous areas in which Jews impinged on public life and concerns in this era. One of the most prominent was education, which we have seen in the previous chapter with respect to Montreal. In 1921 a Toronto *Globe* editorial complained about a Jewish "invasion" of Toronto public schools.[18] The issue that spurred the editorial was that Jews in Toronto had protested over their children being subjected to overtly Christian elements in their educational experience in the city's public school system. Those who protested against compulsory teaching of the New Testament and the singing of Christian hymns in the public schools were accused by a Toronto school trustee of attempting to "dominate" the system, to the detriment of Christian values. The argument that was articulated against the Jewish protest was thus similar to that of Forest in Quebec: Canada is a Christian country and Jews ultimately cannot be citizens of any country except their own, that is, Palestine.[19]

In Montreal the situation for Jewish schoolchildren, who in 1909 constituted approximately 35 percent of the student body of the Montreal Protestant Schools,[20] was hardly better. From the perspective of administrator Irving Elson Rexford of the Montreal Protestant School Board, a "Jewish Problem" existed, and he published an entire monograph on the subject entitled *Our Educational Problem: The Jewish Population and the Protestant Schools*.[21] Jewish children in Montreal Protestant schools were often segregated into separate classes and schools for the avowed purpose of minimizing the effect on Protestant children of Jewish student absenteeism during Jewish holidays.[22] For Rexford, Jewish requests for representation on the Protestant School Board and an end to discrimination against Jewish teachers constituted "attacks on ... the constitutional and religious rights" of Protestants.[23] Indeed, for both Protestants and Catholics in Montreal, the prospect of "even a few Jewish seats on the Protestant Committee or the school commission constituted a prospect to be dreaded."[24] Even more to be feared was the 1930 Quebec legislation, popularly called the "David Bill" after its author, Athanase David, that would have given the Montreal Jewish community its own school board.[25]

The legislation drew considerable criticism from elements in the Jewish community who feared the de jure segregation of Jewish children in their own schools. It also evoked strong and vocal opposition, particularly from the Catholic Church, which was concerned that this measure would be the harbinger of the secularization of Quebec education. Thus Abbé Antonio Huot wrote that the Jews had no right to their own schools, one of the proposed solutions to Montreal's Jewish school problem, since "if we consider the natural and divine law, the Jewish religion has no right because it is corrupted and because according to the expression of God's own will it must give way to the Christian religion ... according to the constitution and laws of our country the Jewish religion has no right either, for the Jews in Canada are immigrants who simply have to accommodate themselves to our laws."[26] In 1938, Roger Duhamel gave a somewhat radical interpretation of this sentiment in *L'Action Nationale* when he advocated the position that a group such as the Jews who wished to preserve their own faith and traditions should simply refrain from participating in public life.[27]

Since many Catholics affirmed the notion that the Jews nursed a profound hatred against the Church and its faithful, asserting, among other things, that "Jews are our enemies according to the prescription of their religious code,"[28] the proposal to create a separate Jewish school board as a solution to the anomalous position of Jewish students in the

Protestant school system was looked upon as "an attack on Catholicism and on the values all French Canadians cherish."[29] The Jewish school issue thus became another excuse for many within the French Canadian intelligentsia to remind Jews that they were guests in Canada who did not have the right to demand equality of treatment.[30]

Canadian Immigration Policy and Jews

One of the first and certainly the most significant political manifestation of public attitudes toward the Jews in post–First World War Canada concerned the development of Canada's immigration policy, which needs to be understood in the context of an economic recession in Canada, which began in 1920, as well as the social dislocations caused by industrialization and urbanization.[31] In 1923 Jews became a "special permit" group for immigration to Canada. This meant that immigration of Jews to Canada from most countries required a special permit, and such permits could only be issued by the cabinet as an act of special patronage.[32] The *Toronto Telegram* expressed a mainstream view of the dangers of an unrestricted Jewish immigration when it editorialized in September 1924: "An influx of Jews puts a worm next the kernel of every fair city where they get a hold ... Jews from all countries should be discriminated against as a race by a poll tax so high that friends in Montreal and Toronto and Winnipeg would have their resources strained to the utmost to lend their tribesmen through foreign post more than enough to bring a baker's dozen per annum."[33]

These sentiments were echoed in French Canada, where petitions against the admission of Jewish refugees in the late 1930s resulted in signatures in the hundreds of thousands. The political leadership of French Canada took this opposition into consideration, contesting most attempts to liberalize the terms of Jewish immigration to Canada.[34] Even though English Canada saw numerous expressions of sympathy with the Jewish refugees from Nazism in the 1930s, there was no accompanying groundswell of support for opening Canada's doors to these refugees in the face of prevailing high levels of unemployment.[35] In these years, the responsibility for overseeing Jewish immigration to Canada on behalf of the Canadian government was a bureaucrat named

Frederick Blair. Blair did not see himself as an antisemite,[36] though he did admit to a strong personal distaste for Jews.[37] As far as he was concerned, the reason Canada should not accept Jewish immigrants was because the country needed farmers, whereas the Jews were "city people" who, whatever they promised in order to obtain a visa to Canada, would not stay on farms.[38]

Jews as a Threat to Society

Jews in Canada were not merely considered by many Canadians to be excluded from the general polity by their race and religion. They were also widely deemed to be an actual threat to that polity. In this connection it is of considerable significance that in Canada, as elsewhere in the world, a document known as the *Protocols of the Elders of Zion*, which came to international public attention in the aftermath of the First World War, was taken so seriously by so many. The *Protocols* presents itself as a record of a series of meetings in which Jews from around the world plot to subvert Christianity and to gain world domination.[39] The work was first published in Russian in 1905. By the early 1920s the book had been translated into English and many other languages and quickly became an antisemitic staple, with the especially active help of industrialist Henry Ford, who distributed 500,000 copies of the book, to which he gave the title *The International Jew*, through his system of automobile dealerships.[40]

Soon enough the *Protocols* was revealed as a forgery concocted by the czarist government on the basis of a nineteenth-century French satire of Napoleon III by Maurice Joly. It was so judged by a Swiss court in 1935, which characterized it as "ridiculous nonsense."[41] Nonetheless, the *Protocols* maintains its position to this day in antisemitic circles as an accurate portrayal of the nefarious Jewish plot to control the world. Abbé Lavergne, writing in *L'Action Catholique* in 1922, reacted to efforts to discredit the *Protocols* with the following logic: "Are the *Protocols* false? Who says so? The Jews themselves! And one can scarcely rely upon their word. Thus the Protocols must be authentic."[42] This expression of a continuing antisemitic will to believe in the truth of the *Protocols*, despite widespread and well-publicized denials of its authenticity, parallels the words of Adolf Hitler: "How much the whole existence of these people [the Jews] is based on a permanent falsehood is proved in a unique way by the *Protocols of the Elders of Zion*, which are so violently repudiated by the Jews ... With moans and groans the *Frankfurter Zeitung* repeats again and again that these are forgeries. This alone is evidence of their authenticity."[43]

Jewish Stereotypes

A second related factor to consider when examining the way Jews were dealt with in interwar Canada concerns the profound distrust felt by many Canadians of radicals and foreigners. This is a subject which will be discussed in detail in the next chapter. A third factor is the widespread attribution to "the Jews" of "control" over "international finance." An example of this attitude is to be found in the following comment that appeared in the 1927 *United Church of Canada Yearbook*: "Wherever the Jew has settled in any part of the world he has created new problems, political, social, economic, and religious ... The power these people wield among the nations is out of proportion to their numbers. They have attained positions ... enabling them to mould thought and public opinion and to influence the life and destiny of nations."[44] In particular, the Canadian Social Credit Movement, which flourished especially in western Canada in the interwar period, tended to blame the "international Jewish financier" for the world's, Canada's, and Alberta's economic and political ills.[45] Many Canadian Social Creditists thus followed their ideological leader, Major C.H. Douglas, the British founder of the Social Credit movement, into expressions of overt antisemitism.[46]

Denials of Antisemitism

As we note the various anti-Jewish expressions on the part of a number of Canadians, it is instructive to see how many of those who openly espoused antisemitic sentiments, like Lionel Groulx and Frederick Blair, were in denial of their antisemitism even as they expressed it. Norman Fergus Black noted this phenomenon in 1944 when he stated: "At the present time and in most parts of this country no single responsible citizen could be induced publicly to proclaim himself an apostle of antisemitism. But there is a poisonous miasma in the air."[47]

A further example of this phenomenon is Alberta's first Social Credit premier, William "Bible Bill" Aberhart. On the one hand, Aberhart publicly denounced anti-Jewish attitudes. In one instance, he stated, "I should like our people to know the Social Credit movement as we understand it is not only opposed to anti-Semitism but condemns it in the strongest possible terms." On the other hand, a number of his comments on international finance and its baneful influence retained a definitely antisemitic ring.[48] And on a symbolic level, he visited two major American purveyors of antisemitic rhetoric, Father Charles Coughlin and Henry Ford, soon after his election.[49] When, in 1943, his successor as Alberta Social Credit premier, Ernest Manning, was in his turn challenged on the movement's antisemitism, he gave the following equivocal reply: "It has been brought to my attention that an erroneous impression has been created in certain quarters that the Social Credit Movement is anti-Semitic. Nothing could be further from the truth ... Social Credit is not opposed to any race or religion as such. It is only when the adherents of any religion, or the people of any race take collective action as a group to attack the principles of Christianity and democracy which are fundamental to Social Credit that conflict arises."[50] Yet another Social Credit official who tried to explain why Social Credit was not antisemitic was Solon Low, who stated on January 9, 1945:

> I am sure that our fellow Canadians of Jewish origins recognize that a truly democratic and Christian society ... alone will give them the social objectives that they seek in common with all Canadians ... Anti-Semitism is spreading because people cannot fail to observe that a disproportionate number of Jews occupy positions of control in international finance, in revolutionary activities, and in some propaganda institutions ... This gives people the impression that therefore there must be a Jewish conspiracy to gain world control.[51]

It was not merely Social Credit—which, despite its dominance of Alberta politics, might be dismissed as politically marginal to the country as a whole—that espoused such ambivalent views. Quite similar views were held by the prime minister of Canada, William Lyon Mackenzie King. According to his biographer, King "thought of [Jews] as aggressive and clannish and disturbingly prominent in international finance, although at the same time he deplored any overt discrimination against them."[52] King confided to his diary on February 20, 1946:

> I recall Goldwin Smith feeling so strongly about the Jews. He expressed it at one time as follows: that they are a poison in the veins of a community ... I myself have never allowed that thought to be entertained for a moment or to have any feeling which would permit prejudice to develop, but I must say that the evidence is very strong, not against Jews, which is quite wrong, as one cannot indict a race any more than one can a nation, but that in a large percentage of the race there are tendencies and trends which are dangerous indeed.[53]

Anti-Jewish Discrimination

It seems, therefore, that in speaking of Canada between the wars, it is possible to describe a "quite routine anti-Semitism," as Jacob Neusner phrases it.[54] How did this "quite routine" antisemitism express itself in the daily lives of Canada's Jews? Louis Rosenberg, one of the most perceptive contemporary observers of Jewish life in interwar Canada, put it this way: "Anti-Jewish discrimination in social life is frequent in Canada ... In some cases, this discrimination is tacit, but in many cases it is open and unashamed ... It is in the economic life of Canada, however, that anti-Jewish discrimination is most marked and most serious in its results. In seeking employment in public bodies, a Jew must be so outstandingly brilliant that his qualifications swamp the obstacles raised by his birth."[55]

Anti-Jewish discrimination in social life certainly encompassed occasional harassment and bullying, as described at the beginning of this chapter. It also included restrictive covenants barring the sale of property to Jews and others, like blacks, who were deemed undesirable. Advertising terms like "exclusive" and "restricted" were universally understood as referring to these undesirable groups.[56] The restrictive covenants encompassed city neighbourhoods as well as beach and resort areas.[57] It was basically understood by most Canadians in this era that landlords and resort owners had a right to discriminate by race and religion, and this discrimination was considered natural and acceptable.[58]

The presence of Jews at areas of public recreation sometimes led to protests against Jewish use of public beaches, as was the case with the members of the Balmy Beach Swastika Club of Toronto in 1933, who roamed the boardwalks of Balmy Beach and neighbouring Kew Beach warning that these facilities should be enjoyed by gentiles only and not spoiled by the allegedly offensive behaviour of Jews.[59] Similarly, in that decade a number of French Canadians in places like Ste-Agathe, a resort town north of Montreal, felt the need to protect their town against the Jews, who were accused, among other things, of loitering in the town's streets and obstructing both traffic and pedestrians.[60]

Sports events with Jewish participants could turn into brawls, as happened in August 1933 during a baseball game at Toronto's Christie Pits, where a battle between Jewish young men and swastika-bearing youth took place, resulting in a riot that lasted for six hours and injured scores of people.[61] This phenomenon was hardly unique to Toronto. In 1936, a Winnipeg YMHA football team was assaulted in Regina with cries of "beat the Jews."[62] In those years, similar confrontations took place in Winnipeg and Vancouver.[63] Canadian Jewish athletes, such as boxer Sammy Luftspring, regularly received antisemitic jeers from the stands.[64]

A 1937 report by Canadian Jewish Congress summarized the impact of social discrimination on Canadian Jews:

> During the past few years we have witnessed an amazing growth of anti-Semitism. Manifestations of an intensified anti-Jewish sentiment have been springing up everywhere … Jews have been barred from hotels, beaches, golf courses and parks … many signs posted in front of parks and beaches to the effect that Gentiles only are admitted … a startling increase in the number of individuals and companies who refuse to rent living quarters to Jews … a spreading policy of not employing Jews; the boycott of all Jewish firms; the sporadic attempts by various organizations to involve Jews in disturbances and violence.[65]

On the subject of discrimination in employment, the *Jewish Post* (Winnipeg) editorialized in 1928: "There are establishments which make a point of inquiring the nationality of applicants to office or sales positions, so that if the answer is 'Jewish' the position is 'already filled' … There are places where Jews are employed accidentally … until the discovery is made that they are Jewish. There are a number of shops … which will not take in Jewish apprentices … It is often harder for a Jew to get a job … simply because he is a Jew."[66]

In a survey taken in the United States in 1938–39, almost half of the respondents described Jewish businessmen as less honest than others.[67] This sentiment was replicated in Toronto, described by Jewish philanthropist Sigmund Samuel as "one of the most quietly bigoted cities in Europe or America."[68] In a 1933–34 survey, 70 percent of Toronto businessmen surveyed indicated that they would not deal with Jewish firms.[69] Many non-Jewish businessmen also evidently thought that employing Jews would adversely affect the prestige of their firms and cause friction with their other employees.[70] In this sort of atmosphere, Ottawa police detective Jean Tissot's accusation that Jewish businessmen were plotting to drive Christians out of business was given a respectful hearing in some circles.[71]

This tendency to segregate Jews even in the Canadian business world had significant consequences. While it should be noted that only Jews among all Canadian ethnic groups were represented at all in the Canadian business elite in that era, it is also clear that nearly all prominent Jewish businessmen entered the economic elite through creating their own firms located in the sectors of trade and real estate. There was simply not much participation by Jews in the private world of the Canadian economic elite. They were certainly not invited into the exclusive clubs of Montreal or Toronto. Jews had their own clubs, like the Montefiore in Montreal, which they could and did join. The Jewish business elite therefore led much of its social and recreational life within the Jewish community; they were separate yet interlocked in a peripheral way with the Canadian Anglo-dominated elite.[72]

A 1938 Canadian Jewish Congress report fleshes out the employment discrimination against Jews even further. The report found that in the educational sector, there were few Jewish teachers and no school principals. In Toronto, it was accepted that Jewish high school teachers would not be hired unless they first got experience in outlying Ontario towns, if even then.[73] Banks, insurance companies, and many industries did not hire Jews. No Jewish salespeople were to be found in department stores like Eaton's.[74] Jewish doctors could not get positions at hospitals. No Jewish judges were appointed. Practically no Jewish university professors were hired. Governments took on few Jewish civil servants. The employment situation was almost impossible for Jewish nurses, architects, and engineers.[75] The profession of engineering, in particular, was known to be unreceptive to Jewish applicants. Jewish students in this era were thus routinely advised to avoid engineering studies.[76] Rev. Claris Silcox, a Protestant minister who was to become a prominent Canadian advocate for Jewish refugees fleeing from Nazism, stated in 1934 the common Canadian perception that "the Jew is essentially an urbanite who 'doesn't take' to engineering and agriculture."[77]

In other professions, like law, it was clearly understood that Jews only articled with Jewish firms and that for the most part only Jewish clients employed Jewish law firms.[78] Most Jewish lawyers suffered from the restricted hiring practices of larger law firms. In Montreal, as Alan Gold stated: "It was a well-accepted fact that English firms would not hire Jewish students. Some may have been taken on a volunteer basis, however, with the understanding that they wouldn't be kept on at the end of their articling stage. It was not normally the practice for French firms to hire Jewish law students but this was mostly because of a language issue."[79]

The situation was similar in Toronto.[80] The barriers facing Jews who wished to make the law their profession in that city are apparent from a letter in which Caesar Wright, a professor at Osgoode Hall Law School of Toronto, wrote in 1937 concerning future Chief Justice of Canada Bora Laskin's prospects in Canada: "I am afraid that in the limited field in this country there would be, unfortunately, a certain prejudice against him which he would find it difficult to overcome."[81] In 1939, Wright further wrote concerning Laskin, "Unfortunately he is a Jew. This may be fatal regarding his chances with you. I do not know. His race is, of course, proving a difficulty facing him in Toronto so far as obtaining a good office is concerned."[82]

Discrimination in Canadian Universities

In the interwar period, Canadian universities, as elsewhere in North America, were widely seen as entryways to the professions and the economic elite. It will come as no surprise, therefore, that elite Canadian universities, like those in the United States, were desirable educational goals for upwardly mobile Jewish students. It is equally no surprise that Canadian universities, like their counterparts in the United States, moved in various ways to restrict admission of Jews.[83] Anticipating the well-publicized 1920s debate at Harvard over restricting Jewish admissions,[84] the principal of Queen's University in Kingston, Ontario, R. Bruce Taylor, stated that he was happy that "Queen's ... was not situated in a great centre of population (mostly Jews) and of wealth (mostly held by Jews)," and that "the presence of so many Jews tended to lower the tone of Canadian universities."[85] At McGill it was observed that in the 1924–25 academic year nearly 25 percent of the first-year students were Jewish.[86] In response, a policy was put in place that discriminated against Jewish applicants with the object of diminishing the Jewish percentage in the student body.[87] In 1926 McGill began with an "informal" policy of not admitting "Hebrews" from outside Quebec. In 1929 it instituted a double standard in the university matriculation examinations: to achieve a passing grade, Jews had to score 700 (70 percent) and gentiles 630.[88] This double standard worked more or less as planned. From 1925 to 1935, the percentage of Jewish students at McGill College dropped from 25 to 12 percent.[89] Dean Ira Mackay of McGill wrote of the Jewish students he administered:

> The simple obvious truth is that the Jewish people are of no use to us in this country. Almost all of them adopt the following four occupations, namely merchandising, money lending, medicine and law, and we already have far too many of our own people engaged in these occupations and professions at present ... [While I have] the highest regard for the better class of Jews, some of whom are our best citizens ... as a race of men their traditions and practices do not fit in with a high civilization in a very new country.[90]

Many Canadian university students seemed to agree with this assessment. In a 1933 survey, 80 percent of the University of Toronto's non-Jewish students expressed a preference not to admit Jews into their clubs.[91]

With respect to the study of law, McGill's Faculty of Law was not similarly restricted. As Alan Gold recalls: "I should say even though those were the years when they still had a quota on Jewish students, the Faculty of Law did not. It was only the undergraduate school, arts and science that did, so I had no problem wondering whether I would be admitted or not."[92] Nonetheless, McGill Principal Sir Arthur Currie reported in 1933 that he was pleased that there was only one Jew in an incoming law school class numbering thirty-nine because other prospective Jewish students had chosen the law school of the Université de Montréal.[93] In the 1930s, standards for Jewish applicants to McGill were tightened still further, and Jews were required to score 750 on their matriculation examination while gentile students had to score only 600.[94] At the French-language Université de Montréal, because there were relatively few Jewish students (no more than 69, or 4.4 percent of the student body in the academic year 1935–36),[95] no quotas were imposed and the presence of the few Jews on campus was not opposed by the administration, though the legitimacy of their presence at a Catholic university was the subject of protest by members of the university's French Canadian student body,[96] as well as by some French Canadian politicians.[97] These politicians included MP Samuel Gobeil, who spoke in the House of Commons on February 26, 1934, against the presence of both lay professors and Jewish students at the Université de Montréal. On March 17, Gobeil made a similar speech at Lac Mégantic that was published as a pamphlet entitled "La griffe rouge sur l'Université de Montréal."[98]

The Université de Montréal administration's consistent answer to the critics of a Jewish presence at their university was well expressed in 1941 by its then vice-rector, Mgr Émile Chartier. Responding to the question, "Does our Catholic university fulfill its national duty by giving the advantage and opportunity to foreigners to study in the various sciences that lead to the liberal professions? Won't these foreigners do harm to our people one of these days?" he replied:

> Your letter proceeds from the idea that the University of Montreal is Catholic and French Canadian. From the fact that it is Catholic, two things follow: that its teachers and their teaching must also be Catholic … It does not follow from it that one must be Catholic in order to be accepted as a student. As to your other departure point, I must indicate to you that our institution is neither French-Canadian nor French. It is a Quebec institution: this means that it is situated in the Province of Quebec, and that it is supported, in part, with provincial funds. As the provincial government is also supported by those you call foreigners, as much as by the money of French-Canadians, the University cannot close

its doors to anybody that the Province has admitted to live among us …
When admitting these students, the University believes that it follows a
course of action that is anything but an antinational one.[99]

In the field of medicine, restrictions on the entrance of Jews were
well known and expressed in various ways across Canada. In 1938, eight
places in the McGill Medical School's incoming class were reserved for
Jews. This quota was set by the university administration "after con-
sulting with Jewish students and graduates and several prominent Jewish citizens of Montreal," who thought the quota "generous," keeping in
mind "the difficulty Jews have in securing hospital internships."[100] This
quota, like other restrictions against Jews at McGill, was "purely admin-
istrative" in nature and was not brought in any "official" way before the
University's Faculty and Senate, which would have had to take a public
stand on the issue.[101] At the University of Manitoba the percentage of
Jews in medicine declined from 28 percent in the 1920s to 9 percent in
1944, a situation which was so notorious it provoked a provincial royal
commission. The Canadian situation entirely paralleled trends in the
United States, where, between 1920 and 1940, the percentage of Jews
enrolled in Columbia University's College of Physicians and Surgeons
dropped from 46.94 to 6.45.[102] Even though the 1944 Manitoba Royal
Commission's findings were dismissed as a "whitewash," the situation
did begin to improve. In the first graduating class of the University of
Manitoba Medical School after the quota was ended (1950), twenty-
three Jewish students graduated as opposed to an average of seven in
the previous years.[103] A partial exception to this generally bleak picture
is Dalhousie University in Halifax, where almost 20 percent of the student body was Jewish and where, in 1939, fourteen of thirty-six medical
school graduates were Jews, all but one of them American.[104]

It must be noted, however, that despite all the obstacles put in their
way during the period from 1921 to 1941, the number of Jewish doctors
and lawyers in Canada increased more than five times, the number of
Jewish dentists more than tripled, and Jewish nurses in Canada almost
quadrupled in number.[105]

Until the post–Second World War era, no Jewish doctor was able
to obtain a clinical position at the University of Toronto or, with one

exception, an indoor staff position at a teaching hospital in Toronto.[106] The exception to this rule was Toronto General Hospital, which, from the year 1929 on, admitted one Jewish intern a year.[107] This was likely in response to a public accusation by Toronto Rabbi Ferdinand M. Isserman in 1927 that it was practically impossible for Jews to obtain either a medical internship or nursing training in Toronto hospitals.[108] In response to the exclusion of Jews from opportunities in the medical professions in this era, the Jewish communities of Montreal and Toronto were impelled to sponsor their own hospitals.

Jewish women studying physiotherapy at the University of Toronto were also not allowed to do regular clinical training at Toronto General Hospital.[109] In the 1940s, the dean of the University of Toronto Medical School, like his counterpart at McGill, approached Jewish community leaders, asking them to "voluntarily" reduce Jewish numbers in the medical faculty.[110] In this period, the University of Toronto School of Dentistry weeded out otherwise qualified Jewish applicants through the use of a dexterity test. Those Jewish students who did make it into the dental program found themselves subject to abuse by their professors.[111]

The University of Toronto's Library School in 1934 rejected an application from a Jew on the grounds that he would not find employment as a librarian and would thus "spoil the placement record of the school."[112]

Discrimination in Medical Practice

In Saskatchewan in this period, the Regina General Hospital refused to hire two Jewish doctors because they were deemed "unacceptable" to the staff and the public.[113] However the most notorious case of exclusion of Jewish medical personnel in Canada occurred in Montreal in 1934. In May of that year, Dr. Samuel Rabinovitch, the highest-ranking graduate of the medical faculty of the Université de Montréal, had been appointed an intern at Montreal's flagship French Canadian hospital, Hôpital Notre Dame. His appointment was considered a provocation by the hospital's French Canadian interns, who went on strike. The interns' strike was widely publicized and soon turned into a *cause célèbre*, with support for the strikers coming from interns at several other

Catholic hospitals in Montreal.[114] The striking interns expressed concern about working together with Dr. Rabinovitch as well as the conviction that Catholic patients would find it "repugnant" to be treated by a Jewish physician.[115] There was strong support for the strike on the part of French Canadian nationalists, represented by the Société Saint-Jean-Baptiste.[116] Though there were certainly voices within the French Canadian community condemning the strike, most notably Edmond Turcotte in Montreal's liberal journal of opinion *Le Canada* and Olivar Asselin in *L'Ordre*,[117] it was clear that while most French Canadians did not approve of the strikers' actions that endangered patients, they did respect the principle of "Canada for Canadians."[118] The strike was ultimately settled when Dr. Rabinovitch resigned his position and obtained an internship in a hospital in the United States.

Rabinovitch was clearly up against more than simple professional prejudice. His appointment at a leading French Canadian hospital had touched a very sensitive nerve, well expressed by numerous letters received by the hospital. All French-language letters took the side of the strikers. One such letter emphasized the fact that "our French-Canadian people has been too long exploited under the banner of 'tolerance.'" Another asserted that "the honor of the French-Canadians demands the exclusion of this stranger [whom] High Finance sustains." A third decried the fact that the Jews had unfortunately become masters of many areas, and concluded that the only way to resolve the Jewish problem was to not admit them at all, or else place them apart in a ghetto, as had been done in the Middle Ages.[119]

Discrimination in French Canada

Historian Everett Hughes has observed that French Canadians of that era, no less than Jews, viewed the professions as "one of the favorite and surest ways of upward mobility" and thus tended to be "especially jealous" of perceived encroachment in what they considered to be a French Canadian professional domain. In the same vein, N.L. Nathanson's 1936 appointment to the board of the Canadian Broadcasting Corporation was decried by *Le Devoir* on the grounds that the seat given to a Jew was not being given to a French Canadian.[120] Similarly, Member of Parliament Samuel Jacobs's request to be appointed part of Canada's delegation to the 1936 coronation of King George VI was successfully opposed by Ernest Lapointe and Pierre Casgrain on the grounds that Quebec should not be represented by a Jew,[121] and Samuel Factor's potential cabinet appointment met with the same opposition.[122] This sensitivity was also evident in this era among French Canadian lawyers, some of whom were "among the most bitter and outspoken agitators against English— and Jewish—invasion of the French Canadian domain,"[123] echoing the arguments of antisemites in France.[124]

Another important aspect of this situation is that Jews did not constitute the only target of French Canadian resentment. They were, however, relatively less powerful than other targets. As Hughes stated: "The symbolic Jew receives the more bitter of the attacks which the French Canadians would like to make upon the English or perhaps even upon some of their own leaders and institutions … Against the Jew, however, attack may proceed without fear either of retaliation or of a bad conscience."[125]

In the Quebec of that era, therefore, overtly anti-Jewish manifestations seemed to proliferate, and there was a widespread perception that antisemitism in Quebec was worse than it was in the rest of Canada. As Toronto rabbi and Canadian Jewish Congress leader Maurice Eisendrath, put it: "Here [in Ontario] it [antisemitism] is subtle. There [in Quebec] it is widespread and demonic."[126] In 1937, F.I. Spielman of the Canadian Jewish Congress wrote that "the rising tide of Anti-Semitism in the Province of Quebec has assumed such proportions that it has become imperative for us to strengthen our position for the defence of the community."[127] However, lest we think that Quebec was uniquely antisemitic compared to the rest of Canada at this time, we should heed the words of A.M. Klein, who looked at the phenomenon from the perspective of Montreal: "Editorial writers go out of their way to give the impression that the entire province of Quebec is a domain of intolerance … This is simply not the truth and one has a right to question the motive of such wholesale prosecution … either the pious defence of a discriminated minority is being used as an instrument of denigration against the French-Canadian minority; or the crusader … is pointing to Quebec antisemitism only to draw attention off his own."[128]

Whether antisemitism was worse in Quebec than elsewhere in Canada is debatable; its reality was not. Signs indicating "No Jews," or "Gentiles Only," or "Jews Not Allowed" were increasingly to be found in the Laurentian Mountains, north of Montreal, where many Montreal Jews summered.[129] These Jews faced occasional harassment in resorts like Ste-Agathe and Val Morin, and, in 1935 in Val David a synagogue filled with worshippers was set on fire.[130] In the summer of 1939, French Canadian agitator Adrien Arcand spoke against the Jews in the Laurentian village of Saint-Faustin on July 23. The very next Sunday, July 30, Abbé Charland of Ste-Agathe announced a campaign against the Jewish presence in his community, stating, "we must keep the district French-Canadian, and must remain masters in our own community."[131] During the Second World War, major antisemitic incidents occurred at places of amusement and recreation like Crystal Beach, Ontario, in 1942,[132] and Plage Laval in 1943.[133]

While these incidents were occurring, Canadian Jewish Congress official H.M. Caiserman observed that "neither the French Canadian religious, political or cultural leaders, nor the general press of the province (French and English alike) uttered a single word of disapproval or condemnation of the most irresponsible and libelous accusations leveled against the Jewish population."[134] To the great consternation of Quebec's Jewish community, no single representative of the Quebec Catholic Church publicly condemned antisemitism in the French press,[135] though one churchman did give private assurances to Jewish representatives, like Rabbi Harry Joshua Stern, that he did not sympathize with antisemitism and that he would take action to remedy the situation.[136] Internally, the Quebec Catholic Church was struggling to find a way in which its institutions, especially those institutions of higher education which were partially funded by Quebec taxpayers, including Jews, could accommodate Jews without compromising the "fundamental principles of our scholastic structure."[137]

It was often the political leadership in Quebec that fed fuel to the fire of anti-Jewish public opinion. Thus Quebec political leader Maurice Duplessis, who publicly disassociated his government from antisemitism,[138] spread a rumour in the 1930s that 100,000 German Jewish refugees from Nazism were planning on coming to Quebec to settle on farms.[139]

This set off a veritable wave of resolutions and protests against the idea of settling so many Jews in Quebec, including one at the Montreal City Council in September 1933.[140]

This does not mean, however, that no voices in French Canada spoke out against such antisemitic manifestations. Henri Bourassa, who, as we have seen in the previous chapter, was a strong anti-Jewish voice in the House of Commons debate on the Lord's Day Act, had abandoned his virulent anti-Jewish rhetoric by the late 1920s. It is likely that Bourassa's change in tone was connected to the Vatican's 1926 condemnation of the doctrines of the Action Française,[141] as well as the Vatican's denunciation of antisemitism in 1928.[142] In the 1930s, Bourassa gave speeches in the House of Commons asserting that antisemitism was in fact an absurd monstrosity.[143] Bourassa expressed these views in a 1934 letter to M.S. Bessler: "I deplore as you do the stupid and coarse attacks against the Jews, without distinction between respectable and non-respectable Jews … it seems to me that your compatriots are taking these attacks too seriously. They especially do not distinguish sufficiently between their declared enemies and certain well-intentioned though possibly ill-informed men who are suspicious of a certain number of Jews whose spirit of monopoly is becoming manifest in public or private enterprises."[144] As can be seen from this citation, however, Bourassa's change in attitude and repudiation of antisemitism did not mean that he had no ambivalence about Jews. He fully believed in the "international tendencies of the [Jewish] race, its financial power, and its hold [empris] over the press,"[145] though he refused to believe that all Jews were the same.[146] It is also clear that during the Second World War he lent his name and prestige to the political movement against conscription and spoke at anti-conscription rallies that had distinct antisemitic elements, such as pro-fascist Paul Bouchard's statement, "We don't want to see thousands of young Canadians die overseas to save international Jewry's finances."[147]

The campaign within the French Canadian community against Jewish immigration continued throughout the period in which Jewish refugees fleeing the Holocaust sought refuge in Canada. In 1944, the Société Saint-Jean-Baptiste campaigned against Jewish immigration with a petition that received over 150,000 signatures, a campaign led by a young public figure named Jean Drapeau, who was later to become mayor of Montreal.[148]

Anti-Jewish Boycotts

Proposed boycotts of Jewish shops and businesses was an important aspect of antisemitic activity in Canada in the interwar period. Jewish shopkeepers had by the 1920s and 1930s established a wide variety of retail establishments in Canadian cities and towns, and in many of them they were the only kind of "outsider" who had successfully invaded the field of small retail trade.[149] The boycott proposals were in essence similar to the anti-Jewish boycott proposed in France in the 1890s. In that country a Social Catholic Congress had passed resolutions in 1889 enjoining its members not to marry Jews, not to read Jewish newspapers, and not to have any commercial relations with Jews. By 1898, the French anti-Jewish boycott campaign had become a reality. Not only was it a project of ideologically driven antisemites; it also expressed the sentiments of a substantial fraction of the general population.[150]

In Quebec, the boycott campaign was carried out under the name "Achat chez nous," with the slogan: "If we do not buy from them, then they will leave." It was sponsored by various French Canadian organizations, including L'Action Catholique and the Société Saint-Jean-Baptiste, which attempted to get French Canadians to promise never to buy from a Jew.[151] Lionel Groulx gave eloquent expression to the sentiments behind "Achat chez nous," as well as his continuing ambivalence with the term antisemitism, when he wrote in 1933 under the pseudonym of "Jacques Brassier":

> Antisemitism is not only not a Christian solution [to the Jewish problem], it is a solution that is negative and ridiculous. To resolve the Jewish problem, it would suffice if French Canadians regained their common sense. There is no need of extraordinary legislation; no need for violence of any sort. We will only give our people the order, "Do not buy from the Jews" ... And if by some miracle our order were understood and complied with, then in six months the Jewish problem would be solved, not merely in Montreal but from one end of the province to the other.[152]

In advocating this course, Groulx may well have had in mind Catholic-inspired boycotts of Jewish businesses in Galicia and Ireland that had significant effects on the economic well-being of the Jewish community.[153]

Other figures suggested boycotting Imperial Tobacco, which was owned by Jews, and "smoking Christian" (*fumez Chrétien*) instead.[154] As one group of French Canadians wrote in a letter to Canadian Justice Minister Ernest Lapointe: "How can our businessman succeed while he was raised by his Christian mother to repeat endlessly 'I will not take another's property,' when he competes against the Jew who was always taught take what you can as long as you are not caught."[155]

While "Achat chez nous" does not in its title specifically target Jews, its spokesmen were clear enough. Though in theory the campaign could be directed at anyone who was not French and Catholic,[156] Henri Leroux in 1926 wrote that the organization must "fight against only one foreign race, the Jews."[157] Another Quebec cleric assured an audience in Vancouver that "Achat chez nous" was not directed at English Canadians but solely at Jews.[158]

A number of French-Canadian newspapers assigned substantial space to their support of the "Achat chez nous" campaign. Prominent among them were *Le Devoir*, *L'Action Catholique*, and *L'Action Populaire*.[159] There is some evidence, however, that these calls for boycotting Jewish stores were largely ignored by the French Canadians. Thus, after two strongly antisemitic articles published in *L'Action Catholique* on April 27 and May 5, 1942, Quebec City Jewish merchant Charles Lax reported to H.M. Caiserman of the Canadian Jewish Congress on May 26: "We do not think that the articles published in the *Action* are having any ill-effects on business as the Jewish stores are still doing well and there is plenty of money in circulation."[160] And indeed *L'Action Catholique*, despite its editorial policy, continued taking advertisements from Jewish stores, particularly the Quebec City Department Store owned by Maurice Pollack.[161]

Even liberal French Canadian journals like *Le Canada* were not immune to the presence of anti-Jewish sentiment in their pages. A.M. Klein, in response to an apology by *Le Canada* for such a story, commented: "The management of *Le Canada* ... repudiated Mlle. Oligny's sentiments, saying that those were but an expression of her personal opinion ... *Le Canada* in its apology, if it is intended as an apology, makes reference to favorable articles about Jews that it printed. We must admit that it does not seem much of a defense to us for a newspaper to state that it does not spread its Jew-baiting all over the journal, but reserves it only for a special department."[162]

The concept, though not the name, of "Achat chez nous" was not at all confined to Quebec. In 1912–13 there were boycotts by Ukrainian Canadians against Jews.[163] In Alberta, the Ukrainian Canadian who managed the Vegreville co-op put the following message in Ukrainian on its paper shopping bags: "Let's stick together / Stop going to the foreigner's [Jewish] / Do all your shopping at the Ukrainian store / Let the foreign bastards starve."[164]

As if this were not enough, Jewish shopkeepers across Canada often experienced harassment for opening their establishments on Sunday in contravention of federal legislation mentioned in the previous chapter mandating closure on the "Lord's Day." Even though in Quebec this law had been modified by provincial legislation that did allow Sunday openings, in practice the permission was often interpreted in a restrictive way and was deemed to cover individual proprietors and not corporations.[165] Even so, the exemption became a political issue in the 1936 provincial election when Maurice Duplessis, then the leader of the opposition, attacked the Liberal government for this policy.[166]

The Quebec City Synagogue Affair

Even during the Second World War, Jews in Quebec felt beleaguered. This was symbolized for them by the fate of the synagogue of Quebec City. In the 1940s there was an attempt to build a new synagogue in that city. Unfortunately, Quebec City's Jews ran up against a wave of public opposition from their French Canadian neighbours to the planned new synagogue building. This protest influenced the Quebec City municipality to withhold permission for the building of the new synagogue. On December 3, 1941, Quebec City's English-language daily, the *Chronicle Telegraph*, editorialized: "If it [the opposition to the synagogue] does not imply anti-Semitic sentiment actively, it does so negatively at least; otherwise there would be no objection to Jewish citizens erecting a synagogue for their own use whenever they see fit."[167] The Jewish perspective on this opposition is perhaps best summarized by the words of A.M. Klein: "Our readers will no doubt remember that for the last several years, Quebec Jewry has been desirous of building itself a place of worship in that pious city. Every time a site was purchased, however, the city fathers of Quebec found … that a building permit could not be granted … the synagogue question has already been converted into a political playground."[168]

On the recommendation of the Canadian Jewish Congress, the Quebec City congregation took the matter to court and began building on the site that the Quebec municipality had officially expropriated for parkland. While the matter was before the courts the basement of the synagogue was built.[169] As Rachel Smiley, the synagogue's historian, describes it, "with hostile mass meetings taking place in the adjoining park, the building took shape."[170]

From the perspective of the congregation, the city fathers of Quebec were taking one unconstitutional step after another to prevent the construction of a place of Jewish worship. As A.M. Klein wrote: "They did, in fact, prepare the intellectual (?) background to acts such as finally occurred. When certain influences, week in week out invoked all the shibboleths of mediaevalism and went rampaging in a veritable orgy of Jew-baiting, they did, in fact, without benefit of torch or phosphorous, prepare the milieu for a deed such as was finally perpetrated."[171]

On the eve of the dedication of the new synagogue, scheduled for May 21, 1944, a fire broke out in the synagogue. It was immediately and widely reported that this was a case of antisemitic arson, probably the most notorious antisemitic act ever committed in Canada. Because of the fire, Quebec City acquired a reputation as a city which had officially forbidden the construction of a synagogue and burned the synagogue that had been built in the midst of a war in which the Allies were fighting for, among other things, "freedom of religion."[172]

Facing all of this antisemitic opposition, the Canadian Jewish community was all but stymied. As Jack Lipinsky writes:

> In battling anti-Semitism, [Canadian Jewish] Congress leaders found themselves between the proverbial rock and hard place. The powers of the day would not listen to their representatives, while *amcha* [rank-and-file Jews] demands for marches or demonstrations were anathema to the Uptown controllers of Congress. With no compelling reason to

act, and no groundswell of voter concern, the government did nothing about discrimination against Jews, Blacks, and Asians in employment, education, and housing.[173] Given these realities, and Jewish community division over how to respond, a feeble and underfinanced Congress saw little point in head-on conflict with government.[174]

This was the situation that Canadian Jews faced as the country entered the Second World War. During the war, Jews in Canada readily enlisted to fight against the fascists and the Nazis abroad while simultaneously seeking to engage the antisemites who espoused fascist and Nazi ideas in Canada. These antisemites also accused the Jews of complicity in the other great ideology of the twentieth century—communism. That aspect of the story of antisemitism in Canada will be related in the next chapter.

CHAPTER SIX

The Spectre of Europe:
Communism and Nazism

It seems that almost any problem can be discussed in America except the Jewish problem. The very mention of the word "Jew" is cause for a storm.

—Charles Lindbergh[1]

The twentieth century saw the rise and fall of two hugely influential ideologies, Communism and Nazism, which together exercised a tremendous influence on the course of the century throughout the world. Both ideologies saw themselves as an ideal, scientific way to reorganize society so as to achieve human perfection. Both ideologies related to each other in a dialectical way and most often saw each other as the great adversary to be conquered on the way to achieving its vision of the perfect society. Both ideologies also saw themselves in an adversarial relation to Jews and Judaism, though in somewhat different ways. Nazism saw the Jews as major obstacles to its envisaged perfection of society, and once they gained power in Germany in 1933, Nazis strove to eliminate Jews from German society through discriminatory legislation, expulsion, and, ultimately, annihilation.[2] Communists saw Judaism, along with other religions, as inimical to societal perfection and believed, as Karl Marx had stated in a well-known essay, in the elimination of Judaism from society.[3] As for the Jews themselves, Communists were divided on whether Jews could, in a Communist society, celebrate selected non-religious aspects of their culture and heritage, or whether they should abandon all of their Jewish cultural baggage and join an undifferentiated proletarian society in achieving societal perfection.[4]

In the early twentieth century, Canada did not bear the brunt of these ideologies with the same intensity that continental Europe did. It was,

85

however, deeply marked by the social and political conflicts created to a large extent by these ideologies and their clash, most notably before and during the Second World War. Canada was also the scene of numerous sustained attempts to convey the principles and advantages of these ideologies to its citizens. While in retrospect it is clearly understood that neither Nazism nor Communism per se gained appreciable numbers of Canadian adherents, it is equally clear that many Canadians in the interwar period were positively impressed by many of the achievements of Fascist Italy and Nazi Germany, on the one hand, and of the Communist Soviet Union on the other. Jews in Canada figured largely in the story of the Canadian reactions to Nazism and Communism: as targets and victims, in the case of Nazism, and as proponents and alleged perpetrators in the case of Communism. It is that story that will be told in this chapter.

Jews and Bolsheviks

The 1917 Bolshevik Revolution in Russia, which ultimately caused the demise of the czarist regime in Russia and the rise of the Communist-controlled Union of Soviet Socialist Republics, forcibly brought the ideology of Communism to the attention of the world. On the one hand, the 1917 revolution was merely one of the major upheavals caused by the First World War that toppled imperial regimes in Germany, Austria-Hungary, and Turkey as well. On the other hand, it was decidedly different in that it sought to bring into being an entirely new political experiment—government by the proletariat and an accompanying oppression of the former ruling classes. Moreover the fledgling Soviet regime at first openly sought to export its revolution and effect such revolutionary changes in all countries.

It was certainly not lost on observers of the Bolshevik Revolution and of other Communist-inspired disturbances in the post–First World War period, most prominently in Hungary, that Jews were prominent among the Communist revolutionary leadership. Indeed, Jonathan Frankel points out that for eastern European Jews at the turn of the twentieth century, "their formative years [were] indelibly stamped by the revolutionary experience in the Russian Empire."[5] It was equally well known that there were groups of Russian Jewish radicals—both Communist and non-Communist—in London and elsewhere in the Western world.[6] Moreover, with so many Bolsheviks of Jewish origin in positions of leadership in the early Soviet Communist Party, it was easy for many casual observers to think that all Communists were Jews and all Jews were Communists.[7] In 1919 the American Jewish leader Louis Marshall remarked, "What I greatly deplore is the fact that whenever anyone discusses Bolshevism, the first thing that comes to his lips are that Jews are to be found among the Bolsheviki."[8] As historian Jerry Muller points out, "because the Communist party did not have a broad popular base … even if a tiny proportion of Jews was attracted to Communism, the party appeared 'Jewish.'"[9] Moreover, for those who were inclined to think the worst of Jews, in the immediate postwar period nothing seemed as bad as Communism. Hence Communism had to be "Jewish."[10]

Certainly many people in the British government and elite in 1917, such as Lord Sydenham, believed that Jews backed the Bolshevik Revolution.[11] Even a British statesman like Winston Churchill, who was personally remote from antisemitism, regarded Bolshevism as a disease of the Jewish body politic.[12] As Churchill stated, "The international Jews, the adherents of this sinister confederacy … have become practically the undisputed masters of that enormous empire."[13]

Others, who tended to think of Jews more directly as the enemies of Christian civilization, quickly concluded that Bolshevism was little more than a malignant transmutation of the essence of the Jewish soul.[14] In Canada, these sentiments connecting Jews and Bolshevism were echoed. Denunciations of "foreigners" who were attempting to import the Bolshevik Revolution to Canada were numerous.[15] Newspapers like the *Toronto Telegram* frequently equated Jews and Bolsheviks.[16] Abbé Nadeau, writing in Quebec City's *L'Action Catholique*, denounced the Judeo-Masonic coalition that controlled the revolution.[17] So did communities of anti-Communist Ukrainians and Mennonites in western Canada who provided audiences for speakers who claimed that 90 percent of Soviet commissars were Jews.[18]

Many of those who viewed the Russian Revolution and its aftermath with dismay found plausibility in the antisemitic forgery *Protocols of the Elders of Zion*, which portrayed the Jews as plotting to undermine Christian civilization.[19] *The Protocols* achieved its first mass notoriety

in the postwar period. As Arthur Goldwag comments: "In 1920, when
the *Protocols* first exploded into general view, the established order of
the Old World was literally coming apart at the seams ... There was a
disturbingly widespread consensus that the Jews—not just overt revolutionaries like Trotsky but plutocrats like the Rothschilds in Europe and
Paul Warburg and Jacob Schiff in the United States—were responsible
for the Russian Revolution."[20]

The Winnipeg General Strike

Canada, like the United States, experienced a major wave of xenophobia
and paranoia in the period following the Bolshevik Revolution, and for
many observers at the time, the Jews constituted nothing less than a cadre
of revolutionaries out to undermine Canadian society as a whole.[21] This
was particularly so in the aftermath of the 1919 General Strike in Winnipeg in which militant workers seemed for a time to threaten an actual
takeover of the reins of power in a major Canadian city. The Winnipeg
General Strike, like the Boston Police Strike of the same year, appeared
to form part of a wide pattern of potentially revolutionary labour unrest
in North America. Responsibility for the Winnipeg General Strike was
widely attributed by many in authority to Jews, who were believed to be
bent on the revolutionary destruction of Canadian society and all it stood
for.[22] In the aftermath of the General Strike, an agent of the Royal Canadian Mounted Police, which had been assigned to investigate "radicals,"
made the claim that rich Jews had financially supported the strikers and
that, in doing so, they were fulfilling a mission for the "higher up Bolsheviks." Winnipeg police magistrate Hugh John Macdonald also claimed
that a large section of Jews "had Bolsheviki ideas."[23] Colonel J.P. Rattray,
commissioner of the Manitoba Provincial Police, charged in 1922 that
Jews were plotting with the Japanese and the Prussians to destroy Christian civilization.[24] It is in this atmosphere of fear and uncertainty that
legislation, known popularly as "Section 98," was passed by the Canadian
Parliament. "Section 98" amended the Canadian Criminal Code to make
it a criminal offence, with a maximum penalty of twenty years in prison,
to be a member of, or even attend a meeting of a group that advocated
the use of force to bring about a change in the government of Canada.[25]

Jews and the Communist Party of Canada

The numerous Canadians who shared the idea that Jews were behind the revolutionaries seeking to undermine the Canadian way of life were able to point to the undeniable fact that Jews were prominent in the Communist Party of Canada and that there were people readily identifiable as Jews who believed in the remaking of Canada on Communist principles.[26] It is fair to say that among many Canadians of this period there existed a general attitude that, while perhaps most Jews were not Communists, many, or even all Communists were in fact Jews.[27] The simplistic conflation of Jews and Bolsheviks thus became common among many Canadians.[28] Where those who accepted the Jewish conspiratorial message of the *Protocols* went beyond this general opinion was in their belief that the Jews were in fact the main cause as well as the directors of the entire international Communist conspiracy.[29] This attitude can be seen in the words of Solon Low, a leader of the Alberta Social Credit movement. Low's 1946 anti-Jewish statement ties together all of these elements:

> Do you know that the same group of international gangsters who are today scheming for world revolution are the same people who promoted the world war? Do you know that these same men promoted and financed the Russian revolution? Are you aware that these arch-criminals were responsible for the economic chaos and suffering of the hungry thirties, for financing Hitler to power, for promoting World War Two with its tragic carnage? Do you know that there is a close tie-up between international communism, international finance and international political Zionism?[30]

Many members of the Social Credit Party, which came to power in Alberta in the 1930s, basically accepted the antisemitic positions taken by the founder of the Social Credit movement, Major Douglas. Though prominent leaders within the Alberta Social Credit Party, like William Aberhart and Ernest Manning, publicly repudiated these positions, others, like Social Credit members of Parliament Norman Jacques and John Blackmore publicly expressed these antisemitic sentiments in the House of Commons and elsewhere. In particular, Norman Jacques, who, like many of the antisemitic personalities cited in this book, did not think of himself as an antisemite,[31] alleged that because nearly all Jews were Communists, their attempt to raise the "bogey" of antisemitism was really nothing more than a "communist smokescreen."[32]

It is evident that the broad spectrum of mainstream Canadian political figures in the interwar period opposed Communism. It is equally fair to say that they often had Jews as Communists in mind when they made some of their policy recommendations. This is clearly illustrated by the 1930 Jewish school issue in Quebec politics. We have seen in the previous chapter that in that year the Quebec government enacted legislation to address the anomaly of the Jewish presence in the province's Protestant schools by creating a Jewish School Board. While there was vehement public opposition to granting a separate school board for Jews in Montreal from a variety of people and for numerous reasons, one of the reasons had to do with the widespread notion that Jews were a prime source for the Communist subversion of the Canadian system. Thus the Archbishop of Quebec, Cardinal Félix-Raymond-Marie Rouleau, wrote Quebec Premier Louis-Alexandre Taschereau that if there were to be a Jewish School Committee, there would be no guarantee "against the encroachments of Bolshevik propaganda, when even with the current provisions for supervision it is said that there are Jewish—or Russian Jewish—schools with Bolshevik tendencies in this very province."[33] In this statement, Rouleau was echoing the sentiments expressed by his colleague, the primate of Poland, Cardinal August Hlond, that "it is a fact that the Jews fight against the Catholic Church, they are freethinkers, and constitute the vanguard of atheism, bolshevism and revolution."[34] This attitude on the part of the Quebec Catholic Church hierarchy doubtless informed its decision to recruit the antisemitic journalist Adrien Arcand to oppose the Jewish school board legislation, which marked the real start of Arcand's long career of antisemitic journalism and activism.[35] French Canadian nationalist leader Lionel Groulx demonstrated that he shared this attitude toward Jews as Communists when he wrote, "Many reputable authors believe that … [Jews] cultivate [Communists] in larger quantities than others, and this gives us sufficient grounds for wariness."[36] André Laurendeau, leader of the Jeune Canada movement likewise wrote in Le Devoir of April 27, 1933, that the Jews constituted a social danger to the country because of their internationalism and their Communism.[37]

Communism, along with other societal ills like chain stores, department stores, high finance, and the burden of mortgages, were often popularly blamed by French Canadians on the Jews.[38]

It is apparent, therefore, that the issue of Communism often impinged largely on relations between Canadian Jews and their neighbours in Quebec during the interwar period, even though the absolute number of Jewish Communists in the province was relatively small. Thus it is estimated that there were only some sixty Communist Party activists in Quebec in 1928, of whom some were certainly French or English Canadians.[39] Despite these small numbers, however, Jews had become so identified with Communists that in a meeting of Jews and French Canadians in the 1930s, the Jewish participants were pointedly asked the question, Why are so many Jews Communists?[40]

In the case of Quebec, the relationship between the government and Communism was particularly fraught. In 1935, the Canadian federal government had repealed article 98 of the Criminal Code, under which, as has already been stated, membership in a "revolutionary" organization or even attending a meeting of such an association was considered a criminal offence.[41] However in Quebec in 1937 the provincial legislature, at the urging of Premier Maurice Duplessis and with the approval of Cardinal Villeneuve,[42] enacted an Act Concerning Communist Propaganda, popularly known as the "padlock law." This law allowed police to close any house, school, or building used by Communists to spread their propaganda. This legislation was widely used against leftist unions, political groups,[43] and even cultural events by Communist-linked groups such as the United Jewish People's Order.[44] In this atmosphere of great suspicion, even labour organizations that were decidedly anti-Communist in their politics, such as the International Ladies Garment Workers Union, were perceived as part of a plot by "international Jewry."[45]

Adrien Arcand

The same Jewish School Commission Bill of 1930 that had created grave concern among those who feared the spread of Communist influence by Jews in Quebec gave antisemite Adrien Arcand the impetus to begin his virulent campaign against Jews in his publication *Le Goglu*. One of the major themes in Arcand's antisemitic publications was the connection between Jews and Communism. Arcand thus described the Russian Communist leader, Vladimir Ilyich Lenin, as a man of "Judeo-Mongol origin" who spoke fluent Yiddish and who had declared the Jewish Sabbath as the official day of rest in Soviet Russia.[46] He also sought to use the Communist issue as a springboard for an assault on the legal status of Jews in Canada, thus going beyond the bound of "respectable" French Canadian journalistic opposition to Jews.[47]

While Arcand shared a fear of Communism with many other French Canadians, he came to his opposition to "the Jews" from a somewhat different direction. He was also an admirer of Nazism in Germany and of its leader, Adolf Hitler. He similarly admired Italian fascism and its leader, Benito Mussolini. Arcand was not alone in his admiration of Mussolini. The pride felt by many Italian Canadians in what Mussolini had done for his country was carefully cultivated by the Italian consular corps in Canada.[48] The fact that Mussolini was ultimately supported by the papacy also gained him support in French Canada.[49]

The juxtaposition of pro-Nazism, pro-fascism, and anti-Communism found in Arcand's thinking is not accidental. It was in fact central to Nazi mythology. As Muller points out: "The myth of Jew as Bolshevik ... became central to the Nazi program of ideological anti-Semitism, and helped inspire the collaboration of non-Germans throughout eastern Europe in that program's murderous execution during World War II."[50] Thus, insofar as anti-Communists saw in fascism the most effective opposition to the Communist menace, many of them tended to give support to fascist causes in the 1930s.[51] Thus *L'Action Catholique* remarked editorially that while Adolf Hitler may have made mistakes, he had saved Germany from falling to the Communists, many of whom, in Germany as in Russia, were Jews.[52] Arcand tried to harness this anti-Communist and anti-Jewish sentiment to further his cause. In the public meetings he organized, in the newspapers he edited— which included, at various times, *Le Goglu, Le Miroir,* and *Le Chameau*—as well as in his organizations, notably l'Ordre des Goglus, the Parti national social Chrétien (1934), and the Parti de l'unité nationale (1938),[53] Arcand concentrated largely on "the Jewish problem," spreading fear and hatred of Jews.[54]

The influence of Arcand's antisemitic propaganda can be illustrated by the following incident. In the course of the 1931 Quebec provincial election, Dr. Raoul Poulin, a candidate for the Conservative Party in a rural riding, brought up the accusation that the Talmud commands Jews to kill Christian children, and when a passing Jewish peddler attempted to protest, he was barely saved from an angry mob.[55]

Of all Canadian antisemites of his era, Adrien Arcand was probably the most notorious. He was, in short, a man for whom antisemitism had become practically a religion.[56] He wrote in a 1933 pamphlet: "Jewry because of its very essence, because of its destructive instincts, because of its ancient atavism of corruption, because of its exclusively materialist feelings, constitutes the real danger for the peoples whether materially or spiritually. This is why the Jewish Question needs to be at the foundation of any true fascism, of any serious movement of national regeneration."[57] Arcand further wrote: "Jews are like cockroaches and bugs. When you see one you can be sure that there are dozens around, and when you see a few around in the cities and in all the streets don't be fooled. There are more around. It is too bad we cannot exterminate them with insecticide."[58] It was clear to Arcand, whose publications often reprinted the virulently anti-Jewish images and texts of the German Nazi periodical *Der Stürmer*,[59] that there was no crime that the Jews were not capable of and that they did not actually commit. Thus Arcand alleged that the notorious kidnapping of the child of Charles and Anna Lindbergh in 1937 had been committed by Jews seeking to use the child's blood in Jewish rituals.[60]

In the 1930s Arcand developed a noticeable following in Quebec, and, to a lesser extent, in the rest of Canada. The number of his followers may have been relatively small, but they were considered a potentially dangerous force and were thus investigated by agents of the Royal Canadian Mounted Police who had hitherto confined their reporting to leftist threats to Canada's security. RCMP reports in the late 1930s indicated that Arcand's supporters were in the process of infiltrating factories and government agencies. In particular, it was reported that at the Montreal customs house pro-fascist activities took place quite openly.[61] By the late 1930s, Arcand's political organization le Parti de l'Unité Nationale boasted approximately 6,000 members, of whom 5,000 were in Quebec, and the movement gained considerable publicity in Canada as well as in the United States.[62] Arcand attempted to go beyond his base in Quebec and to create links with pro-Nazi groups in other parts of Canada. He thus spoke to a large crowd in Massey Hall in Toronto in 1938.[63] The audience that came to hear his message in Massey Hall presumably came from among those who had joined the Ontario "Swastika Clubs" that had arisen to declare that certain public beaches in the Toronto area should be free of Jews.[64]

Pro-Nazi Sentiment in Canada

Arcand could draw support from other groups in Canada in the 1930s. As early as 1933, pro-Nazi pamphlets were being widely distributed in Toronto.[65] Louis Rosenberg, writing in 1939, identified numerous antisemitic and fascist groups in Quebec, Ontario, Manitoba, Saskatchewan, British Columbia, and the Maritime provinces that had sprung up in Canada since the Nazi takeover of Germany in 1933.[66] Other than Arcand, perhaps the best-known Canadian Nazi sympathizer was William Whittaker in Winnipeg, who was responsible for the publication of the newspaper the *Canadian Nationalist* as well as small-scale violence on the streets of Winnipeg as Whittaker's men confronted their leftist and Jewish opponents. Whittaker's movement received considerable support from strongly anti-Soviet Mennonites in western Canada.[67] As well, many Canadians of German origin, particularly in western Canada, had become enthusiastic supporters of Hitler.[68]

In the Canada of the 1930s, one did not need to be a devotee of fascism or Nazism to have positive views of either Nazi Germany or its leader. Canadians in this era experienced a relentless pro-German and anti-Jewish propaganda campaign inspired (and perhaps funded) by Nazis that had a definite influence on public opinion and discourse within Canada. No less than the prime minister of Canada, William Lyon Mackenzie King, visited Adolf Hitler in 1937 and was favourably impressed with him. [69] As King wrote in his diary: "I am convinced he [Hitler] is a spiritualist—that he has a vision to which he is being true ... I believe that the world will yet come to see a very great man-mystic in Hitler ... His dictatorship is a means to an end ... much I cannot abide in Nazism—the regimentation—cruelty—oppression of Jews ... but Hitler ... will rank some day with Joan of Arc among the deliverers of his people."[70]

Canadian Jews saw these developments and grew afraid. As the *Canadian Jewish Chronicle* stated in an editorial, "Nor are we sure that the brand of anti-Semitism in Quebec is any less virulent than that of Germany. The dynamite is here, merely waiting for a Canadian Hitler to explode it."[71]

There were many other discouraging straws in the wind for those Canadians who sought to arouse sympathy and support for the persecuted Jews of Germany. Powerful forces in society seemed massed against them. Zionist leader Chaim Weizmann in 1936 aptly expressed the plight of world Jewry, particularly that of the increasing numbers of Jewish refugees from Nazism, when he said that "the world seems to be divided in two parts—those places where the Jew cannot live, and those where they cannot enter."[72] Fear of a coming war in the late 1930s did not necessarily result in support for the increasing number of Jewish refugees from Nazism. In December 1938, the Anglo-Canadian press magnate Lord Beaverbrook described the "big position" the Jews had in the press and then stated: "The Jews may drive us into war ... Their political influence is moving us in that direction."[73]

Nazi Persecution of Jews: Canadian Reactions

At the moment when Jews and their Christian sympathizers in Canada were decrying the plight of persecuted German Jewry, they were met with press reports like those published in the *Toronto Evening Telegram* in 1933 that asserted that anti-Jewish terror in Germany was much exaggerated.[74] When Jewish leaders in Montreal organized a protest rally against Nazi anti-Jewish atrocities, they were met by a counter-demonstration in April 1933 organized by André Laurendeau, leader of Jeune Canada, which rebuked those French Canadian politicians who had shown sympathy for the plight of the Jews in Germany.[75] Laurendeau and his organization made this counter-protest because of Laurendeau's belief, obviously influenced by the antisemitic ideas that were commonplace in this era, that "the Israelites aspire—everyone knows this—one happy day when their race will dominate the world,"[76] and that the persecution of the Jews in Germany was a pretence put forward by the Jews for their own purposes.[77]

These same sentiments, which had also animated the anti-Jewish actions of antisemitic students in France,[78] inspired a group of students from the Université de Montréal to demonstrate against the Jews on Montreal's St. Catherine Street on September 29, 1933.[79] Rowdy anti-Communist riots by these students in which antisemitic slogans were heard as well, also took place in October 1936.[80] Similar antisemitic outbreaks occurred in 1942 in the midst of the referendum campaign over the issue of conscription of Canadian men for overseas military service. A meeting of the anti-conscription League for the Defense of Canada, of which Laurendeau was a leader, resounded with cries of "down with the Jews." Laurendeau later claimed that the antisemitic manifestations at the meeting were met with a strong protest from the podium by an Ontario labour leader, Landon Ladd. According to Laurendeau, Ladd's protest got a round of applause from the crowd that was, however, not mentioned in any newspaper report. Laurendeau also attributed these anti-Jewish slogans to Adrien Arcand's followers, who had come to the meeting he had organized solely in order to make trouble.[81] He further claimed that it was Arcand's people, and not his supporters, who subsequently demonstrated on Saint-Laurent Boulevard, scuffling with young Jews and smashing windows of Jewish shops.[82] One of the people who participated in that riot was a medical student at the Université de Montréal, Jean-Louis Roux, who was to become Quebec's lieutenant-governor and was forced to resign after admitting he wore a Nazi swastika as a youngster. Roux admitted drawing a swastika on his lab coat in 1942 as a pre-medical student and participating as a nineteen-year-old in an anti-conscription protest which degenerated into vandalism against shops believed to be owned by Jews. Roux attributed his actions to youthful bravado and stated that he was not a Nazi supporter.[83]

Laurendeau himself began to have second thoughts about the Jewish issue when he visited Europe in the mid-1930s and publicly expressed regret for his beliefs much later.[84] Looking back on his actions as leader of Jeune Canada in 1933, Laurendeau claimed: "I can remember to the last detail how we got the idea for each of our political meetings, except for that one in particular, which we baptized "Politicians and Jews" ... But we held it just the same, because a cloud of anti-Semitism had polluted the atmosphere ... everyone was looking for a scapegoat."[85]

The cloud of antisemitism referred to by Laurendeau was acutely felt by Canadian Jewish Congress official H.M. Caiserman. Caiserman expressed contemporary Jewish community fears of antisemitism, particularly in the light of the ascendance of Nazi Germany, in the following way: "The most frightening development in Canada during the 1930s was the transition from sporadic and unorganized types of anti-Semitism to organized activities sponsored by national organizations directed by professional agents of Nazi Germany."[86]

Canadian Jews in the 1930s saw a stark analogy between themselves and the Jews in Germany, especially with respect to Quebec. The cry went out from a Jewish member of the Ontario legislature: "Unless something is done quickly, the Jewish people may well meet the same fate in Canada that the Jews are meeting in Germany ... No fire is so easily kindled as anti-Semitism. The fire is dormant in Canada, it has not yet blazed up, but the spark is there. Germany is not the only place with prejudice. Look at Quebec."[87]

In 1936, the editors of *Fortune* magazine published a book on the Jews in America which stated that "leading members of the Jewish community in the United States—men who had previously looked to the future with complete confidence—have been shocked into fear."[88] A 1937 Canadian Jewish Congress report reiterated this perspective: "During the past four years an entirely new type of antisemitism has assumed prominence in this country. There has been a transition from the sporadic and unorganized type of anti-Jewishness to national organizations directed by professional agents. It is this professional aspect of anti-Semitism which has given an entirely new status to anti-Jewish functions, has aroused unprecedentedly anti-Jewish feeling, and has brought the Jewish community face to face with a situation somewhat familiar: the situation of Germany in the early years of the Nazi movement."[89]

During the Second World War

When Canadian Jews attempted to respond to the charges brought against their community by antisemites, they were met with distrust. Antisemites tried to delegitimize the statements and arguments of Jewish authorities in their fight against racism as being made by "special interests."[90] Thus in 1943, when the magnitude of Hitler's Final Solution of the "Jewish Problem" was just beginning to impinge on public consciousness, a *Le Devoir* editorial commented on the magnitude of the catastrophe but wondered whether "the Jews are not exaggerating these numbers in an oriental or Talmudic fashion."[91] In the same year, H.M. Caiserman of the Canadian Jewish Congress wrote to the editor of the *Victoria-Inverness Bulletin* (Truro, NS): "We have read your editorial in your issue of December 25, 1942 entitled 'Fantastic Fallacy' with a great deal of interest. We feel that your reaction towards the report of the massacres of Jews in Europe is a very natural one; decent men are inclined to dismiss as incredible reports from however responsible sources that any organized society of mankind can perpetrate such tremendous crimes on an incredibly large scale."[92] In English Canada, the *United Church Observer*, in a similar fashion, acknowledged the enormity of the destruction of European Jewry in its issue of September 15, 1944, but admitted that it had previously been reluctant to accept at face value the anti-Jewish atrocities perpetrated by the Nazis "perhaps ... because we were defending ourselves against propaganda."[93]

These ideas were taken to an extreme by certain elements within the Alberta Social Credit movement during the war. Jews were accused of being Communist conspirators who were able to extend their activities in North America under the cover of their refugee status. Jews were accused ultimately of being behind Germany's war against the Allies, and it was the Jews who were to blame for the Holocaust, which was essentially a Jewish fabrication.[94]

During the Second World War, in which Canadians found themselves fighting on the side of the Allied powers against Nazi Germany, antisemitism in Canada did not cease. On the contrary, Watson Kirkconnell, a prominent Canadian Baptist, noted that "Anti-Semitism is still being vigorously propagated. The Toronto police have had to deal with pretended drunks who systematically boarded street-cars and proclaimed in loud and inebriated tones that: 'Of course the Jews are behind this war. Their motto is "Onward Christian soldiers.""'[95]

These attempts to discredit the Jews for being the cause of the war and for not doing their share of the fighting were often repeated during the Second World War.[96] There were reports of discrimination against Jews in enlisting in certain units of the military and in certain sectors of the war industry.[97] During the war anti-Jewish tropes were heard in Quebec political campaigns in which the provincial Liberals were derided as Jew lovers in the newspaper *Le Bloc* with the slogan "A vote for Godboutsky [Quebec Liberal leader Adélard Godbout] is a vote for Abraham, Isaac and Jacob."[98]

Attempts at Legal Redress

In response to the grave charges and prejudices laid against them, Jews in Canada attempted to utilize the political process to create laws against spreading such hatred against them or other identifiable groups. These efforts, predictably, ran into problems.

In response to Adrien Arcand's antisemitic libels of the early 1930s, the two Jewish members of the Quebec Legislative Assembly, Peter Bercovitch and Joseph Cohen, introduced a bill in the legislature against "the publication and distribution of outrageous subject matter against any religious sect, creed, class, denomination, race, or nationality" that was clearly aimed at Arcand's publications.[99] The legislation received extensive criticism in the Quebec press, both French and English, and there appeared little support for the bill outside the Jewish community. In the end, Liberal Premier Louis-Alexandre Taschereau, while strongly condemning antisemitism, announced that he could not support the bill and that the proper redress for Arcand's diatribes was through the courts. The bill thus died in committee.[100]

The Jewish community then looked to the courts. A 1932 test case (*Abugov v. Menard*), however, proved that existing law did not give Jews adequate recourse. The judge vigorously condemned the defendants, calling Arcand's publications "anti-Christian, anti-social, and anti-national," but lamented the fact that he lacked legal authority to issue more than a moral injunction.[101] Premier Taschereau then prepared an amendment to the Quebec Civil Code dealing with issues of hate speech directed against identifiable groups only to withdraw it when Arcand's newspapers stopped publication due to bankruptcy in 1933.[102]

In 1932, John J. Glass, an Ontario Liberal MPP, wanted to introduce legislation in the provincial legislature that would make the slandering of groups illegal on the same basis as slandering individuals, but he was persuaded not to introduce his bill.[103] In the same year, E. Frederick Singer, another member of the Ontario Legislature representing the heavily Jewish riding of St. Andrews, introduced a bill to prohibit discrimination in the granting of insurance policies "which discriminates unfairly between risks ... because of the race or religion of the insured." This bill passed and has the merit of being the first human rights legislation adopted in Canada.[104] In 1937, Glass again attempted to introduce legislation protecting against group libel but was persuaded to withdraw the bill.[105] The Ontario Racial Discrimination Act, which prohibited the publication of anything that advocated racial discrimination, would be passed only in 1944.[106]

In 1934 the Manitoba legislature passed the "Hyman Bill," named after Marcus Hyman, which was the first successful group anti-defamation legislation in Canada. With the full support of the Manitoba government, the opposition, and the local mainstream press, this legislation allowed legal action against "any person, firm, or corporation directly or indirectly responsible for the authorship, publication, and circulation of such libel," which was defined as "the repeated publication of a libel against any race or creed likely to expose persons belonging to such race or professing such creed to hatred, contempt, or ridicule."[107] That which had been tried and failed to pass in Quebec and Ontario was now successful in Manitoba.[108] As we have seen, however, the goodwill inherent in the legislation, and its successful application in a test case in Winnipeg against William Whittaker's publication the *Canadian Nationalist*[109] did not seem to relieve the gloomy atmosphere within the Jewish community, which was afraid because of the plight of Jews abroad and traumatized because of continuing assaults on their probity and character from within Canada.

In the final analysis, there seems to be a scholarly consensus that, however vicious Canadian antisemitic movements were in the inter-war period, particularly but not exclusively in Quebec, there existed no unified and effective antisemitic movement with actual political power. Though antisemites like Adrien Arcand and William Whittaker no doubt dreamed of the day when Jews' rights as Canadian citizens and British subjects were limited, this was never a realistic possibility in interwar Canada.[110] Nonetheless, it can be said that antisemitism was part of the climate of opinion existing in Canada that—directly or indirectly—made it virtually impossible for Canada's political leadership to materially aid the multitude of European Jews put in harm's way by Hitler's "final solution" when that aid became literally a matter of life or death.[111]

PART FOUR

POSTWAR CANADA (1945–PRESENT)

CHAPTER SEVEN

Canada and Antisemitism in the Second Half of the Twentieth Century

Canadians as well as all other people of the world have to be told, and told again, what gruesome savagery Nazism had reached and what unbelievable, inhuman, monstrous crimes were committed against our people.

—J.B. Salsberg[1]

This chapter will discuss general trends in attitudes toward Jews in Canada from the end of the Second World War in 1945 until the beginning of the twenty-first century. The next two chapters will deal more specifically with issues related to the impact of the Holocaust and its denial (chapter 8) and the impact of the State of Israel and the Israel–Arab conflict (chapter 9) on the phenomenon of antisemitism in Canada. Finally, chapter 10 will be devoted to a discussion of issues and approaches to antisemitism in twenty-first-century Canada.

The period after the Second World War was crucial for the development of Canada as a nation with a strong sense of itself. It is in this era in particular that Canada emerged as a country that was no longer in the shadow of Great Britain and that had definitively made a place for itself among the nations of the world. In the postwar era as well, Canadians began to acquire a much clearer sense of their own developing literature, culture, and history, which led to a stronger appreciation for the country's cultural and linguistic diversity.

It was in the postwar period that Canadian Jews came to a certain maturity and sense of themselves as a community. The first factor that facilitated this process was that the generation of Jews that had emigrated to Canada at the turn of the twentieth century with nearly

empty pockets had, by the 1940s, largely established itself economically, socially, and communally. Another major factor that spurred the
development of Canadian Jewry was the full revelation at the end of the
war of the magnitude of the systematic destruction of European Jews by
Nazi Germany that would become known as the Holocaust. The Nazi
destruction of six million Jews, along with their communities and institutions, meant that the Jews of Canada were called upon in the postwar
period as never before to aid their stricken overseas brethren. The task
before them was to try to bring as many of them as possible to a country
that had throughout the war remained mostly indifferent to the Jewish refugees' cries for help.[2] Canadian Jewry's efforts ultimately resulted
in a major postwar immigration of Jewish Holocaust survivors to Canada, an immigration that was to highly influence the development of
the Canadian Jewish community.[3] Nonetheless, even in the period after
1948, when the doors of Canada were once more opened to large-scale
immigration, Jews did not constitute more than a small percentage of
the total immigration to Canada.[4]

Canadian Jews in the immediate postwar era also needed to respond
to the challenging call of the *Yishuv* (Jewish community) of British-
mandated Palestine to aid in the struggle to create and sustain the Jewish homeland promised in the Balfour Declaration. The result of this
effort was the creation of the State of Israel in May 1948, an event that
was to have an immense impact on all Canadian Jews.

Postwar Public Opinion and the Jews

The Jews of Canada took on both of these major tasks while at the same
time engaging in a struggle with the significant heritage of negative Canadian attitudes toward Jews and Judaism that had still not disappeared
with Canada's September 1939 declaration of war on Nazi Germany. By
the end of the war in 1945, public attitudes toward Jews across Canada
had seemingly not really changed from the decided negativity that had
characterized the prewar Dominion. Thus fairly soon after the war was
over, a public opinion poll in Canada asked respondents to compare and
rank potential immigrants to Canada. The poll results indicated that

Canadians seemed to prefer almost any type of immigrant—including their erstwhile enemies, the Germans—to Jews.[5] Similar results could be gleaned from a Canadian Gallup poll, taken in October 1946, which indicated that almost half (49 percent) of the respondents held negative views of Jews. In that poll, only the Japanese at 60 percent were higher in negative evaluation than the Jews.[6] These negative attitudes in Canada were similar to the results of concurrent polling in the United States. A US survey indicated that respondents' belief in a "Jewish threat" rose to a peak in June 1944,[7] and Jews polled consistently higher than Germans and Japanese as a "menace" to the country.[8] The results of these polls were noted by Lord Halifax, the British ambassador to the United States, who reported to his government that "the United States is so strongly anti-Semitic that anti-Semitism at home is an ever present problem for every American Jew."[9] Indeed, as late as the mid-1950s, North American pollsters remained aware of a substantial negativity toward Jews. For example, a 1955 survey in the United States showed that many respondents would strongly object to having a Jewish neighbour.[10]

Harassment

Jews in Canada felt much the same sentiment from their non-Jewish neighbours. As a rule, they continued to live in a profoundly Jewish solitude, both by choice as well as for reasons of exclusion.[11] In those years, many Canadian Jewish children faced similar issues of bullying and social exclusion as those faced by Jewish children in the interwar era. Lynda Lemberg, born in Oshawa, Ontario in 1950 thus recalls: "My experiences of being chased en route to school … by stone-throwing, insult-slinging youths were transformed into recurring nightmares … I remember the confusion and searing pain when a classmate explained to me that I couldn't come to her home for lunch or she to mine because I was a Jew."[12] Bernie Farber also remembers: "As a young boy growing up in Ottawa in the 1950s and '60s, it was at times a tough place to be Jewish. Often I was one of only a couple of Jewish children in my school and the religious-based anti-Semitism was in your face. Anti-Jewish taunts leading to schoolyard fights were almost a daily occurrence."[13]

Postwar Prospects for Jewish Immigration to Canada

If public opinion toward Jews in Canada had seemingly not changed much since the thirties, the same could be said for the short-term prospects of the immigration to Canada of those who had survived the Nazi plan to create a "Final Solution" to the "Jewish Problem" in Europe. In the period immediately after the war, stringent Canadian restrictions on Jewish immigration, which had made certain that Canada received relatively few Jewish immigrants in the 1930s,[14] remained largely in place, though there was definitely a bit more "give" in the system. Thus, in 1948, when an orphaned Holocaust survivor's application to join her relatives in Canada was denied, Manitoba CCF Member of Parliament Stanley Knowles investigated. The Canadian official who had refused her application allegedly told Knowles, "We don't want any more of these people, you know." However, when Knowles threatened to raise the case in Question Period in the House of Commons and to quote the official by name, the visa was hastily approved.[15]

Ironically, at that time it seemed to be easier for Germans and former European fascists to enter Canada than Jews.[16] Thus immediately after the war, the Canadian government became a compliant partner in a British-American plan to settle German scientists in Canada so as to keep them out of Soviet hands. A number of French collaborators with the Nazis, including Count Jacques de Bernonville, condemned for war crimes during the Vichy regime in France, as well as Jacques Duge and Georges-Benoît Montel, both associated with Klaus Barbie's atrocities in Lyons, were brought illegally to Quebec in the late 1940s. They were allegedly protected and supported by a number of prominent French Canadians including Montreal mayor Camilien Houde, historian Robert Rumilly, Father Lionel Groulx, Louis St. Laurent, and Maurice Duplessis.[17] Esther Delisle asserts that the Canadian embassy in Paris was connected with this escape operation.[18]

Perception of Change for the Better

Despite this lingering negativity, the Canadian Jewish community was able to see some evidence of change for the better. In 1947, for example, a Canadian poll found that 64 percent of those surveyed approved of legislation designed to combat discrimination in employment, and the positive percentage actually increased when Jews were specified in the question as opposed to the original group-neutral "race, colour, or religion."[19] Another positive sign was the public opposition to prejudice against Jews in Canadian society in mainstream Canadian periodicals such as *Maclean's*, in parallel with major exposés against antisemitism appearing in the United States, such as the award-winning film *Gentleman's Agreement* (1947).[20] In the November 1, 1948, issue of *Maclean's*, Pierre Berton published an exposé of anti-Jewish job discrimination in Canada while noting that a "rash of books, plays, movies, and radio broadcasts" were appearing that condemned antisemitism.[21]

In the postwar era, the public status of Judaism in North America continued to undergo a transformation and came to be considered part of the established North American "Judeo-Christian" religious mainstream along with the Protestant and Catholic churches.[22] This change did not happen without a struggle, however. Prior to the war, many people commonly referred to the "Christian" civilization of Canada, and there is considerable evidence of a continuation of this feeling well into the 1950s. Public education in Ontario and Quebec was still decidedly identified as Christian. In 1950 a controversy arose over the propriety of Jewish children being required to sing Christmas carols and recite the Lord's Prayer in Ontario schools, observances that marked the Christian character of public instruction in that province. Public opinion in this case was mostly opposed to the Jewish protest. Toronto's *Globe and Mail* seemed to summarize the majority opinion when it stated in an editorial: "Nobody should ask [the majority] to give up their right to be Christians in the full expression of that word, just to avoid the minority's feelings."[23]

The Canadian Jewish Congress, ever vigilant in its campaign against all manifestations of antisemitism in Canada, acknowledged in January 1946 that "overt acts of anti-Semitism are rarer today than they have been."[24] The very next year, the Congress published an article in its *Bulletin* of May 30 indicating a subtle but distinct change for the better in the relationship between French Canadians and Jews:

Since ... January 1945 there has been a series of developments whose import cannot be exaggerated. This is not to say that racial or religious prejudice has disappeared from this part of Canada any more than from any other part. Nor is it implied that there has been a volte face or a

change of policy or of doctrine among this section of the Canadian people. Rather might it be said that the friends whom we have always had
among them [French Canadians] have become more active in the presentation of their views ... The change has been great although its symptoms
are intangible.[25]

It is also important to note that the onset of the Cold War in the
mid-1940s and the consequent suspicion of all things Communist in
North America did not seem to adversely affect the Jews. This occurred
despite the fact that in the prewar period many Canadians attempted
to make an issue of Jewish support of Communism,[26] despite the fact
that Jews continued to constitute a recognizably large group within the
Canadian Communist Party through the 1950s,[27] and despite the efforts
by the radical right in Canada to brand prominent Canadian Jews, such
as Toronto Rabbi Abraham Feinberg, as Communist.[28]

Yet another sign of a positive shift in public opinion was the 1947 passage in Saskatchewan of a law outlawing discrimination on the basis of
race or religion.[29] Not only was discrimination against Jews now against
the law, but many areas in professional life that had been closed to Jews
were now opening up. For example, 1948 saw the appointment of the
first Jewish lawyer to the Council of the Montreal Bar, while 1950 saw
the first Jewish judicial appointment in Quebec.[30] In sum, Saul Hayes
of the Canadian Jewish Congress was able to report in May 1949 that
"antisemitism does not present an immediate menace to the Jewish
community today."[31]

The Impact of the Holocaust

The 1950s trend toward greater social acceptance of Jews seemed to
go hand in hand with the Canadian postwar generation's growing dis-
enchantment with antisemitism.[32] One of the major reasons for this
change in Canadian attitudes was surely the public revelation of the
enormity of the Holocaust. In 1952 André Laurendeau, who prior to
the war had been at the forefront of those who opposed Jewish immigration to Canada, stated: "After the assassination of six million Jews
under Hitler's reign, one must have a too delicate stomach to swallow
these fanatical denunciations without heaving. Such anti-Semitism is so

stupid that it turned us into philosemites."[33] To grasp the full implications of Laurendeau's statement we need to understand that attitudes in French Canada in the 1950s were changing on many issues, and that a large number of traditional assumptions were being questioned and abandoned in the years prior to the onset of Quebec's "Quiet Revolution."[34] In addition, Harold Troper reminds us that Canada as a whole, along with other Western nations, was caught up in a human rights revolution symbolized by the 1948 United Nations Universal Declaration of Human Rights.[35] All this seemed to bode well for the future of the Jewish community in Canada.

Gradually Crumbling Barriers and Persistent Discrimination

Surveys taken in the late 1940s indicated that in many areas the prewar pattern of excluding Jews from resorts and residential areas was being maintained.[36] However, by the early 1950s, "restricted" residential areas, like the Montreal suburb of Hampstead that had for more than twenty years maintained a "gentlemen's agreement" barring Jews from buying or renting homes within its boundaries began receiving an influx of Jewish homeowners. The process of integrating these neighbourhoods did not always go smoothly, however. The pioneer Jewish homeowners in Hampstead soon discovered that the local Protestant elementary school, the Hampstead School, would not admit Jewish students, and a vigorous protest was required to rectify the situation, a protest complicated by the rule that Jews were still not able to be elected as members of the Montreal Protestant school boards.[37] Not until the 1960s would Jews have the right to vote for and be elected to Montreal Protestant school boards.[38]

In the 1950s, a sociological survey of suburban Toronto found that most of the Christians who sent their children to private schools, which still severely restricted the admission of Jews, did so because they did not wish their children to be in the same class as Jews. One respondent stated, "I think that all of them [Christians] would be in private schools if the parents could afford it."[39] The same survey found a widespread tacit assumption that Jewish boys should not "date" gentile girls and that gentile boys must not "date" Jewish girls.[40] It is this attitude that provides the drama in Canadian writer Gwethalyn Graham's celebrated 1944 novel *Earth and High Heaven*, whose plot hinges on the complications of a love affair between a Jewish man and an Anglo-Canadian woman and the adamant opposition of her family to the match.[41]

There was much activity on the Canadian legal front in the immediate postwar period. In 1945 the Supreme Court of Ontario, on the basis of the 1944 Ontario Racial Discrimination Act, found restrictive covenants barring Jews and other minority groups from acquiring and owning certain properties, or the use of language referring to "Jews or other persons of objectionable nationality," to be illegal.[42] This was followed in 1950 by the decision of the Supreme Court of Canada in the case of *Noble and Wolf v. Alley* that found such "racial covenants" invalid (*ultra vires*).[43] An attempt by the Toronto-area Municipality of York Township to deny a building permit to a synagogue, recalling the notorious issue of the new synagogue to be built in Quebec City in the 1940s discussed in chapter 5, was contested by the congregation and the case resolved in favour of the synagogue in 1950.[44] Ontario's Racial Discrimination Act was followed in 1951 by the province's Fair Employment Practices Act, which banned employment discrimination in Ontario. This act put an end to such overt discrimination as requiring job applicants to specify their religion on job applications.

In 1955 a Jewish man, Nathan Phillips, ran for mayor of Toronto and won. While a Jew being elected to political office in Canada was hardly unprecedented, the election of Phillips to head Canada's then second-largest city was of special significance. During the electoral campaign, Phillips's opponent had pointedly called on Toronto voters not to elect a Jew as mayor, but that electoral strategy failed and Phillips's election marked an important stage in the transition of Toronto away from the political and economic domination of the Orange Order.[45]

Yet another positive development in these years was the weakening of the quota system that had limited the access by Jewish students to many parts of the Canadian university system. As we have previously seen, the Jewish quota at the University of Manitoba medical school, which in some years had resulted in the admission of as few as nine Jewish medical students,[46] was successfully challenged in 1944.[47] By the late 1940s, McGill University was publicly proclaiming that there was no religious discrimination in admissions.[48] Nonetheless McGill's quota system had not completely disappeared, and until the 1960s the McGill medical school continued to maintain a strict 10 percent quota on Jewish students while the University of Toronto medical school likewise kept its restriction on Jewish admissions in this period.[49]

Despite all these positive signs of Jewish social acceptance in Canada, in the 1950s antisemitism remained a recognizable feature of Canadian Jewish life. In Toronto in 1947, despite the existence of the Ontario Racial Discrimination Act, an ice rink refused to permit Blacks and Jews to enter. It took a vigorous protest by Jews and others to induce the Toronto Board of Police Commissioners to adopt a ruling which forbade racial and religious discrimination in public places.[50] In 1948 in Val Morin, Quebec, a man described as an "anti-Semitic maniac" burned down eighteen summer houses belonging to Jewish residents.[51] In 2012 a similar incident occurred in Val Morin with incidents of antisemitic vandalism at several Hasidic-owned summer cottages.[52] In the Laurentian region, Jews continued to report occasional exclusion from hotels,[53] while as late as 1960 Jews were barred from numerous Ontario resorts.[54]

In the area of employment, Jews still found it difficult to obtain positions in numerous fields. For example in Toronto in 1946 a Jewish war veteran who had obtained employment in a hardware store was dismissed at the request of customers who preferred not to be served by a Jewish salesman.[55] In education, job prospects for Jewish applicants often remained bleak. According to Saul Hayes's Canadian Jewish Congress report of May 1949, "legally there exists no basis for restrictions against the appointment of Jewish teachers. Nevertheless, Jewish applicants find it very difficult to secure appointments on the staffs of public schools in Canadian cities." Merely one example of a widespread practice can be found in Toronto's *Globe and Mail* of July 28, 1945. In that issue there appeared fifty-three classified advertisements for teachers, twenty-eight of which either specified "Protestant" as a job qualification, or asked the applicants to specify their religion.[56] The CJC report also noted that "it is common knowledge that the Medical Associations, Dental Associations and Pharmaceutical Associations do not look with great favour upon the increase of Jewish doctors, dentists, and pharmacists." The report further stated that "a study, made in Toronto in 1946 … indicated that there is not a Jewish white collar worker employed by a Toronto bank office and no Jew or Negro on the City Police Force."[57] In 1950, a study by sociologist John Porter found that there was no Jewish director in any of the nine Canadian chartered banks.[58] In 1961 Canada's banks continued to be accused of employment discrimination against Jews.[59]

Discrimination, or anticipation of discrimination, still profoundly influenced the occupation distribution of Canadian Jews. Thus, for example, into the 1950s in Toronto opportunities for Jewish lawyers at many established law firms just did not exist,[60] and "senior management positions in companies controlled by members of the predominant British or French groups [were] closed to them." This situation tends to explain, at least partially, the vocational choices of Canadian Jews, which led to the predominance of Jews in such occupations as real estate development.[61]

In mid-twentieth-century North America, membership in elite businessmen's clubs was "a major requirement for eventual assimilation into any major city's business establishment."[62] Into the 1950s, Jews in the Canadian economic elite tended not to belong to the same clubs, were not members of the important trade associations, and their philanthropic activities rarely overlapped with those of other members of the Canadian business elite.[63] Yet even in the exclusive world of elite men's clubs the situation was evolving. In 1952 the Lawyers' Club of Toronto eliminated a clause in its thirty-year-old constitution requiring its members to be "white and Christian."[64] Other such clubs followed suit more or less voluntarily. In 1964, the Rideau Club in Ottawa, which had an "informal" no-Jews policy enforced by blackballing, ended its discrimination not because of any pressure from Jews but because of an in-house revolt by younger members.[65] By the late 1960s, the Granite Club in Toronto had also eliminated discriminatory membership.[66] Harold Troper asserts that the opening of the Granite Club to Jews was symbolic because in the late 1960s the Canadian Jewish community wished to serve notice that social discrimination was no less wrong than discrimination in housing, employment, and education.[67]

Inevitably, however, there were still holdouts. As late as the 1980s anti-Jewish discrimination continued in the Manitoba Club and the St. Charles Country Club in Winnipeg[68] and another country club in Scarborough, Ontario.[69] Breaking into certain areas was still an uphill battle for Jews.

As Morton Weinfeld stated: "It remain[ed] easier for Canadian Jews to amass wealth than to rise to the top of a major public corporation. [Wa]s this the result of anti-Semitism, or simply an indirect exclusion resulting from an old boy's network?"[70] For Izzy Asper, the answer to this question would certainly be antisemitism. Asper strongly expressed his feeling that his progress in the Canadian television industry had been hampered by antisemitism. As he said: "I lectured my family very carefully, very thoroughly on anti-Semitism because nothing's changed. Before we became involved in broadcasting, no Jew had owned anything in network television. It wasn't done. It was an exclusive WASP domain."[71]

The Late Twentieth Century

In Canada, as Harold Troper asserts, the 1960s was the "decade in which barriers to Jewish participation in the larger Canadian social, political, and economic mainstream slipped away."[72] Nonetheless, for all the social progress Jews experienced in the postwar period, it remained patently clear that certain deep-seated prejudicial attitudes in Canadian society remained; antisemitism's sting may have been significantly blunted, but it was still a lived reality for Jews in postwar Canada. In 1963, André Laurendeau described a conversation he had with a man he described as a successful Jewish businessman, who told him: "You are a French Canadian. I am a Jew ... The others keep reminding us of it constantly— even perfect gentlemen, even those who denounce racial prejudice." Laurendeau concluded that there was a secret place within his Jewish acquaintance that had never ceased to suffer.[73]

An example of the sort of phenomenon Laurendeau's Jewish acquaintance was referring to was provided in 1963 by Canada's Prime Minister, John Diefenbaker, by all accounts a politician who consistently denounced racial prejudice "based on colour, creed or racial origin."[74] Nonetheless, after author Peter C. Newman wrote a biography that Diefenbaker felt was critical of him, he was heard referring to Newman as "that Viennese Jew."[75]

The social distance that had existed between Jews and French Canadians earlier in the twentieth century remained largely unchanged during the Quiet Revolution which began in earnest in the 1960s. This was

a period which coincided with the Second Vatican Council's proclamation of *Nostra Aetate* (1965) in which the Roman Catholic Church
formally repudiated antisemitism.[76] Later, Pope John Paul II would call
antisemitism "a sin against God and humanity." As well, the condemnation of antisemitism had by this time become a tenet of every large
Protestant church in Canada, whether liberal or conservative.[77]

In 1965, French Canadian journalist and political leader Claude Ryan
made a statement about relations between contemporary French Canadians and Jews: "I know of very few French Canadians who maintain
friendly private relations with Jews or who have any serious knowledge
of the mentality, the real problems, the frustrations and the aspirations
of the average Jew … or who care about such things."[78] Ryan added that
many French Canadians believed in the stereotypical idea that the Jew
is still first and above all a money-maker who "will do practically anything in order to make a fast dollar," and that the myth that Jews killed
Jesus Christ was still very much alive among them.[79] Ryan continued:
"French Canadians have observed that Jews speak French more than the
English do in Montreal. In the legal profession, for instance, practically
all the members of Jewish background speak French and have French
customers and clients, and can deal with French Canadians pretty easily.
But French Canadians believe that they do this because of self-interest
rather than because of any genuine interest in French Canadians, their
way of life and their culture."[80]

The conundrum faced by Jews in Quebec with respect to their integration into the social and political life of a province that was experiencing an aggressive empowerment of francophones was well stated by
Gérard Bouchard, who points out that there is essentially no means by
which a non-French Canadian, regardless of his or her expertise in the
French language, can truly become a "Canadien français," unless that
person renounces completely his or her cultural and linguistic past.
Even then he or she may be left in a state of quasi-marginality.[81]

Historian Richard Menkis notes an ambivalence and unresolved ten-
sion between French Canadians and Jews in this era as expressed in
the work of Quebec scholar Denis Vaugeois, who wrote on the early
history of the Jews in Quebec. In Vaugeois's 1968 book *Les Juifs et la
Nouvelle-France*, Menkis understands the author to have been engaged

in an effort to confront antisemitism in Quebec, particularly the sort of antisemitism that feared the "international connections" of the Jew. Vaugeois worries that some parts of his work might provide ammunition for those who believe that Jews are behind all wars, or be interpreted as proof that international Jewry and freemasonry were at work in Quebec. On the other hand, Menkis notes Vaugeois's argument that these charges of antisemitism "[are] easily fed by the tireless activity of the Diaspora Jews." Menkis thus argues that even while Vaugeois was attempting to reject antisemitic myths, the major myth of the international control of finance by the Jews had retained some residual force in his thinking. Menkis concludes that Denis Vaugeois's work "speaks eloquently ... about inherited myths regarding the Jews, and the process of dismantling them in mid-twentieth century Quebec."[82]

In Canada as a whole, there was a growing realization by the end of the 1960s of the progress of Jewish social integration in Canada in the postwar period. Writing from the perspective of the United States in the mid-1960s, Charles Stember notes: "Evidence of antisemitism has become increasingly scarce and ambiguous, the facts of Jewish acceptance seem to speak for themselves."[83] In that period antisemitic attitudes in Canada seemed in many instances to consist largely of remarks about "Jews having all the money" or a vague feeling on the part of Jews of being personally regarded and treated "as somewhat different."[84] Even so, there was continuing anxiety. Rabbi Reuben Slonim of Toronto expressed it this way: "Jews applaud the gains, but wonder how secure they really are. Jews do not see anti-Semitism as just another prejudice. Its long, long, history and deep, deep bias, culminating in the scientific destruction of more than one-third of their people, makes it a plague that will not soon be eradicated."[85]

Even in the 1970s issues like abortion rights evoked accusations against Jews. In 1976, Camille Samson, a leader of the Quebec Social Credit Party, singled out Jewish physicians who performed abortions as "artisans of destruction," threatening the people of Quebec.[86] The condemnation of Jewish doctors as abortionists manifested itself again in the 1990s, also in Quebec, in a campaign directed against Dr. Henry Morgentaler, a Jewish physician and a leading abortion rights advocate who was accused of leading a conspiracy to kill Christian babies through abortions.[87] At about the same time in New Brunswick, Malcolm Ross, whose Holocaust denial publications we will discuss in the next chapter, wrote *The Real Holocaust: The Attack on Unborn Children and Life Itself* in which he accused Jewish physicians of threatening "Christian civilization" by performing abortions.[88]

The 1980s saw significant changes in the nature of antisemitism in Canada, with much attention being paid to issues relative to both the denial of the Holocaust and the State of Israel and its alleged misdeeds. These issues will be dealt with in detail in the next two chapters of this book. Largely because of these issues, there was a growing recognition both in the Jewish community and among law-enforcement officials that there was "a need for stronger security measures at Jewish synagogues and other Jewish institutions."[89] It is symbolic of this change that in 1982 B'nai Brith Canada's League of Human Rights presented the first of its series of annual reviews of antisemitic activities in Canada. The first report remarked on the fact that many of the issues reported "do not fit the traditional definitions of anti-Semitism. But … they are likely to have a special effect on Jewish well-being, and in combination they testify to the continuing presence of anti-Semitism in Canada."[90]

Public opinion polls in the 1980s that attempted to understand the issue of antisemitism in Canada consistently found a small but significant number of Canadians who expressed antisemitic feelings. General levels of antisemitism were measured in a survey conducted by the League for Human Rights of B'nai B'rith from 1983 to 1985 and published in 1986. This survey indicated that in 1983–84 approximately 13 percent and in 1985 about 16 percent of the total Canadian population could be considered antisemitic, with the proportion in Quebec higher at about 22 percent.[91] A 1984 Goldfarb poll indicated that 6 percent of Canadians saw themselves as antisemites and another 20–25 percent admitted to some degree of prejudice against Jews.[92] In that same year, a Canada-wide survey showed that 14 percent of the respondents had expressed negative attitudes toward Jews.[93] In response to questions in a 1987 survey, 19 percent agreed that "Jews just care for themselves," 34 percent agreed that Jews are "pushy," and 23 percent were of the opinion that Jews use "shady practices" to get ahead.[94] All of these polls indicated a fairly consistent and statistically significant higher level of antisemitism in Quebec, for which there have been several explanations.[95] Sociologist Taylor Buckner attributed the difference to lack of contact between francophone Québécois and the Jewish community,[96] while Paul Sniderman put forward the hypothesis that the reason for the statistical difference is the great value francophone Quebec places on "conformity as a sociocultural norm."[97]

No matter how low the levels of antisemitism elicited by the various public opinion surveys, Jews in Canada tended to feel beset by antisemitism. Thus a survey of Jewish attitudes in Toronto conducted by public opinion specialist Martin Goldfarb for the *Toronto Star* in the 1980s found that 85 percent of the respondents believed that there was prejudice against Jews, while 55 percent said they had personally experienced prejudice or discrimination.[98] These responses tend to complement a 1984 poll of Jews in the United States, in which 92 percent of respondents said Jews must be alert to stop all signs of antisemitism and a decided majority rejected the notion that antisemitism was not a serious problem.[99]

L'Affaire Outremont

The large and growing Hasidic community of the Montreal suburb of Outremont, which had developed into one of the largest concentrations of Hasidic Jews in the world, experienced a series of unpleasant encounters with its French-Canadian neighbours and their municipal government starting in the late 1980s. These encounters mushroomed into serious and widely publicized accusations of antisemitism. It is important in this context to note that, other than Hasidic Jews, Outremont is largely populated by an upscale francophone elite, a group which a 2002 survey found to possess more antisemitic attitudes than the general Quebec population.[100]

In that period, the Outremont city council twice rejected the Viznitz Hasidic community's petition to rezone a property in order to allow for the construction of a synagogue. Opposition to the Hasidic request was led by Gérard Pelletier, a member of the Outremont council. "L'Affaire Outremont," as the controversy became known, escalated significantly when one of Montreal's major French newspapers, *La Presse*, ran a front-page story stating that Outremont had a "Jewish problem." The Montreal Jewish community denounced the article, while *La Presse* apologized for using the term "Jewish problem" but not for the content of its story. *La Presse* editorialist Alain Dubuc argued that this was a misunderstanding and yet another manifestation of "tensions between the francophone majority and groups that have chosen English as their language of usage." For his part, columnist Gerald LeBlanc accused the Jews of failing to integrate into the French milieu and opposing the survival and protection of the French society.

There were also French Canadian voices raised in defence of the Hassidim of Outremont. These included Quebec's immigration minister, Louise Robic, and Education Minister Claude Ryan. As well, several attempts at dialogue in Outremont were undertaken in an effort to get the two sides to communicate and to defuse the situation.[101] However "the situation" in Outremont refused to go away completely. In subsequent years tensions remained high after repeated incidents of assault and robbery against Hasidim in Outremont that were characterized by some Jewish observers as "a pogrom" that "stirs grim memories." The aftermath of these incidents was also unsettling to Montreal's Jewish community when radio personality Claude Jasmin, in discussing the incident on his program, charged the Jews with being "the most racist" people in the world and blaming the Hasidim for refusing to integrate into Quebec society. Jasmin was ultimately rebuked by the management of the radio station and ordered to desist from such inflammatory statements.[102]

Attempts by the Hasidic communities of Outremont to create a symbolic boundary (*eruv*) in order to enhance their Sabbath observance drew significant objections on the part of French Canadians. Valerie Stoker, who has studied the Outremont *eruv* controversy, asserts that the French Canadian opposition to the eruv "tended to view Outremont's public image in the same terms as its physical territory, that is, as a substantive, material, and therefore finite entity whose 'use' and/or 'occupancy' had to be carefully monitored and apportioned. Outremont *eruv* opposition therefore tended to presume that the proper management of religious and cultural diversity occurs through the privatization of difference by minority members in the interests of protecting a dominant cultural community that is uniquely entitled to mark Outremont's landscape and shape its public image."[103]

While tensions have considerably subsided, Outremont activist Pierre Lacerte in his writings and on his website meticulously points out every Hasidic zoning infraction and disregard of traffic ordinances and the like. Lacerte's activities were deemed by many Hasidim to constitute harassment, and he was sued. In 2013 the court found that Lacerte's activities did not constitute harassment and he was exonerated of the charges.[104]

To show that French Canadian perceptions of Jews "taking over" territory in Quebec is not confined to Outremont, it is instructive to examine the reaction to the town of Hampstead's 2011 noise ban on the Jewish high holidays. The Quebec French media coverage was deemed by several observers to have been a "grotesque overreaction," while radio personality Benoit Dutrizac encouraged his listeners to go to Hampstead and make noise to show "that it is not the Jewish community that leads Quebec."[105]

Quebec Nationalism and the Jews

The great issue in Quebec (and for the rest of Canada) for the past half-century and more has been the resurgence of Quebec nationalism and the possibility of Quebec separation from Canada. This issue has caused profound disquiet among Jews in Quebec and has brought to public attention many of the "inherited myths" about Jews in Quebec to which Menkis referred.[106]

In December 1971, Quebec separatist leader René Lévesque spoke to a Jewish audience in Toronto to reassure his listeners who were concerned about the future of Jews in an increasingly nationalist Quebec. Lévesque stated:

> I know that eighty to ninety percent of the Jews of Quebec are nervous about the effects of separatism. I know that history shows that a rise of nationalism means Jews get it in the neck. But what can I do about it? I can't change your history. But I also know that anti-Semitism is not a significant French-Canadian characteristic. The more serious problem for the Jews is that Jews in Quebec are closely related to the English community. If they choose to put in with them, what can I do?[107]

Despite Lévesque's attempts to reassure Canadian Jews, and despite data from the mid-1980s indicating that Quebec nationalists were not necessarily any more antisemitic than non-nationalists,[108] a number of incidents from the 1960s and 1970s demonstrated that antisemitic ideas were alive in Quebec nationalist circles. In February 1969, during demonstrations of Quebec separatist groups demanding the "francization" of McGill University, antisemitic slogans such as "Death to the Jews" and "The Nazis have not cremated enough Jews" were heard.[109] Similarly, during the October Crisis of 1970, the radical Front de Libération du Québec (FLQ) published a manifesto that included a virulent attack on the financial power of the Montreal Jewish community. During the House of Commons debate on the War Measures Act designed to combat the threat represented by the FLQ, Jean Marchand, a minister in Prime Minister Trudeau's cabinet, utilized these FLQ statements in order to brand it as "anti-Jewish."[110] Raymond Villeneuve, a convicted terrorist who advocated for Quebec's separation from Canada and threatened violence against his opponents, was the author of a number of statements of concern to Jews. In a September 1996 issue of *La Tempête*, the newsletter of his Mouvement de libération nationale du Québec, Villeneuve accused Montreal's Ashkenazic Jews of playing a leading role in the opposition to Quebec separation and to laws giving sole official status to the French language. He went on to name several individuals in the Jewish community, implying that they might face retaliation after independence was achieved. He also suggested in a radio interview with respect to the English community that "it could come to bombs, or more simple methods like Molotov cocktails."[111]

Less radical nationalist voices accused Jews in Quebec of racist behaviour, aloofness, hostility to the French community, and a failure to assimilate into the Quebec milieu.[112] In 1990, prominent Quebec businessman Pierre Péladeau was quoted in an article in the Quebec newsmagazine *Actualité* as having stated "I have great respect for Jews but they take up too much room [*ils prennent trop de place*]."[113]

These individual statements seemingly reflect the sentiments of a substantial segment within Quebec society. As we have already noted, public opinion surveys show a consistent and significant difference on Jewish-related issues between English and French Canada. Twice as many French Canadians as English Canadians responded positively to survey questions asking whether Jews have too much power, caused the

Holocaust, or exaggerated the number of Jews who perished at the hands of Nazi Germany.[114] A survey taken in the early 1990s similarly indicated that 64 percent of francophones and 37 percent of anglophones in Quebec were in agreement with the proposition that Jews had too much power over business in Quebec.[115]

Jews in Quebec, the majority of whom identified with Quebec's anglophone minority, were further disquieted by statements like that of Parti Québécois Premier Jacques Parizeau, who famously attributed the narrow failure of the 1995 referendum on Quebec sovereignty to "money and the ethnic vote." Parizeau subsequently clarified his statement to refer specifically to the activities of the Canadian Jewish Congress, then the face of the Jewish community in public affairs, as well as those of Greek and Italian community organizations who supported the "No" option in the referendum.[116] This sort of uneasiness certainly contributed to a Jewish exodus from Quebec in which an estimated 30,000 to 40,000 Jews left Quebec for elsewhere in the decades following the Parti Québécois's first electoral victory, leaving a Quebec Jewish community much diminished in numbers from its demographic peak in the early 1970s.[117]

In the early 1990s, Esther Delisle published a book which spoke of a virulent antisemitism in Quebec in the interwar years as expressed especially by Lionel Groulx.[118] Her conclusions were adopted and given wide publicity by writer Mordecai Richler in a prominent *New Yorker* article later issued as a book.[119] The claim expressed in Richler's book that French Canadians were more susceptible to antisemitism than other Canadians was the subject of vehement denunciations in the French-language media of Quebec[120] and some of these criticisms of Delisle and Richler caused considerable consternation within the Jewish community.[121] In several media appearances Richler was characteristically unrepentant, attacking his critics for "intellectual dishonesty, hysteria, and vulgarity" and continually expressing his contempt for Quebec's language policies. Furthermore, Richler insisted on his characterization of French Canadian antisemitism, arguing that "we are riding dark, tribal horses. It could be unpleasant … We are playing dangerous games." Ruth Wisse, then a McGill University professor of Jewish studies, also expressed her concern at that point that Quebec seemed to be departing from the model of tolerance of Jews and Judaism that characterized North America. As she stated, "Quebec is the first place in North America to use the 'protection of the collectivity' as an excuse to limit certain rights of its citizens ... Quebec, then, may be a test case of minority influence in North America."[122] It is a testimony to the heated emotions elicited by this controversy that at the height of Deslisle/Richler affair, Gary Caldwell, who identified with the opposition to Delisle and who had himself been involved in research on the Quebec Jewish community, wrote that he was "well aware that, according to the contemporary definition of antisemitism I can do no other than to pass as an antisemite."[123]

The Turn of the Twenty-First Century

By the 1990s antisemitism in Canada had become, in the words of a 1994 survey, "a marginal phenomenon ... unacceptable in mainstream society."[124] In a Canadian poll of the late 1980s, some 6 percent of Canadians admitted to being antisemitic, while another 20 to 25 percent displayed varying degrees of anti-Jewish prejudice.[125] This trend concurred with a finding of a 1992 Anti-Defamation League survey in the United States that revealed that whereas roughly 20 percent of Americans held "a collection of views about Jews which are unquestionably anti-Semitic," there had been "a steady decline in US acceptance of the classical ethical stereotypes traditionally attributed to Jews."[126] It is perhaps a sign of the relative decline of classical antisemitism in Canada at that time that B'nai Brith Canada's 1998 survey of antisemitism in Canada moved to broaden the definition of "antisemitism" to include the activities of missionaries and messianic churches targeting Jews for conversion to Christianity.[127]

In this decade, despite the relative calm, certain antisemitic incidents did make the headlines, including a 1992 incident in which Michael Lubin resigned from the Reform Party alleging widespread antisemitism and racism within the party. Reacting to these allegations, the party expelled four members of the White Supremacist Heritage Front, including the group's leader, Wolfgang Droege.[128]

In 1993 an attempted revival of the musical *Showboat* in Toronto was met with accusations that the play was racist and an insult to Blacks. The rhetoric of the opposition to *Showboat* at times focused on the Jewishness of the show's producers, leading Professor Howard Adelman, who analyzed the "Showboat Affair," to comment: "The same people who associated opponents of the [*Showboat*] boycott with being in power or in the pay of those in power ... easily slipped into antisemitic remarks."[129]

At the beginning of the twenty-first century, the al-Qaeda attack on the World Trade Center and other targets on September 11, 2001, resulted in a number of antisemitic incidents: graffiti, bomb threats, synagogue and cemetery desecrations, and verbal and written abuse. Of the 286 anti-Semitic incidents audited by B'nai Brith Canada for 2001, fully 35 percent occurred during September and October in the immediate aftermath of the 9/11 attack. In Toronto, 41 percent of the year's incidents were concentrated in those two months, including the spray painting of graffiti against Jews and for Osama bin Laden on the walls of Shaar Shalom Synagogue in the suburb of Thornhill, as well as a rash of antisemitic graffiti at Ryerson University.[130] Also in the aftermath of 9/11, physical assaults on Jews became common enough that the B'nai Brith Audit, which previously had included violent antisemitic incidents in the category of "harassment," now began listing violent incidents as a separate category.[131]

An Environics poll conducted the next spring (April 2002) showed that less than one in five of the Canadian population believed that antisemitism was on the increase, though, true to historical patterns, the figure for Quebec was somewhat higher, around one-fourth. The respondents, both nationally and in Quebec, were nearly evenly split over how to evaluate the cases of antisemitic vandalism that continued to occur. Were they merely random acts or part of a trend?[132] Cogent arguments were put forward on both sides of this issue.

In 2002, the Jewish community in Canada was shocked to hear of the cold-blooded murder of David Rosenzweig, a man who was obviously an Orthodox Jew in appearance, in front of a kosher pizza parlour in Toronto on a Saturday night in July. The killer, Christopher Steven McBride, appeared to be a skinhead. Among Jews there was a widespread perception that Rosenzweig had been targeted because he was Jewish. Witnesses reported that the killer had shouted obscenities at Jews shortly before the attack. Ed Morgan, Ontario Region Chair of the

CJC, asked, "Why else would a skinhead be at a kosher restaurant other than to harass the Jewish customers? When an Orthodox man is killed for no reason whatsoever, it seems like a hate crime." Nonetheless, neither the police nor the prosecution felt that a hate crime had occurred and basically accepted Mcbride's contention that the murder was the result of a drunken rage.[133]

The great hesitation by law enforcement authorities in declaring crimes against Jews as "hate crimes" extended further than the Rosenzweig murder. After a Toronto Jew was assaulted after leaving a synagogue late at night in 2003, police treated the case in a similar manner. B'nai Brith Canada commented on this case: "The circumstances of this assault, including the absence of any robbery attempt, leads to the assumption that this was a hate crime. Yet … this incident has not been classified as a hate crime by the police. This underscores the necessity for an independent agency like the League to ensure that such attacks are recorded and classified for their antisemitic content."[134]

The perceived increase in anti-Semitic incidents in the first years of the twenty-first century induced Canadian synagogues, schools, and other Jewish institutions to take measures to increase their security despite the extra costs and the strains on already-stretched budgets.[135] It also induced a number of non-Jewish executives from Canada's largest corporations, led by Tony Comper, president of the Bank of Montreal, and his wife, Elizabeth Comper, to establish an organization called Fighting Anti-Semitism Together (FAST) in May 2004. An immediate goal of FAST was to develop a program about antisemitism designed for the public schools. FAST's inaugural announcement stated that "2004 was the worst year in more than half a century for vicious anti-Jewish activity in this country," and promised the Jews of Canada that "they are not alone and on their own." Mrs. Comper was quoted by the *Canadian Jewish News* as stating that "this isn't just a Jewish issue. This is an issue of every single person living in Canada." For his part, Mr. Comper stressed the importance of educating young people so that Jewish children would no longer have to "grow up in fear of the people around them."[136]

In December 2004, the Quebec government announced that it would increase funding for secular studies provided in Jewish day schools from 60 to 100 percent of the public school level, a move that would have brought as much as an additional $10 million per year to the Jewish community's schools. This announcement, however, aroused a tremendous backlash in the province, and considerable public pressure was brought to bear against the government. Polls showed that 90 percent of the province opposed the plan. The Quebec government under Liberal Premier Jean Charest soon rescinded the measure. From the media coverage it was clear that many saw this funding as a reward by the Liberals to "a powerful Jewish lobby." One Quebec newspaper went much further and openly questioned the propriety of special funding to "a community that controls a good part of the Western economy and supports without reservation its political leader, the criminal Ariel Sharon, whose country legalizes torture and carries out genocide."[137] As McGill history professor Gil Troy commented: "Rather than debating the program's merits, too much innuendo and invective demonized the Jewish community, revealing ugly pools of anti-Semitism festering provincewide. Cartoonists depicted Quebec's Education Minister as a big-nosed Hasidic Jew. Editorialists complained that a rich community which donates $15 million annually to Israeli schools should not be grabbing $10 million from Quebec's deserving, desperate schoolchildren."[138]

In June 2005 lawyer Guy Bertrand argued before the Supreme Court of Canada that his client, Leon Mugesera, who had been accused of war crimes in Rwanda, was the victim of a conspiracy that involved prominent Canadian Jewish leaders Irving Abella, Irwin Cotler, and David Matas. Bertrand alleged that these people conspired to appoint Irving Abella's wife, Rosalie Abella, to the Supreme Court of Canada in "what appeared … to be a conspiracy hatched to organize a powerful network of influences." The Supreme Court chastised Bertrand for "expressing anti-Semitic sentiment and views that most might have thought had disappeared from Canadian society, and even more so from legal debate in Canada."[139]

The Bouchard-Taylor Commission

In 2007, the Quebec government appointed a commission headed by Gérard Bouchard and Charles Taylor to investigate the issue of "religious accommodation" in Quebec, and it quickly became clear that the Quebec Jewish community was strongly implicated in the controversy. The debate that followed seemed to a number of observers to go beyond

previous bounds, and some feared that it might lead to "serious persecution of minorities, particularly religious minorities."[140] Calls for a crack-
down on open displays of non-Christian religions in public spaces[141]
ultimately led to the divisive 2013–14 controversy over the Quebec
Charter of Values promoted by the Parti Québécois government.

While a major focus of the Bouchard-Taylor Commission's delib-
erations was the Quebec Muslim community,[142] a significantly large
number of submissions to the commission concerned the Jewish community in Quebec. Issues related to the Jewish community included the
Hasidic community, kosher food, visible Jewish symbols such as male
head covering (kipa, yarmulke), Jewish schools, and the Jewish character of publicly funded health institutions such as Montreal's Jewish
General Hospital.

Despite the Jews' long presence in Quebec, the Quebec Jewish community remains largely isolated from and mysterious to the surrounding
francophone milieu in Québec.[143] This isolation was reflected in a 2007
poll in which a large minority of francophones in Quebec (41 percent)
responded positively to the statement "The Jews want to impose their
customs and traditions on others," while only 31 percent said yes to the
proposition "Jews want to participate fully in society."[144]

Francophone Quebec society's reaction to the perceived crisis of "reasonable accommodation" was captured by politician and academic Louise Beaudoin, who explained Quebec's societal malaise in the following
way: "Possibly this reaction was provoked by the request formulated by
other communities to reintroduce religion in the public sphere."[145] An
example of the sort of issue discussed by Beaudoin, and one certainly
very much on the minds of the public, was equality of the sexes, which
was perceived by many as being in danger from resurgent religion in the
public space on the part of "d'autres communautés." Thus the Quebec
Council on the Status of Women, a group appointed to advise the Quebec government on women's issues, recommended that "public employees … remove visible religious signs when on the job."[146]

While it can be argued that most Jews (and Muslims) are well inte-
grated into Quebec society, the focus of the testimony before the commission revolved around those areas in which Jews became a visible
minority to many Quebecers, and in which they were alleged to have

made concrete (and excessive) demands for religious accommodation in Quebec. Kosher food, which differentiates observant Jews from their fellow citizens, became one such issue. Thus, some presenters to the commission, echoing the claims of American white supremacist organizations,[147] charged that the Jewish community was forcing food companies to pay for kashrut certification, change their formulas, and raise their prices in order to obtain kosher certification, thus making everyone pay higher prices for their food.[148] This charge has persisted in Quebec, and propaganda against kosher food remained active in certain areas of the province in 2014.[149]

One presenter, Pierre Lacerte, whose activities in Outremont we have already discussed, charged that the Hasidim are "powerful, stubborn and pugnacious," and are granted "special privileges." Others described them as "money-driven profiteers of the immigration system, determined to force their archaic ways on the Quebec majority with their kosher foods, large families, loud prayers, and separate lives."[150]

The official response of Quebec's Jewish community to the widespread nature of the controversy was determinedly low key. Montreal's Federation CJA chose not to formally present a public statement but rather to be represented through the Canadian Jewish Congress, Quebec Region.[151] The then president of Federation CJA, Marc Gold, stated that his organization was determined "not to respond publicly to every comment made ... believing it would not serve the best interests of the community."[152] The brief presented by the Canadian Jewish Congress was an attempt to answer charges that had been raised against Jews and Judaism during the hearings, such as the alleged prevalence of Jewish "wealth and influence"[153] and the higher cost of kosher food. As well, the brief opposed the precedence of gender equality over religious freedom and supported the right of workers in public institutions to wear religious symbols. The main spokesman, Dr. Victor Goldbloom, tried to underline the community of values shared by the Jewish community and Quebec as a whole.[154] The brief presented by the Jewish General Hospital likewise accentuated the positive and presented an image that is captured in the title of the brief, "Care For All." The hospital presented itself as an institution that has practised "reasonable accommodation" for decades, and emphasized that the concept "is a sound one, as long as it is sensibly applied, fairly administered, and able to balance the rights and needs of the minority with those of the majority."[155] Allegations against the hospital were passed over in silence.

The commission officially released its report at the end of May 2008.[156] It recommended a number of measures that might have a potential impact on the Jewish community. In particular, it recommended that government employees who "embody the state," such as judges and police officers, should not be allowed to wear religious symbols, such as kippot, while other public employees, such as physicians, could be allowed to wear them. Thus Bouchard-Taylor, rather than calming the waters as its advocates had hoped, led directly to the 2013–14 controversy in Quebec over the proposed "Charter of Values," which proposed that wearers of religiously based garments, such as the Jewish kippot, should not be allowed to wear such garments while working for the Quebec public service or in parapublic roles such as physicians in hospitals. The controversy over the "Charter of Values," which has subsided at least for the moment by the Liberal victory in the April 7, 2014, provincial elections, was characterized by Gérard Bouchard in the following way: "I think that the debate will be very heated, unpleasant and useless because (the proposed charter) will go nowhere ... It will divide Quebecers and it will (pit) the majority against the minority."[157]

In 2012 an antisemitic theme intruded in Winnipeg politics after the distribution of a poster accusing the mayor, Sam Katz, of corruption and malfeasance by using pointedly antisemitic tropes.[158] Beyond charging Mayor Katz with funnelling "hundreds of millions of dollars" through "untendered contracts and shady land deals" to a list of thirteen Jews, including some of the most prominent in the Winnipeg community, the poster predicted: "His cabal of cockroaches will be clutching their dirty money and running for cover."[159] The author of the posters, Gordon Warren, was not indicted because the police concluded that there was no incitement for hatred.[160]

The pattern that we have seen throughout this chapter—that actions perceived by members of the Jewish community to constitute antisemitic hate crimes are not defined as such by law enforcement authorities—will be seen to continue as we examine issues of Holocaust denial and anti-Zionism in the next two chapters.

CHAPTER EIGHT

The Holocaust and Its Deniers

The Zionists cannot say the Jew is an innocent victim being put in concentration camps.

—James Keegstra[1]

It is hard to overestimate the impact of the Holocaust on postwar Canadian Jews. As Morton Weinfeld states (with specific reference to Quebec): "To understand Jewish fear of anti-Semitism one must not only take into account the historical record of Quebec society, but supranational events such as the Holocaust. At present, perhaps 20–25 percent of Montreal's adult Jewish population are postwar immigrants, survivors of the Holocaust. These Jews cannot help but remain forever alert to the possible dangers."[2]

From the perspective of Canadian Jews, there thus exists a deep-seated fear that "it can happen here." This factor, as Evelyn Kallen remarks, has caused significant numbers of Canadian Jews to become sensitized to the slightest nuance of anti-Jewish discrimination. They are convinced that anti-Jewish incidents provide clear indicators of a manifest social problem with which they must be concerned.[3]

The possible fears and anxieties felt by postwar Canadian Jews, to which Weinfeld and Kallen have referred, are numerous. They certainly encompass occasional incidents of vandalism against Jewish property and sacred places, such as took place in August 1953, when a synagogue in Winnipeg was trashed and its Torah scrolls were desecrated.[4] Such incidents of violence carried out against Jews through property damage or, more rarely, through physical assault against Jewish people, were hardly unknown in Canada in the postwar period, as we have seen.

However Canadian Jews became collectively astonished at the relatively large-scale revival of such incidents in the late 1950s and early 1960s as part of a worldwide phenomenon.

Revival of Nazism in the Early 1960s

In December 1959, Canadians became aware of a seemingly spontaneous epidemic of antisemitic incidents, beginning in Cologne, Germany, and swiftly moving to South and North America.[5] In the course of this epidemic, identifiably Jewish buildings, monuments, and, above all, tombstones in several Canadian cities were defaced with swastikas. Anti-Jewish slogans, clearly instigated by people who supported the Nazi regime and its anti-Jewish actions, were found in Montreal and Toronto.[6] Prominent Jews in Canada became the targets of this kind of harassment. For example, in Toronto in 1960 Meyer J. Nurenberger, the editor of the newly founded Jewish community weekly *Canadian Jewish News*, received verbal threats from neo-Nazis, a swastika was painted on his garage door, and his daughter was obliged for a time to walk to school with a police escort.[7]

By the mid-1960s Canada was experiencing a wave of public pro-Nazi white supremacist activities as a new generation of neo-Nazis, many of them taking inspiration from Nazi and other white-supremacist groups in the United States, demonstrated against Jews and Blacks in Toronto and elsewhere. These demonstrations were often accompanied by multiple incidents of antisemitic vandalism, one of the more prominent of which extended over a period of three weeks in Toronto in May 1963. At that time, swastikas and slogans like "Jew die" were painted on the Shomrei Shabbat and Anshe Apt synagogues in downtown Toronto, and black swastikas were plastered on the Borochov Center, a building housing several Jewish cultural and educational institutions, as well as on a Jewish-owned variety store several blocks away.[8] In July of the same year, in Winnipeg Beach, Manitoba, several anti-Jewish incidents appeared to have been triggered by a Dominion Day disturbance. An unidentified car was driven along the Winnipeg Beach lakefront on which a loudspeaker was mounted. From the vehicle someone calling himself "Adolph Eichmann" broadcast the message: "Jews, get out of the Beach, Go Home.

You'll be killed."[9] Swastikas on synagogues and Jewish cemeteries were also to be found in Vancouver and in Winnipeg in 1966.[10]

Events of this nature particularly traumatized Holocaust survivors, who made up a major component of the Canadian Jewish community. As Toronto Rabbi W. Gunther Plaut, himself a refugee from Nazi Germany, put it: "To them a public Nazi rally meant the possibility of a repetition of what they had barely lived through: gassings, inhuman treatment, murder and rapine, mutilation, starvation and torture."[11] This sort of "in your face" antisemitic activity, in the aftermath of the well-publicized and much-discussed trial and execution of Nazi war criminal Adolph Eichmann in Israel, pointedly reminded Canadian Jews of the trauma of the Holocaust. By bringing back memories of that era, these incidents had by the mid-1960s created a growing fear of the revival of antisemitism in Canada and abroad despite the clearly small prospects of a Nazi takeover of Canada. What to do about the problem of neo-Nazism became a primary concern among the rank and file of Canadian Jews. The issue brought to the fore basic differences in both strategy and tactics that caused a serious split within the Canadian Jewish community.[12] The time-honoured approach of the Canadian Jewish community had been to quietly lobby the Canadian government for redress of perceived wrongs. This approach offered a possible way forward, and Jewish community representatives did lobby the government to amend Canada's Criminal Code and thus stop the activities of the neo-Nazis. The other way was for Jews to take direct militant action against the Nazis in their midst.[13] Those Toronto Jews who did not wish to wait for government action, therefore, conceived and carried out "a systematic campaign of harassment and physical confrontation"[14] against Nazi leader William John Beattie and the militants of the Canadian Nazi party, who apparently never numbered more than fifty.[15]

Laws against Hate Speech

The neo-Nazi disturbances and the enormous media publicity they generated spurred the Canadian government to respond to the underlying issue of hate propaganda that targeted Jews and other minorities. In 1965, therefore, federal Minister of Justice Guy Favreau appointed a

Special Committee on Hate Propaganda in Canada in order to study the issue and make recommendations for its legal prohibition. The committee was chaired by Maxwell Cohen, then dean of McGill University's Faculty of Law. Political figures like Pierre Elliott Trudeau and Mark MacGuigan, as well as Saul Hayes, national executive vice-president of the Canadian Jewish Congress, were among its members.[16] In its final report, the Cohen Committee called for an anti-hate law designed to protect the community from the "corrosive effects of propaganda." The Cohen Committee's report ultimately led to legislation that passed in 1970. The legislation added three sections (318–320) to the Criminal Code of Canada that criminalized the promotion of hatred via print and speech.[17] Trudeau doubtless spoke for the other members of the committee when he commented: "Let this law be one step towards the society we seek to build."[18] At that point it was not yet clear that the great challenge this legislation would face would not in fact be further incidents of graffiti, overturned Jewish tombstones, and vandalism directed at synagogues and Jewish schools. Instead, the mettle of the anti-hate-propaganda legislation would be most severely tested by the phenomenon of Holocaust denial and the rights Holocaust deniers claimed to freedom of speech in a Canadian society which treasured that principle.

Holocaust Denial

Holocaust denial posits that the genocide of European Jewry by Nazi Germany during the Second World War never took place. Advocates of Holocaust denial claim further that the Nazis did not, in fact, have any specific policy to exterminate Jews. The phenomenon of denial obviously arose in the postwar period in order to exculpate the Nazis of the guilt placed upon them for the mass destruction of six million Jews and, in a sense, to posthumously victimize Jews who had died in the Holocaust by denying them recognition in death just as the Nazi death machine denied them life. Holocaust deniers, or, as they often preferred to call themselves, "historical revisionists," asserted through their lectures and publications that the Holocaust was nothing but a hoax perpetrated by an international Jewish conspiracy in order to gain sympathy for the

Jews and support for the State of Israel. The culmination of this aspect of Holocaust denial is to withhold from Jews the status of victims. Jews are seen by deniers as the perpetrators of an essentially false accusation, victimizing those brave revisionists who dare to stand up for the truth.[19]

It can readily be seen, therefore, that Holocaust denial is in many senses a late-twentieth-century continuation of a rather old anti-Jewish and antisemitic trope: that you cannot believe that the Jews speak the truth. Thus, for example, the *Diary of Anne Frank* has been declared a forgery.[20] Holocaust denial builds on a history of practically two millennia of accusations of lying against Jews. In the premodern period, both Christians and Muslims often asserted that the Jews were not simply innocent people with faulty theological interpretations who should be persuaded to see the truth. On the contrary Jews were widely believed to be conscious liars in the service of satanic powers for evil purposes whose word could not and should not be trusted. They used their prevarications in order to advance their nefarious schemes of world domination.[21]

In Canada, this sort of denial of Jewish claims of persecution found ample expression even prior to the Second World War in the Social Credit movement. In the 1930s Alberta Social Credit Premier William Aberhart could be heard to echo Social Credit founder Major C.H. Douglas's claim that despite widely publicized Jewish claims that they were persecuted in Nazi Germany, it was in reality a Jewish group of financiers in Germany who were responsible for the persecution of the Jews in that country while they themselves remained unscathed and prospered economically, and that the allegations of persecution constituted a smokescreen to insert German agents abroad.[22] In the postwar period, a significant number of Alberta Social Crediters, despite the well-publicized public repudiation of antisemitism by party leader Ernest Manning, persisted in thinking of both the Holocaust and Zionism as components of an international Jewish plot for world control.[23] That these ideas had some staying power is shown by the case of Stephen Stiles, a Conservative MLA in Alberta in 1983 who was publicly repudiated by the Alberta legislature for having cast doubt on Jewish persecution by the Nazis.[24] As we will see, Social Credit–style antisemitism constituted one of the prime intellectual sources of one of the most prominent of late-twentieth-century Canadian Holocaust deniers, James Keegstra.

However beyond Social Credit there existed another important postwar Canadian intellectual source for Holocaust denial, one that also stretched back into the prewar period—Adrien Arcand. We have examined Arcand's many pre-war antisemitic writings and activities in chapter 6. Though Arcand was interned by the Canadian government during the Second World War for these activities, upon his release in 1945 he resumed his antisemitic writings and his political activities as leader of the Parti de l'Unité Nationale. Arcand actively carried on these activities until his death in 1967. During this period, like many of the antisemitic figures we have previously examined, he did not wish to publicly label himself an antisemite. However, in his description of his political movement, his opposition to the Jews is obvious. As he stated: "The PUN is not antisemitic, it is pro-gentile and pro-Christian. It fights the error of Communism which is the work of the Jews and supports the suppression of the chapters of the Talmud that sow hatred of Christians."[25]

Arcand was a Holocaust denier[26] who attempted to place the blame for all the world's ills on the Jews. As he said, "the only real spreaders of hate are the Jews, because the moment you say one word against them, they brand you as an antisemite."[27] His ideas would continue in the next generation through the career of yet another prominent Canadian Holocaust denier, Ernst Zundel, who considered himself a disciple of Arcand, as was John Ross Taylor, who became the leader of the Western Guard in 1976.[28] The activities of both Keegstra and Zundel made sensational headlines and helped keep the issue of Holocaust denial in front of the Canadian public for much of the late twentieth century.

During the 1970s, increasing attention was paid to the Holocaust and its memorialization among Canadian Jews, symbolized by the dedication of the Montreal Holocaust Memorial Centre in 1979. By the mid-1980s Holocaust curricula were established in the two largest school boards in Ontario, and a Holocaust Centre was opened in Toronto as well.[29] In that sort of atmosphere, there was a greater readiness on the part of Canadian Holocaust survivors to tell their stories in public. Groups of Jewish Holocaust survivors, especially in Toronto, began asserting themselves and pressured the established Jewish community over the issue of getting the Canadian government to legislate against Nazi war criminals in Canada as well as Holocaust deniers.[30]

Nazi War Criminals in Canada

Although there is no direct connection between the complex issue of Nazi war criminals in Canada and postwar manifestations of antisemitism in Canada, the fact that many of the same activists on both sides were often deeply involved in both issues makes it worthwhile to address them together in this chapter.

The Simon Wiesenthal Center for Holocaust Studies website claims that, in the aftermath of the Second World War, some 2,000 Nazi war criminals came to Canada and were, for the most part, not noticed by the Canadian government.[31] Whether these people actually numbered in the thousands or the hundreds involves basic issues of definition that are well beyond the scope of this discussion. For our purposes it will suffice to say that a significant number of people who actively served on the Nazi side in various capacities during the Second World War did come to Canada illegally after the war, mostly in the first few years after its end, but some as late as 1983, when a senior member of the RCMP admitted two alleged Nazi war criminals into Canada because he "regarded the war criminals issue as blown all out of proportion by the Jewish lobby."[32] Prominent Nazi hunter Simon Wiesenthal publicly accused the Canadian government of not acting on evidence of Nazi war criminals in Canada, and reportedly announced that he would refuse to set foot in Canada until decisive action was taken against Nazi war criminals in that country. He held both the Canadian government and the organized Jewish community to blame for the current state of affairs.[33]

In 1982, the well-publicized extradition trial of Helmut Rauca, wanted in West Germany for participation in the extermination of the Jews of Kaunas, Lithuania, in 1941 and who had lived in Canada since 1950 (as a Canadian citizen since 1956) gave credence to these allegations.[34] It should also be noted that while the Rauca extradition trial was under way, the publication of Irving Abella and Harold Troper's *None Is Too Many*, which offered a carefully documented study of the ways in which Jewish immigration to Canada was severely discouraged in the interwar period, "inadvertently set up a contrast between the conscious Canadian refusal to offer sanctuary to the victims of Nazi brutality and a growing realization that Canada may have given haven, perhaps unknowingly, to their murderers."[35]

There was certainly growing pressure on the Canadian government to do something about this issue. From the perspective of Prime Minister Trudeau, the presence of war criminals in Canada did not seem to constitute a basic human rights issue that needed to be urgently addressed. On the contrary, as he saw it, the issue appeared to be a parochially Jewish issue. If acted upon by government, it might prove disruptive to the Canadian body politic, because taking action on the allegations of the presence of Nazi war criminals in Canada might well inflame the situation further, most particularly because the issue was liable to strain and upset relationships between different ethnic groups in Canada and to encourage other ethnocultural groups to pursue similar issues of their own.[36]

This was certainly the case with the Canadian Ukrainian community, which both feared and resented accusations of antisemitism against it. As John Gregorovich of the Civil Liberties Commission of the Ukrainian Canadian Congress put it in 1986: "The situation in the English speaking world, indeed in the Western world, is such that the slightest indication of criticism of Jews is automatically classified as anti-Semitism. Once a statement is classified as anti-Semitism … credibility is completely lost. No mainstream media person, academician, government official or politician will have anything to do with the person making the statement."[37]

However, when Brian Mulroney and his Progressive Conservatives decisively won the 1984 elections, one of his first steps as prime minister, unexpectedly and seemingly without overt pressure from the Canadian Jewish community, was to announce that he would create a commission to investigate the war criminals issue, to be headed by Jules Deschênes.[38] For our purposes it is not necessary to review in detail the recommendations of the Deschênes Commission. It is also not within the scope of this account of antisemitism in Canada to detail the extensive history of the actions and inactions of the Canadian government with respect to the prosecution of Nazi war criminals in Canada.[39] It is, however, of great importance for us to clearly understand that all the extensive publicity accompanying the war criminals issue did serve to concentrate Canadian public attention on the existence of antisemitism within Canadian society. It further highlighted the nexus between the issues of prosecuting war criminals and fighting against the perceived increase in Holocaust denial in Canada, in that activists in both areas tended to see the Canadian justice system as the preferred solution to the problems.

The well-publicized prosecution of Imre Finta from 1987 to 1990 was the first major test of the Canadian war crimes legislation. The failure to convict Finta, which largely stymied the ongoing prosecution of alleged Nazi war criminals in Canada, can nonetheless serve as an example of this nexus. Commonalities between the Finta case and the Holocaust denial trials include the fact that Finta was publicly supported by Holocaust denier Ernst Zundel and defended by attorney Doug Christie, who was deeply involved at that time in defending several prominent Holocaust deniers. David Matas notes as well that Christie, in his defence of Finta, attempted to assert the moral equivalence of Jews and Nazis to the members of the jury. In his defence arguments, Christie emphasized several arguments that Matas felt had antisemitic features. He thus pointedly cited the New Testament at length, implied that the Jewish witnesses testifying against Finta were both mercenary and vengeful, and highlighted Jewish sympathies with Communism.[40]

The Keegstra Affair

James Keegstra was a rural Alberta high school teacher and an activist in the Social Credit Party. As was mentioned earlier, he had absorbed teachings of an antisemitic nature inculcated within the Social Credit movement. He believed and taught his high school students in Eckville, Alberta, that an international Jewish conspiracy had manipulated the course of history for centuries, moving behind the scenes and manipulating events in order to secretly bring about the destruction of Christianity and the establishment of a single world government under Jewish control.[41]

Keegstra taught his students that the Holocaust did not happen but was yet another Jewish-Zionist fraud created by the Jews in order to gain sympathy for their cause and, especially, for the State of Israel.[42]

Antisemitism itself, in Keegstra's world view, was thus to be understood
as merely another Jewish fraud and smokescreen to be utilized for the
same purpose of advancing the Jews' campaign for world domination.[43]
As one of Keegstra's students wrote in an essay that was entered into evidence at his trial, "the Jews believe that by the year 2000 they will control
the world ... with the headquarters in Israel."[44]

Keegstra was charged in 1984 with promoting antisemitism and
Holocaust denial under Canada's hate crime laws, which had been
enacted as the result of the recommendations of the Cohen Committee.
His ensuing court battle was to become a landmark in Canadian juris-
prudence. At his original trial, Keegstra was convicted. However that
conviction was overturned by the appeals court after his lawyer, Doug
Christie, argued that the law under which he was convicted was unconstitutional because it violated the provisions of the Canadian Charter of
Rights and Freedoms which guaranteed Canadians freedom of expression. The Keegstra case stayed before the courts for well over a decade
until a 1996 ruling by the Supreme Court of Canada concluded that,
while it was true that the Canadian Criminal Code section on public
incitement of hatred under which Keegstra was convicted did impinge
on Keegstra's Charter rights, nonetheless in this case the infringement
was justified and Keegstra's conviction was upheld.[45]

The Ernst Zundel Affair

The Keegstra case was far from the only prosecution of Holocaust
deniers before the Canadian courts in this period. At the same time as
R. v. Keegstra was making its way through the justice system, the media
and public were also fixated on the sensational case of Ernst Zundel.
Zundel had been born in Germany and immigrated to Toronto in 1958.
He was attracted to antisemitic ideas and causes. In the course of his
antisemitic networking, Zundel had contacted and befriended Adrien
Arcand, who ultimately bequeathed to him his extensive collection of
antisemitic publications which Zundel utilized extensively.[46]

By the 1970s, Zundel had established a publishing house, Samis-
dat Books, in his Toronto home which became a major publisher and
distributor of Holocaust denial literature on a world scale.[47] He also

participated in the challenge to the authority of a course on the Holocaust presented in the Department of History at the University of Toronto.[48] Zundel was becoming well known to the Jewish community, and, in a seemingly jocular gesture, he applied for a job advertised by the Canadian Jewish Congress for director of its National Holocaust Project.[49] He placed a classified ad in the *Toronto Star* in 1981 before the High Holidays wishing all his Jewish friends a happy New Year.[50]

Zundel's publications on antisemitic subjects were exported to forty-two countries around the world.[51] In his own writings, and in the writings of other authors he published and distributed, Zundel argued that the systematic extermination of European Jews by Nazi Germany never happened. The Holocaust was rather a hoax perpetrated by the Jews in order to inflict guilt on the Western world and thereby help promote the establishment of the State of Israel.[52] Kristallnacht, the well-known November 1938 Nazi pogrom against the Jews, their synagogues, and their property in Germany was described by Zundel as the work of the Jews themselves. As he stated: "Mysterious people wearing SS uniforms suddenly appeared out of nowhere, set fire to the synagogues, and just as suddenly and mysteriously vanished. The same tactics the Zionists used against Germany as partisans, as maquis and as members of the Jewish Brigade; false uniforms, false documents, etc."[53]

Zundel was charged with "spreading false news" for publishing a pamphlet in 1974 entitled "Did Six Million Really Die?" contrary to section 181 of the Canadian Criminal Code, which states that "every one who willfully publishes a statement, tale or news that he knows is false and causes or is likely to cause injury or mischief to a public interest is guilty of an indictable offence and liable to imprisonment."

At his trial in 1985 Zundel was defended by Finta's and Keegstra's attorney, Doug Christie, whose defence strategy was to place the Jewish people and the reality of the Holocaust on trial.[54] Fellow Holocaust denier James Keegstra testified in Zundel's defence.[55] Zundel was convicted. However the appeals court ordered a new trial due to procedural errors during the original trial in the admission of evidence and in the instruction of the jury. Zundel was retried in 1988, and once again convicted. This conviction was upheld by the Cout of Appeal, at which point Zundel appealed his case to the Supreme Court of Canada.

The issue at law before the Supreme Court of Canada, which heard the case in 1992, was whether section 181 of the Criminal Code infringed "the guarantee of freedom of expression in s. 2(b) of the Canadian Charter of Rights and Freedoms and, if so, whether s. 181 is justifiable under s. 1 of the Charter." The majority opinion of the Supreme Court was written by Justice Beverley McLachlin. The court found that Zundel's publication had indeed violated section 181. The court observed that Zundel's pamphlet had "misrepresented the work of historians, misquoted witnesses, fabricated evidence, and cited non-existent authorities." However, the court also found that Criminal Code section 181 was in violation of section 2(b) of the Canadian Charter of Rights and Freedoms. Justice McLachlin's opinion noted that section 2(b) of the Charter protects all expression of a non-violent form, and as such, the fact that the content itself was false is irrelevant. The protection provided by the Charter encompasses the expression of minority beliefs even in those instances which the majority of the population may consider false. The imposition of imprisonment for such expression would have a severely limiting and unreasonable effect on freedom of expression in Canada. McLachlin further found that the restriction of freedom of speech concerning all expressions "likely to cause injury or mischief to a public interest" was far too broad.[56]

In the aftermath of Zundel's Supreme Court exoneration, observers began to re-evaluate whether the hate propaganda laws, which Doug Christie had characterized as "instruments of oppression,"[57] and which many considered a threat to freedom of speech, were a viable means of solving the problems of Holocaust denial. Alan Borovoy, general counsel of the Canadian Civil Liberties Association, thus advocated the law's repeal and stated his opinion that bringing Ernst Zundel to trial in the first place was "foolish" and had only earned Zundel wider publicity.[58] Shimon Fogel, CEO of the Centre for Israel and Jewish Affairs (CIJA) also stated in retrospect: "What was intended as a shield against hate has become a sword ... What it has really done is create difficulties for those who might legitimately want to raise questions about groups or ideas that in fact are a threat to the Jewish community or Israel. In effect, the act has become an instrument to chill critical debate about important issues like radical Islam."[59]

Some activists within the Jewish community who were disappointed with the Supreme Court decision attempted to continue their campaign against Zundel by lodging a complaint against him in the Canadian Human Rights Tribunal for promoting hatred against Jews on his website. Zundel continued to live in Toronto until 2000, when he left to live in the United States. He returned to Canada and was eventually deported to Germany in 2005 after a Canadian judge ruled his neo-Nazi and white supremacist connections made him a threat to national security. He was convicted in Germany for denying the Holocaust and was freed from a German prison in 2010 after serving the maximum five-year sentence.[60]

During Ernst Zundel's numerous trials and frequent court appearances to face the charges against him and to argue for his freedom to express his antisemitic perspectives in books, pamphlets, and on his website, he enjoyed a great deal of publicity, particularly in English Canada.[61] This extensive media coverage not infrequently descended to the level of a media circus which Zundel sought to exploit. As well, because the court in his first trial did not take "judicial notice" of the fact of the Holocaust, Zundel's defence was able to present "expert witnesses" who attempted to cast doubt on the Holocaust's reality. Zundel also tried to go on a counter-offensive with an unsuccessful attempt to prosecute one of his severest critics within the Jewish community, Saul Littman.[62]

Zundel expressed the opinion that his court appearances had created tremendous publicity for his ideas. Many of his opponents were inclined to agree, and there existed an apprehension among a number of observers who feared that Zundel might well be able to gain more followers in the court of public opinion.[63] These apprehensions were certainly fuelled by a 1985 poll that stated that only 50 percent of Canadians agreed that six million Jews had been killed in the Holocaust, and that 16 percent of the respondents were of the opinion that the Holocaust was partly the Jews' fault.[64] However, after the Zundel trial, another public opinion survey indicated that despite fears that publicity from the Zundel trial would create an antisemitic backlash, interest among the general public in the Holocaust had increased and support for Holocaust denial had declined.[65]

On the other hand, while it is not possible to directly connect this with the Zundel publicity, the year 1985 did see a significant rise in the number of overt antisemitic incidents, including the firebombing of Vancouver's Temple Shalom, arson attacks against a Jewish funeral home and a kosher butcher shop in Vancouver, and a number of anti-Jewish incidents of vandalism in Toronto.[66] Moreover, B'nai Brith Canada noted a tripling of reported incidents of antisemitic harassment and vandalism between 1987 and 1989. Though this significant increase could at least partly have resulted from B'nai Brith's improved networking which enabled the organization to have better access to reports of antisemitic incidents Canada-wide, B'nai Brith dismissed this interpretation and concluded that it had "little bearing ... on the significant increases over the last three years."[67] The fact that Nazi and Holocaust denial manifestations did not go away is also underlined by the fact that in 1988 a number of antisemitic incidents, many of which were connected to Nazism or the Holocaust, occurred at Canadian universities such as Concordia, York, Ryerson, McMaster, Western, and the University of Toronto.[68]

The Malcolm Ross Affair

In the 1980s, Atlantic Canada, which had witnessed incidents of antisemitism in the form of fliers in apartment mailboxes, letters, and swastikas in driveways,[69] had its own Holocaust denial *cause célèbre*. Malcolm Ross was a New Brunswick high school teacher with clearly antisemitic opinions. Ross published *Web of Deceit*, whose key message is that the Holocaust is a hoax and part of a world conspiracy on the part of the Jews—whom he characterizes as a "deadly poison"—to eliminate Christianity on behalf of Communism, financiers, and Zionism. [70] As well, Ross published *The Real Holocaust: The Attack on Unborn Children and Life Itself* in which he accused Jewish physicians of threatening "Christian civilization" by performing abortions.[71] Ross also wrote a series of letters to the *Moncton Times* in which he accused Jews of controlling international banking and of duping "much of Christendom into believing they were God's chosen people."[72]

Ross's publications shocked and dismayed the small local Jewish community, causing a Jewish parent, David Attis, to initiate a complaint to the New Brunswick Human Rights Commission. The Commission ordered Ross's employer, New Brunswick School District 15, to remove him from the classroom. Ross, who, like both Keegstra and Zundel, was represented by Doug Christie, appealed the decision, and the New Brunswick Court of Appeal ordered that the commission's decision be reversed on the ground that it contravened both his freedom of expression and freedom of religion. Like those of Keegstra and Zundel, the Ross case was eventually heard by the Supreme Court of Canada. In its 1996 decision, the Supreme Court held that the New Brunswick School District's removal of Ross from the classroom had been justified, but that the gag order which threatened him with dismissal from the non-teaching position to which he had been assigned, should he publish further antisemitic material, was unjustified.[73]

More Recent Issues of Holocaust Denial

Further evidence that Holocaust denial remained alive in Canada included the appearance, in early 1997, of articles published in some Canadian Arab community newspapers that, at one and the same time, denied the reality of the Holocaust perpetrated against the Jews and suggested that Jews were in fact planning a holocaust against North American Arabs.[74] In that same year, Doug Collins, a British Columbia journalist, also continued in the path of Holocaust denial when he cast public doubt about the veracity of the Holocaust and accused Hollywood's "powerful Jewish influence" of Holocaust propaganda at the time of the release of the motion picture *Schindler's List*. Collins was brought before the British Columbia Human Rights Commission, which affirmed that his columns were antisemitic but nonetheless dismissed the complaint against him, though in 1999 a similar complaint against him was upheld by the commission and was sustained on appeal.[75]

The David Ahenakew Affair

Another sensational Canadian case with a strong Holocaust theme, though it did not involve "denial" as such, was that of David Ahenakew. Ahenakew was a Canadian First Nations leader whose significant legacy of achievement, including a term as Chief of the Federation of Saskatchewan Indian Nations, and another as National Chief of the Assembly of

First Nations, was compromised by the accusation that he harboured antisemitic feelings. This accusation led to two trials on charges of promoting hatred of Jews and the revocation of his membership in the Order of Canada in 2005. His trials also have much to say about the nature of antisemitism in Canada as well as the limitations of the judicial process in combatting antisemitism.

The roots of Ahenakew's attitudes toward the Jews likely stem from his experience in the Canadian Forces from 1951 to 1967. During this period, he was stationed in Germany, where, according to his account, he was exposed to a German antisemitic narrative that he accepted as truth. According to this narrative, as he related it: "The Second World War was started by the Jews … The Jews damn near owned all of Germany prior to the war. That's why Hitler came in. He was going to make damn sure that the Jews didn't take over Germany, or even Europe. That's why he fried six million of those guys, you know. Jews would have owned the goddamned world." Ahenakew was also stationed in the Gaza Strip as a UN peacekeeper, where it is not unlikely that he adopted an anti-Israel narrative. As he stated, "And look what they're [Jews] doing now; they're killing people in Arab countries."

These remarks, which triggered Ahenakew's first trial, were made in a question-and-answer session after a lecture he gave at a meeting of the Federation of Saskatchewan Indian Nations on December 13, 2002. His comments were reported by the *Saskatoon Star-Phoenix* and were quickly picked up by the Canadian national media. Because of these remarks Ahenakew was charged in June 2003 with promoting hatred. In a magazine interview published soon afterward, he accused the media, which he held responsible for his troubles, of being controlled by Jews (another key element in the antisemitic narrative): "When a group of people, a race of people, control the world media, something has to be done about it."[76]

When he was put on trial in July 2005, Ahenakew attempted to excuse his remarks, blaming them on his diabetic condition, a change in medication, and his having drunk some wine previous to the lecture. He was convicted of promoting hatred against Jews and fined $1,000. However, one year later, in June 2006, the Saskatchewan Court of Queen's Bench overturned his conviction and ordered a new trial on the grounds that while Ahenakew's remarks were "on any standard ... shocking, brutal and hurtful," the judge had failed to properly take into account the context of Ahenakew's antisemitic statements that came out in an angry confrontation with a reporter, and therefore may not have constituted "willful" hatred.[77]

A new trial was held in 2008, as a result of which Ahenakew was acquitted of the charges against him. In the judgment, issued in February 2009, Judge Wilfred Tucker characterized Ahenakew's antisemitic remarks as "revolting, disgusting and untrue," but basically accepted the defence's contention that the confrontational context of the remarks did not constitute an "intent" to incite hatred.[78]

One thing the Ahenakew affair brings into focus is the presence of antisemitic attitudes among First Nations in Canada. Although a number of First Nations leaders like Matthew Coon Come condemned his antisemitism, other First Nations voices supported Ahenakew. For example, Manitoba Aboriginal leader Terry Nelson, who has himself accused the Canadian government of attempting to commit genocide against First Nations, publicly asserted that David Ahenakew was a victim of a Jewish-controlled media. In response to the Ahenakew affair, the Canadian Jewish communal leadership has devoted some attention to the First Nations community and has sponsored several trips to Israel by Aboriginal leaders.[79]

The second matter of importance made clear by the Ahenakew affair is the difficulty Canadians have found in prosecuting those accused of fomenting hatred against Jews. Indeed, in the wake of the Ahenakew case, the entire process of prosecuting Canadians under Criminal Code section 319 (2) has come under question. As a *National Post* editorial on the 2012 Saskatchewan trial of neo-Nazi Terry Tremain stated: "Canadian Society does an awfully good job of simply ignoring and marginalizing hateful messages without the law getting involved. We know this from the racist and anti-Semitic letters that we (and all newspapers) occasionally receive: the writers inevitably complain to us that their views are being 'ignored' by the 'mainstream media.'"[80]

More recently, prominent incidents of Holocaust denial have not resulted in litigation, possibly because they involved universities and the issue of academic freedom. Thus in 2005 Holocaust denier Lenni

Brenner was allowed to address a student group at the University of Waterloo.[81] In 2006, Professor Shiraz Dossa of Nova Scotia's St. Francis Xavier University attended an Iranian Holocaust denial conference. In the face of criticism at his university and in the Canadian media, Dossa attempted to reverse the accusations. He accused his critics of Islamophobia and complained that he was being denounced as a "Muslim professor" and a "Muslim Holocaust scholar … who also happens to be an outspoken critic of Israel's brutality in occupied Palestine." He was publicly defended by James Turk, executive director of the Canadian Association of University Teachers, on the basis of Dossa's academic freedom and "the right of academic staff to speak the truth as they see it without repression from their institution, the state, religious authorities, special interest groups or anyone else." Turk strongly chastised Dossa's critics as engaging in an "aggressive attempt based on very little information to denigrate Prof. Dossa and to vilify him."[82]

The Dossa case illustrates the intimate connection between the Holocaust denial issue and the equally if not more controversial subject of the State of Israel and the Israeli–Arab conflict. It is not a unique connection. In the emotional heat caused by the Gaza campaign in the summer of 2014, one can find references in anti-Israel polemic to the "alleged killing of millions of Jewish people in Nazi gas chambers."[83] In the next chapter we turn to a further consideration of the connection between Zionism, Israel, and antisemitism in Canada.

CHAPTER NINE

Zionism and Israel

Everything that happens today in the world has to do with the Zionists.
— Mikis Theodorakis[1]

We have seen in chapter 6 that in the interwar period the major ideological conflicts on the world stage involving Communism and Nazism had their impact on the course of antisemitism in Canada. It is therefore not at all surprising that Zionism, one of the most controversial ideologies of the twentieth century, has also strongly influenced antisemitism in Canada. Moreover, the establishment of the State of Israel in 1948 and its decades-long conflict with the Arab and Muslim world has also impacted strongly on the way antisemitism in Canada has been experienced, as we will see in this chapter.

Anti-Zionist Rhetoric and Antisemitism

The rhetoric on both sides of the conflict concerning Zionism and Israel has been polarized for so long that many of the highly committed antagonists in this arena seem to be unable to communicate directly to each other, or even to agree on basic facts, but rather most often tend to speak past each other. It is thus no surprise that the opposing sides in this conflict cannot agree on whether opposition to Zionism is or is not related to antisemitism. One aspect of this issue was addressed by Charles Stember as early as the 1960s. Stember said at that time: "Where antisemitism occurs it is so often entangled in other motives and issues ... that one grows uncertain in his beliefs that habitual prejudice against Jews is involved in any salient way."[2]

The sheer complexity of the factors involved in the nature of the anti-Zionist phenomenon makes Canadian scholar Michael Marrus argue for a careful, nuanced examination before deciding definitively whether anti-Zionism and antisemitism are one and the same phenomenon. Writing in 1986, Marrus was skeptical if "this emotional spasm warrants the term antisemitism."[3] In the first decade of the twenty-first century he reiterated a plea for caution in this area: "What is happening now seems to be the work of highly diverse, globally oriented bedfellows who occasionally promote a Jewish theme, rather than a recrudescence of ancient hatreds. Not every anti-Semitic expression is a reflection of the hoary anti-Semitic tradition, not every incident should evoke the Holocaust, and we need to be as clear-eyed as possible in judging just what it is, as a society that we face."[4] Gil Troy has also expressed his opinion that "it is hard sometimes to criticize Israel without appearing anti-Semitic."[5]

Part of the "entanglement of motives and issues" we must face is also connected to the fact that, as we have already had ample occasion to observe, antisemites more often than not have tended to vehemently deny that their views should be defined as antisemitic. Most certainly, anti-Zionists and opponents of Israel's existence consider accusations of antisemitism by their ideological opponents both false and little more than a political ploy designed to deflect what they consider legitimate criticism of Israel and its policies. Thus, as Bernard Harrison states:

> When a specific accusation is made with a view of demonstrating an instance of the new anti-Semitism, the person accused will almost always reply that he or she is hostile to *Israel*, or to the actions of one or another Israeli government; but not in the least hostile toward *Jews as such*. It is also very common ... for the accused to remark with considerable irritation that these accusations always seem to come from Jews ... [who] display a discreditable willingness to use accusations of anti-Semitism to deflect all and any criticism of Israel.[6]

Arnold Ages agrees. In his analysis of anti-Zionism he remarks that "anti-Zionism is a marvelous weapon to attack Jews with near impunity. Anyone who is challenged has merely to say, 'You see, if you attack Israel they call you antisemitic.'"[7] This sort of response by anti-Zionists is well represented by Canadian anti-Zionist academic Michael Keefer: "The rhetorical tactics being employed in this attack on free speech are familiar enough. They consist in leveling a charge of antisemitism against anyone who draws attention to the State of Israel's violent, degrading, and (under international law) flagrantly illegal treatment of the Palestinian people ... or who points to the fact that this treatment is motivated by a systematic and likewise flagrantly illegal project of colonization, apartheid treatment of a subject population, and ethnic cleansing."[8]

The perspective of somewhat less virulently anti-Israel Canadians is expressed by Jonathan Sas, who complains: "We resent not being able to talk about—and, yes, criticize—Israel's diminished democratic status without being scolded as naïve, or even ostracized."[9] Quebec journalist Nathalie Collard also asks pointedly whether there exists a space in the media to criticize Israel without being condemned by pro-Israel Jewish organizations like B'nai Brith.[10]

On the other hand, historian of antisemitism Robert Wistrich, a keen observer of contemporary antisemitic phenomena, tends to believe in the existence of the anti-Zionism/antisemitism nexus. As he states: "Even when presented in an impeccably anti-Zionist wrapping, such [anti-Israel] views all too often have reflected anti-Semitic bias, whether overt or covert. Unfortunately much of the European intelligentsia prefers to deny this fact, reducing anti-Semitism to a mere card played in bad faith by Israel and world Jewry. Since Jews are a priori deemed to be powerful, even addressing anti-Semitism as a serious problem tends to be seen as suspect in certain quarters or, worse still, as a Jewish invention."[11] Wistrich believes that "hatred for Israel more often appears to be the *result* [emphasis in original] of Jew hatred, rather than the reverse.[12] Canadian scholar Irving Abella certainly agrees with Wistrich when he says: "Antisemites ... try to prove that Zionism, or, more correctly, Judaism, is itself racist ... 'Zionist' is a synonym for 'Jew.'"[13] Similarly, Canadian legal scholar and member of Parliament Irwin Cotler is of the opinion that:

> the old antisemitism denies Jews their full rights as citizens, discriminates against them, and at times actively persecutes them. This has now been largely overshadowed by a new antisemitism that denies Jews their national rights and peoplehood. Discrimination against Israel and attacks

on Israel's existence deny Jews equal national rights. Israel is the only state in the world today—and the Jews are the only people in the world today—that are the object of a standing set of threats from governmental, religious, and terrorist bodies seeking their destruction.[14]

Finally, Canadian Prime Minister Stephen Harper, in his January 20, 2014, speech to the Israeli Knesset, showed in a lengthy portion of the address that he had fully assimilated the idea that some forms of opposition to Israel constitute a "new" antisemitism. For Harper, opposition to the policies of the State of Israel, while legitimate in a context of freedom of speech, can and does lead to antisemitic consequences:

And so we have witnessed, in recent years, the mutation of the old disease of anti-Semitism and the emergence of a new strain. We all know about the old anti-Semitism. It was crude and ignorant, and it led to the horrors of the death camps. Of course, in many dark corners, it is still with us. But, in much of the western world, the old hatred has been translated into more sophisticated language for use in polite society. People who would never say they hate and blame the Jews for their own failings or the problems of the world, instead declare their hatred of Israel and blame the only Jewish state for the problems of the Middle East. As once Jewish businesses were boycotted, some civil-society leaders today call for a boycott of Israel. On some campuses, intellectualized arguments against Israeli policies thinly mask the underlying realities, such as the shunning of Israeli academics and the harassment of Jewish students. Most disgracefully of all, some openly call Israel an apartheid state. Think about that. Think about the twisted logic and outright malice behind that: a state, based on freedom, democracy and the rule of law, that was founded so Jews can flourish, as Jews, and seek shelter from the shadow of the worst racist experiment in history, that is condemned, and that condemnation is masked in the language of anti-racism. It is nothing short of sickening. But this is the face of the new anti-Semitism. It targets the Jewish people by targeting Israel and attempts to make the old bigotry acceptable for a new generation. Of course, criticism of Israeli government policy is not in and of itself necessarily anti-Semitic. But what else can we call criticism that selectively condemns only the Jewish state and effectively denies its right to defend itself while systematically ignoring—or excusing—the violence and oppression all around it? What else can we call it when, Israel is routinely targeted at the United Nations, and when Israel remains the only country to be the subject of a permanent agenda item at the regular sessions of its human rights council?[15]

Those who support the legitimacy of Zionism and the State of Israel are invariably careful to differentiate between what they perceive as "legitimate" criticism of Israel and the sort of criticism they deem "illegitimate." Israeli scholar Yehuda Bauer thus defines the issue as follows: "Opposition to individual policies of the Israeli government, even if fierce and outspoken, is not necessarily antisemitism ... Opposition in principle to Jewish independence and to national rights for Jews, however, or opposition to Zionism as a national movement coupled with acceptance of all other national movements as legitimate, does constitute antisemitism."[16]

Former Canadian Prime Minister Brian Mulroney agrees that "one can strongly disagree with the policies of the government of Israel without being called an antisemite."[17] Similarly, on a policy level, the Anti-Defamation League in the United States has adopted the following guideline in defining an antisemitic action: "The ADL does not count critiques of Israel or Zionism as anti-Semitic incidents, unless such criticism invokes 'classic anti-Jewish stereotypes or inappropriate Nazi imagery and/or analogies' ... It does, however, count 'public expressions of anti-Israel sentiments that demonize Jews or create an atmosphere of fear or intimidation for U.S. Jews.'"[18]

It may be said that this principle has fostered the emergence of a kind of consensus among the majority of Canadian Jews that excessively one-sided criticism of Israel and certainly the rejection of Israel's right to exist or defend itself comes close to being antisemitic, if not in motivation then in outcome.[19]

Pre-1948 Anti-Zionism in Canada

While the controversy over whether antisemitism and anti-Zionism can be one and the same plays out in the op-ed columns and blogs of the twenty-first century, the relationship between antisemitism and the Jews' connection to the land of Israel is not new and its history can be traced back to well before Israel became a state in 1948. In Canada, the special connection between Palestine and the Jews was not lost on antisemites. We have already noted that in the nineteenth century Goldwin Smith argued that Jews who did not wish to entirely assimilate and who thus desired to remain "Jewish" should leave Canada and go to Palestine.[20] Camillien Houde, mayor of Montreal, addressing a meeting in Quebec City in 1930 on the Montreal Jewish school question, utilized the very same antisemitic trope. The issue of the place of Jewish children in Montreal's Protestant schools, as we have seen, had aroused a great deal of anti-Jewish feeling, and Houde was reported to have declared to his audience: "They [the Jews] have a new country and if they won't meet your demands they can go to Palestine, their country."[21]

When the Zionist movement began to create a Jewish homeland in British Mandate Palestine in the interwar years, the Zionists' project, which culminated in the declaration of Israel's independence in 1948, posed a significant challenge to the classic Christian conception of the supersession of Judaism by Christianity. Supersession left no room for a Jewish claim to a sovereign state or for the Jewish people to play any national role in contemporary history.[22] As Eugene Korn observes, this attitude makes it possible to understand that: "vehement and unbalanced Protestant criticisms against Israel are rooted in traditional Christian biases against Jews and Judaism. Because Israel is the public face of the Jewish people today ... unjust attitudes toward Israel often indicate a continuing underlying animus to Jews and the Jewish people."[23] This meant that a number of churchmen tended to look upon the rise of the State of Israel with considerable misgiving. An important Canadian example of this phenomenon is Rev. Claris Silcox.

During the 1930s, Silcox had been one of Canada's most prominent opponents of Canadian government policies that refused to allow desperate Jewish refugees from Nazism into Canada.[24] Although he was widely known as a sympathetic advocate for the Jews, he showed himself to be more than ambivalent on the subject of Zionism, especially as a Jewish state in Palestine came closer to realization. In 1947, the year of the United Nations General Assembly resolution calling for the creation of a Jewish state in Palestine, he stated, "with some hesitation," that the

Jews' nostalgia for Palestine was a cause of antisemitism in almost every age and militated against the Jews' complete identification with the people among whom they were temporarily living. For Silcox, therefore, Zionist efforts in Palestine were "creating a new focal centre of anti-Semitism."[25] Silcox considered the 1917 Balfour Declaration a terrible mistake, and the United Nations plan to partition Palestine into Jewish and Arab states was for him "utterly stupid." He also believed that the establishment of a Jewish state would bring about "a more bitter anti-Semitism than this world has ever known."[26] Once Israel was founded, Silcox became severely critical of the actions of the State of Israel and was obviously stung by adverse Jewish reactions to his criticisms. In 1956, at the time of the Sinai campaign, Silcox complained that anyone critical of the behaviour of the Zionists "invite[s] the charge of being anti-Semitic."[27]

The Canadian Social Credit movement, which, as we have seen, harboured within it distinct antisemitic tendencies, demonstrated that Zionism was one of the areas of alleged Jewish malfeasance that attracted its attention. For Alberta Social Credit MP Norman Jacques, anti-Zionism constituted one of the recurring antisemitic themes in his speeches in the House of Commons. He thus stated that political Zionism and Communism were "the only real threat to the peace of the world.[28] Indeed, for Jacques, Zionism was an integral part of a Jewish plot, and "the struggle for Palestine [is] the key to [Jewish] world control."[29]

These ideas lingered in the Social Credit movement through the 1950s. At the October 1957 convention of the British Columbia Social Credit League in Vancouver one delegate, Percy Young, made a vehement anti-Zionist address. In that speech Young stated: "Zionism has completely destroyed Christianity and it will destroy Social Credit too unless the people have proper education."[30] The Canadian Jewish Congress immediately protested the speech to Solon Low, leader of the Social Credit Party in the federal Parliament, who at the end of his career became a declared friend of Israel,[31] and to the premiers of the Social Credit governments in British Columbia and Alberta. The CJC, which noted "past disavowals of anti-Semitism by the Social Credit

Movement," received from Low a statement that "Mr. Young was not expressing the views of the Social Credit Association of Canada, and I wish most strongly to disassociate our movement from the references he made to Zionism and the Jews."[32]

The *United Church Observer* Affair

Israel's signal victory in the Six Day War of 1967 provoked a prolonged controversy between the Canadian Jewish community and the United Church of Canada that lasted until early 1973 and flared up again during and after the Yom Kippur War of 1973.[33] Rev. Alfred C. Forrest, editor of the prominent Canadian Protestant periodical *United Church Observer*, condemned Israeli policies in his magazine with such vehemence that he was accused by many Jews of antisemitism.[34] Toronto Jewish philosopher and theologian Emil Fackenheim was one of Forrest's accusers. Fackenheim stated:

> Ever since the Six Day War the most visible and powerful groups in the United Church have behaved toward the Jewish people as though the Church were, indeed, a monolithic body, and their behavior has been hostile. To be more specific, *The Observer* has shown an ever-increasing anti-Jewish bias, and United Church officials, while seeking refuge behind the editor's freedom of speech, have either themselves kept silent or else used their own freedom of speech only to defend the policies of the editor, or even to attack, often vociferously, those who opposed these policies ... No official I know of has used his freedom of speech to oppose the anti-Jewish policies of *The Observer*.[35]

In response to these accusations, Forrest claimed that his opponents within the Jewish community had lost sight of the difference between antisemitism and legitimate criticism of Israel. In evaluating the positions of the two sides, Alan T. Davies concluded that much of the controversy stemmed from fundamental misunderstandings on both sides: "Many Christians ... could not understand why Jews were so touchy when Israel was criticized and they put it down to unreason; Jews could not understand why Christians could not see what was perfectly obvious to them. Hence each grew frustrated and increasingly angry."[36]

Toronto Rabbi Reuben Slonim, who was by no means unsympathetic to many of Forrest's positions, attempted to understand the position of Forrest's Jewish opponents in this way: "The Canadian Jew believes his existence is always precarious. Any pressure from without could topple him from his hazardous position. When the *Observer* publishes articles he considers anti-Semitic or anti-Israel and United Church leaders fail to announce their displeasure with the *Observer* stand, he reacts passionately, because he is firmly convinced that his security and status are at stake."[37]

Rev. Forrest, in defence of his anti-Israel positions, adumbrated several key arguments that would be reiterated time and again by Israel's opponents in the decades to follow. One of these arguments is that his presentation was meant to balance the allegedly pro-Israel coverage in the Western media.[38] However in the course of redressing this alleged media imbalance, reminiscent of the frequent antisemitic charge that "the Jews" dominate the media, Forrest also printed out-and-out anti-semitic articles in his periodical such as John Nicholls Booth's "How Zionists Manipulate Your News."[39]

Another often-utilized argument employed by Forrest was that, since some Jews were anti-Zionist, opposition to Zionism could not possibly be antisemitic.[40] Furthermore, Forrest compared Israel to the apartheid regime in South Africa. For Forrest, the Israelis "made the South Africans look like babes in the wood when it comes to practicing apartheid and keeping another race in its place and misleading the world about it." He finally compared Israelis with the Nazis: "I do not like to refer in any way to Israel's treatment of the Arabs as Nazi but the parallels are so numerous and so similar."[41]

Taking all the evidence carefully into consideration, Rabbi Slonim concluded that "if a reader since 1967 were to obtain his information on the Middle East from *The Observer* as his only source, the picture would be distorted beyond recognition. The fault is not ... that Forrest favors the Arabs ... The error, most grievous, is that the editor interposes himself between his readers and the situation to be covered ... [A] ... magazine has a responsibility not to diffuse the dividing line between opinion and fact. In the years 1967 to 1969 that line almost disappears."[42]

Though the overt quarrel between the United Church of Canada and the Jewish community subsided, tensions remained. On antisemitism, the United Church of Canada's policy, adopted in 2002, states that "The Church ... strongly repudiates any suggestion that disagreement with the policies of the State of Israel should lead to attacks on the Jewish people. The United Church of Canada reiterates its passionate prayer for peace, security and justice for all peoples of the region as it recommits itself to denounce antisemitism whenever and wherever it occurs."[43] Despite this clear opposition to antisemitism, however, the United Church has displayed a continuing history of anti-Israel rhetoric and in 2012 voted to back a campaign entitled "Unsettling Goods" to boycott a list of items made by Israeli firms in the West Bank.[44]

The United Church, as well as Canadian Catholic, Anglican, Presbyterian, Evangelical Lutheran, and Mennonite churches have also supported KAIROS, a Toronto-based NGO that sponsors projects "promoting social and economic justice" in Africa, Asia, Latin America, and the Middle East. In 2009, Canadian Immigration Minister Jason Kenney ended thirty-five years of government funding to KAIROS as part of an effort to cut off such funding to antisemitic organizations. KAIROS had been "defunded," Kenney asserted, because it had been prominent in the boycott, divestment, and sanctions campaign against Israel. This was a charge that KAIROS vigorously denied.[45]

Israel and French Canada

The 1967 Middle East war also elicited a number of reactions in French Canada that gave verisimilitude to the 1969 statement of French Holocaust survivor Jean Améry that "antisemitism, which is contained in anti-Zionism as the thunderstorm is part of the cloud, is again respectable."[46] Because Quebec is the sort of place in which religious, ethnic, and linguistic conflicts often manifest themselves in the public square, issues of antisemitism and anti-Zionism are frequently discussed, particularly in its French-language media. The State of Israel and its alleged misdeeds in the post-1967 era provide numerous examples of anti-Israel and anti-Zionist themes in Quebec public discourse that have been interpreted as antisemitic.[47] These include opinions that Jews are all openly or covertly Zionists, that Zionism is a form of colonialism, imperialism, and racism, and that therefore all Jews are colonialists, imperialists, and racists.[48]

In the years following 1967, this trend was evident in Quebec journalism,[49] and Quebec writers of pro-Israel articles often received antisemitic responses from readers. Thus future Quebec premier René Lévesque, then a newspaper columnist, published a pro-Israel article shortly after the Six Day War. In response to this article, Lévesque received a number of anti-Israel letters, one of which included the insinuation that a group of elite Jews was behind the genocide the United States was committing in Vietnam. Lévesque characterized the antisemitism contained in one of these letters in the following way: "One sent me an entire synopsis of the 'Protocols of the Elders of Zion,' saying to me, 'After having read these infamous Protocols written by your friends the Jews, can you dare ask us to love them tenderly? Now be honest: Hitler was right!'"[50]

Anti-Israel sentiment in Quebec was also evident in some radical separatist circles, including the Front de Libération du Québec (FLQ), whose members tended to identify as fellow revolutionaries with the Palestinian cause and which sent some of its members to Algeria and Jordan for training in guerrilla warfare.[51] Even in the less militantly separatist Parti Québécois (PQ), leader René Lévesque confronted a significant body of anti-Israel and pro-Palestinian sentiment, especially among the party's younger members.[52]

In 1975, at the time when Zionism was condemned as racism in a United Nations General Assembly vote,[53] Yvon Charbonneau, then president of the Centrale de l'enseignement du Québec (CEQ) and known as a virulent anti-Zionist, stated that it was incumbent on Quebec teachers to instill anti-Zionist sentiments in the minds of their pupils.[54] The CEQ attempted to distribute in Quebec schools pro-Palestinian material accusing Israel of "genocide" against Palestinian Arabs.[55]

A significant part of the Quebec public discourse critical of Israel was directed at the Montreal Jewish community for its perceived support for Israel's policies. Charbonneau thus raised an accusation against Montreal Jewish community leaders Sam Steinberg and Bernard Finestone for their support of Israel.[56] Political and trade union leader Michel Chartrand, president of the Confederation of National Trade Unions

(CNTU), spoke of a sinister Jewish conspiracy,[57] pointedly referred to Charles Bronfman and Steinberg, prominent Montreal Jewish leaders, among his enemies,[58] and was quoted as saying: "We don't want them [Quebec Jews] to poison the air of this country any more. Israel is now committing the same barbaric crimes against others that were committed against her in her previous history. We are sick and tired of being called antisemites."[59]

The Quebec separatist monthly *Ici Québec* in a February 1978 article written by the magazine's editor-in-chief, accused Israel of racism and called Zionism "the cancer of the world." Lévesque, commenting on the article at a news conference, sought to distance his party from the publication, which had been condemned by the Quebec Press Council, stating that it was "a lousy article … reeking of prejudice." While "it is permissible to criticize Zionism," he noted, "there is a delicate line between anti-Zionism and antisemitism." Levesque insisted that the "Parti Québécois was in no way linked to the magazine." Nonetheless Jean-Marie Cossette, the director of *Ici Québec*, was elected president of the Montreal branch of the party.[60]

René Lévesque, as leader of the Parti Québécois and the first PQ premier, adopted a moderately anti-Israel and pro-Palestinian stance, without, however, calling for the elimination of Israel.[61] He thus wrote that the establishment of Israel was an "incredible political blunder" and that the Palestinian cause was "just."[62] Others within the PQ nonetheless continued to advocate a harder anti-Israel line that appeared to some observers to be antisemitic in nature. Among them was Yves Michaud, who in 2001, pointedly asked the Jews of Quebec how they could reject Quebec sovereignty and yet affirm that of Israel.[63] Michaud further commented: "It's always about you [Jews]. You're the only people in the world to have suffered in the history of humanity. I had just about had it." On efforts then under way to change the name of the Lionel Groulx Metro station in Montreal on the grounds of Groulx's antisemitism, Michaud stated: "It's the B'nai Brith who did that—they're the extremist arm, you know, of international Zionism."[64]

Michaud's remarks were criticized as antisemitic by Parti Québécois Premier Lucien Bouchard and were condemned by the Quebec National Assembly. The subsequent criticism of Bouchard within his party for "l'affaire Michaud" became the official reason for Premier Bouchard's resignation in January 2001.[65]

In February 2003, Ghila Sroka, editor of *Tribune Juive*, launched an attack on the French-language media in Quebec for their anti-Israel bias, singling out Radio-Canada (the French-language network of the Canadian Broadcasting Corporation). The *Tribune Juive*'s special issue was provocatively entitled, "Montréal: Capitale de la Palestine," and in the lead story Sroka wrote of the emergence of what she termed a "judéophobie perverse" in Quebec's universities, media, and unions, where "anti-Jewish ideas circulate freely without encountering the least resistance."[66] She charged that, within Quebec intellectual circles, it had become politically and psychologically acceptable to be antisemitic.[67]

The June 1982 Israeli campaign in Lebanon marked a turning point in the tenor of anti-Israel discourse in Canada. B'nai Brith Canada noted that "after June, 1982, the criticism of Israel [in the media] could no longer be described as merely the expression of opinion, or even of ideology. Criticism of Israel and criticism of the historical position of Diaspora Jewry was firmly established for the purpose of a propaganda campaign against the Jews."[68]

Anti-Zionism and the Left

The anti-Israel campaign in Canada was now starting to be led from the left of the political spectrum, even though for some observers in the 1980s this turn of events was highly surprising. For them, evidence of antisemitism on the left seemed "an odd speculation given that anti-Semitism is generally associated with the right."[69] Just this sort of propaganda campaign was taken to the streets of Montreal with a demonstration against Israeli leader Ariel Sharon, who had come to Montreal in June 1983 to address a Jewish group. The demonstration was led by Canadian Arabs, combined with elements of Yvon Charbonneau's teachers' union as well as the Communist Party.[70]

Concerning the phenomenon of leftist anti-Zionism, Bernard Harrison points out: "The very force of the moral indignation felt on the left on behalf of the Palestinians ... compel some of their more committed supporters ... on the left to feel themselves ... morally obliged to present the situation in progressively more extreme and emotionally heightened terms in an effort to capture the attention of affluent Western audiences."[71] For these leftists, Zionism is a form of colonialism, imperialism, and racism, and thus all Zionists are colonialists, imperialists, and racists, either openly or covertly.[72] Some of their ideologues believe that antisemitism can constitute a most useful weapon in this political struggle.[73] Thus pro-Palestinian academic Michael Neumann of Trent University in Peterborough, Ontario, has stated:

> If an effective strategy [in support of the Palestinians] means that some truths about the Jews don't have to come to light, I don't care. If an effective strategy means encouraging reasonable anti-Semitism, or reasonable hostility to Jews, I also don't care. If it means encouraging vicious, racist anti-Semitism or the destruction of the State of Israel, I still don't care … To regard any shedding of Jewish blood as a world-shattering calamity … is racism, pure and simple; the valuing of one race's blood over all others.[74]

At its extreme, therefore, this leftist anti-Zionism betrays definite antisemitic aspects. Rabbi Jonathan Sacks comments on this phenomenon when he states:

> An assault on Jewish life always needs justification by the highest source of authority in the culture at any given age. Throughout the Middle Ages the highest authority in Europe was the Church. Hence anti-Semitism took the form of Christian anti-Judaism. In the post-enlightenment Europe of the 19th century the highest authority was no longer the Church. Instead it was science. Thus was born racial anti-Semitism, based on two disciplines regarded as science in their day: the "scientific study of race" and the Social Darwinism of Herbert Spencer and Ernst Haeckel … Since Hiroshima and the Holocaust, science no longer holds its pristine place as the highest moral authority. Instead, that role is taken by human rights. It follows that any assault on Jewish life—on Jews or Judaism or the Jewish state—must be cast in the language of human rights. Hence the by-now routine accusation that Israel has committed the five cardinal sins against human rights: racism, apartheid, ethnic cleansing, attempted genocide and crimes against humanity … this is the only form in which an assault on Jews can be stated today.[75]

What this means is that, as Morton Weinfeld points out, in Canada leftist critics of Israeli policies find themselves in a sort of pragmatic alliance "with other demonizers of Israel," who include some of the most "unsavory, undemocratic, violent, dictatorial, misogynist, homophobic and generally illiberal regimes and groups anywhere."[76] It is thus no surprise that some anti-Israel protests draw support as well from white supremacists,[77] who now tend to play up their opposition to Zionism,[78] as occurred in 2012 when a swastika was displayed at an anti-Israel rally in Halifax.[79] The possibility of the furtherance of their antisemitic activities through anti-Zionism was apparent to the Canadian branch of the white supremacist Heritage Front, whose website was cited as stating: "Remember to say 'Zionists,' 'bankers,' or 'Israel Firsters' instead of 'Jews' when making public speeches or writing articles."[80]

For the Jewish community, therefore, the semantic nexus on the part of Israel's opponents between "Jewish" and "Zionist" means that anti-Zionist rhetoric has to be taken as an antisemitic attack against the Jewish people as a whole.[81]

The Dual-Loyalty Issue

By the late 1980s, during the First Intifada, strong criticism of Israel seemed to have gone from extreme radical elements in Canadian society—left and right—toward the mainstream. On March 10, 1988, Progressive Conservative External Affairs Minister Joe Clark spoke at the annual dinner of the Canada-Israel Committee (CIC). In that speech, before strong supporters of Israel, Clark accused Israel of committing grave human rights violations against the Palestinians. For Clark, these Israeli actions were "illegal" and were designed to maintain Israeli control by "force and fear." In response to Clark, CIC chair Sidney Spivak stated that the Jewish community would bear in mind what they had heard at the next election. Many in the audience walked out on Clark, and the CIC issued a press release critical of Clark's position.

While Clark and Prime Minister Brian Mulroney promptly engaged in damage control and reiterated Canada's "unwavering support" and "firm friendship" for Israel,[82] this public dispute resulted in accusations by the *Toronto Star*, Canada's largest-circulation newspaper, of "dual loyalty"—that Jewish citizens of Canada were primarily loyal to Israel and its policies.[83] On March 12, 1988, the *Star* published an editorial praising Clark's speech to the CIC as "a necessary reminder to members of the Jewish community in Canada that they are citizens of Canada, not Israel." This very public raising of the dual-loyalty accusation, seemingly addressed to all Jewish Canadians, exacerbated the CIC–Joe Clark controversy and elicited demands that the newspaper apologize for its remarks, which the *Star* refused to do. Ultimately the Ontario Press Council, acting on a complaint, determined that the *Star* should have made clear that it was not referring to all Canadian Jews, only those who had walked out on Clark.[84]

The sentiments manifested by Joe Clark's speech and by the *Toronto Star* editorial were hardly unique. Polling in the United States between 1964 and 1981 demonstrated a marked increase in agreement on the part of the respondents with the notion that the primary loyalty of American Jews was to Israel.[85] Such feelings were evidently held within the political class in Canada. Pierre Elliott Trudeau stated that Canadian Jews had "opened the way to growing antisemitism" by making their views known on matters related to Israel and anti-boycott legislation.[86] Similarly, a former moderator of the United Church of Canada wrote in the *Toronto Star* that the Jews could cause antisemitism if they continued to attack those who spoke out against Israel.[87] Presumably they felt, like US President Richard Nixon, that because Nixon's foreign policy adviser, Henry Kissinger, was Jewish meant that he should not be involved in policymaking relative to Israel.[88] Thus in 1992 the appointment of Norman Spector, who was Jewish, as the first Canadian ambassador to Israel was subject to criticism on this basis; as well, the entire political career of former Canadian justice minister Irwin Cotler has been marked by allegations of dual loyalty on his part.[89]

The Nazi Comparison

Canadian Jews reacted to this perceived change in atmosphere. In a February 1989 speech in Toronto, historian Irving Abella asserted that severe criticism of Israel was serving as a means to legitimize antisemitism. As he stated, "The poison of anti-Semitism has been decanted from the old

Czarist bottle and put into a new one." In particular, Abella condemned as dishonest the media's use of the Holocaust image in comparing Israelis to the Nazis.[90] As Abella wrote somewhat later, "the victims of the Holocaust, the people slated for destruction, must prove in court not only that they suffered, but that they have not established the successor state to Nazi Germany."[91]

Bernard Harrison concurs with Abella:

> To assert of any group that it is indistinguishable from the Nazis ... is precisely to stigmatize it *as evil* ... that it is so irredeemably bad that ... the only desirable thing ... is that it should be ... expunged from the face of the world ... To attach the label "Nazi" to Israel ... is thus not just to express opposition ... to the policies of one or another Israeli government. It is to defame Israel by association with the most powerful symbol of evil.[92]

Israel thus became, in the rhetoric of its accusers, a Nazi entity—a state so utterly devoted to evil, so far beyond the bounds of human decency as to make suicide bombing a comprehensible reaction on the part of its victims.[93]

Anti-Zionism on Campus

In September 2002, Harvard University president Lawrence Summers publicly warned of the increasing connection between anti-Zionism and antisemitism on campus: "Profoundly anti-Israel views are increasingly finding support in progressive intellectual communities ... Serious and thoughtful people are advocating and taking actions that are anti-Semitic in their effect, if not their intent."[94]

In the same month that Summers issued his warning, events at Montreal's Concordia University gave a Canadian focus to the debate on campus antisemitism. Concordia is a university with a largely commuter student body that has attracted many first-generation Canadians as students, including large numbers of Muslim and Arab students. In the context of the Second Intifada, ongoing since 2000, Solidarity for Palestinian Human Rights (SPHR), a well-organized group founded "to uphold the rights of the Palestinian people in the face of human rights violations and all forms of racism, discrimination, misinformation and misrepresentation,"[95] made Jewish students feel uncomfortable and even intimidated by its activism. In April 2002, the Concordia Student Union (CSU) adopted a resolution on Palestinian Human Rights, voted on by some 1,400 of 20,000 eligible students, that called on the Canadian government to cut political and economic ties with Israel. For the fall 2002 semester, the CSU published a student handbook entitled *Uprising*, which promoted the Palestinian cause. These CSU initiatives caused much disquiet in Montreal's Jewish community.

While the university, led by Rector Frederick Lowy, attempted to keep its discourse on an even keel and tried to deal with community criticisms by deploring the handbook's contents, calling many of its statements "inflammatory and possibly libelous," its hands were substantially tied. The student union was a legally independent entity and not at all under the university's control. It would take new student union elections in order to oust the CSU administration.[96]

In the meantime, Concordia became the site of radical anti-Israel demonstrations by militant Arab students and their leftist allies, creating an atmosphere of hostility and intimidation for pro-Israel students. These students found that they had no help from a CSU that fully supported the Palestinian cause, nor from the university administration, which felt powerless to intervene. Jewish students experienced what they considered to be acts of anti-Zionism and antisemitism, including a provocative display of mock Palestinian gravestones by SPHR strategically placed at a central point in Concordia's main classroom building where thousands of students and faculty passed daily.

In September 2002, then former Israeli Prime Minister Benjamin Netanyahu was invited by Hillel Concordia, which SPHR called "Concordia's Zionist student group,"[97] to provide a strong pro-Israeli voice in response to the plethora of anti-Zionist propaganda emanating from SPHR and CSU. The anti-Israel groups—led by the Quebec Coalition for a Just Peace in the Middle East, with a key role played by Aaron Maté, a vice-president of CSU—determined that they would prevent Netanyahu from presenting his lecture and a violent protest created a situation that neither the campus security nor the Montreal police was able to control. Protesters smashed glass windows, threw various objects at police, and abused and assaulted people on their way into the lecture. The event was cancelled, and the university imposed a moratorium on Middle East–related events that was not to be lifted until late November. Five people were arrested in connection with the riot and the university instituted disciplinary proceedings against twelve identifiable ringleaders. Leaders of the Jewish community criticized both the police and the university administration for failing to provide Netanyahu with adequate security. Netanyahu himself declared that "what we had was a coercive riot to prevent the airing of the truth."[98]

Subsequent to the September riots, the CSU executive moved to suspend Hillel Concordia in an action that was accompanied by several irregularities in procedure and ultimately involved litigation by Hillel against CSU.[99]

Other Canadian campuses saw an increase in anti-Zionist activity in subsequent years. In particular, the University of Toronto in 2005 was the original site of an annual event called Israel Apartheid Week (IAW), which has since spread to many campuses in Canada and elsewhere. The aim of IAW is to portray Israel and Zionism, the ideology that created it, as racist, illegitimate, and comparable with the white supremacist apartheid regime in South Africa. Those protesting to the University of Toronto against the activities of IAW were told that since it operates within the limits of free speech as understood by the university, it could not be banned. While some observers feel that IAW in its first decade has become essentially "a non-event for students" and does not generate either the publicity or the overt tensions of the past, others decry the ways in which it has adversely influenced campus life for identified Jews.[100] The latter would certainly agree with the 2007 statement issued by the University of Toronto Hillel that "the extremist nature of this week does nothing to promote dialogue, cultural understanding, and campus unity. Rather it only serves to promote hatred and intolerance. While we are committed to freedom of speech on campus, we feel this inflammatory week of programs imposes a toxic environment on all students."[101]

Similar tensions have flared up on other Canadian campuses, most strikingly at York University in Toronto, where Jewish and other pro-Israel students felt themselves to be intimidated and besieged by militantly pro-Palestinian demonstrators. Confrontations there in 2009 between pro- and anti-Zionist activists and demonstrators resulted in numerous sensational headlines.[102] In 2012, allegations arose that IAW had created an antisemitic atmosphere at Carleton University in Ottawa.[103] However, some observers, like the *National Post*'s Jonathan Kay, dismissed accusations concerning anti-Zionist agitation at York University as exaggerated and stated that there is no evidence that tensions at Canadian universities like Concordia or York have affected Jewish enrolment in the long run.[104]

The Muslim Community in Canada

There has been a significant increase in the number of Muslim Canadians in the past few decades. Just over one million individuals identified as Muslim in the 2011 Canadian census, representing 3.2 percent of the nation's total population, up from the 2.0 percent recorded in the 2001 census.[105] Given that many Muslims in Canada are relatively recent immigrants from countries in which strongly expressed anti-Zionist and antisemitic rhetoric is frequently to be found, it is of little surprise that some of the anti-Zionist rhetoric emanating from the Canadian Muslim community has been seen as antisemitic, for in their countries of origin Jews and Judaism have become defined for Muslims largely in terms of Zionism.[106] For many Muslims, as Wistrich points out, Jews have also become a metaphor for the dangers of Western domination and immorality.[107]

Mohamed Elmasry, a professor at the University of Waterloo, headed an organization called the Canadian Islamic Congress (ironically paralleling the name of the prominent Jewish organization, Canadian Jewish Congress). On a Toronto TV talk show in 2004, Elmasry argued that any Jew in Israel of military age (over eighteen) could be a legitimate target for terrorists, because they are "not innocent." Though Elmasry later apologized for his statement, his organization's website has featured much negative material on Jews and Israel, as well as justifications for Hamas and for Iran's nuclear program. Elmasry has accused Israel and the Jews of ethnic cleansing, apartheid, instigating the invasion of Iraq, and forming a Jewish "cabal" that effectively runs the Canadian government.[108]

Another organization that made news for its publications on this subject was the Canadian Arab Federation (CAF). In January 2014 Canadian Federal Court Justice Russel Zinn ruled that a government decision to stop funding the CAF over charges of antisemitism was justified. Zinn ruled that "CAF cannot completely disassociate itself from the content of web links it includes in its materials, or from comments, distribution of materials, or attendance at meetings and conference by its executives." The court rejected arguments that Minister of Employment and Social Development and for Multiculturalism Jason Kenney had thereby restricted free expression on the Israeli–Palestinian issue.[109]

In April 2004 the firebombing of the library of the United Talmud Torahs school in the Montreal suburb of Saint-Laurent created great concern in the Montreal community. Flyers left at the scene claimed that the act was in retaliation for the Israeli army's killing of the leader of Hamas, Sheik Ahmed Yassin. The document blamed Israel for crimes against the Palestinians and warned that "this is just the beginning." The perpetrator was a Muslim, nineteen-year-old Sleiman Elmerhebi, who was apprehended and pleaded guilty to arson in a plea bargain.[110]

In September 2006, a Molotov cocktail was thrown into the Skver Hasidic boy's school building in the Montreal suburb of Outremont, home to several Hasidic groups. The resulting fire caused considerable damage to the school.[111] The perpetrators was eventually arrested and turned out to be Omar Bulphred and his accomplice Azim Abigimov, Georgian Muslim immigrants to Montreal who had become Canadian citizens. They had also attempted to set off an explosion at the Montreal YM-YWHA on the night of the Passover Seder in April 2007.[112] Although the police were initially reluctant to describe the incident as a hate crime, the Jewish community considered it to be exactly that, and further investigation by the police showed clearly that antisemitism had been a motivating factor in both cases.[113] Certainly the number of perpetrators of antisemitic incidents who self-identified as Muslims has increased measurably in recent years, up from 16 in 2011 to 87 in 2012.[114]

Beyond physical attacks on Jewish targets by individuals within the Muslim community, some Islamic clerics, such as Sheikh Younus Kathrada, the leader of the Vancouver mosque Dar al-Madinah, have denounced Jews as "the brothers of monkeys and swine," stressing that the Quran depicts Jews as treacherous.[115] In a sermon placed on the Internet Sheikh Kathrada said: "Unfortunately we hear too many people saying we must build bridges with them [the Jews]. No. They understand one language. It is the language of the sword, and it is the only language they understand."[116]

The press of the Canadian Muslim community has also attracted attention. The Royal Canadian Mounted Police Hate Crimes Unit investigated a series of articles appearing in *The Miracle*, a Muslim newspaper in British Columbia. The articles blamed the Jews for both world wars as well as the 9/11 terror attacks. The investigation concluded that this was not hate literature per se, and although the paper clearly intended to promote hatred, that intention was insufficient to prosecute.[117] In addition, antisemitic cartoons[118] and statements of Holocaust denial[119] have appeared in several Muslim community newspapers in Toronto.

Antisemitic comments were witnessed at a 2011 "Al-Quds Day" rally at the Ontario Legislature in Toronto. This rally has become an annual event in Toronto, with Jewish observers decrying its speakers' calls for the elimination of Israel and the killing of Israelis, although the attorney general of Ontario has refused to prosecute the man who publicly called for the expulsion or killing of Jews in Jerusalem.[120] Although the rally was forbidden to use the grounds of the Ontario Legislature itself in 2013, it simply moved to a park a few hundred metres away.[121] Its 2014 event spawned comments caught on video such as "Israel does not believe in humanity. They just believe in the killing. They want to make money with the blood of the human being. They are sucking the blood out of the human being just to make the money" and "We will go from here … and we will kill all Israel."[122]

In the same summer of 2014, Israel's response to Hamas's rocket and missile attacks resulted in anti-Israel feeling that resulted in violent attacks on individual Jews in Montreal and on a small group of pro-Israel demonstrators at an anti-Israel rally in Calgary.[123] In addition, protesters invaded the building of Montreal's Federation/CJA, asserting that the Canadian Jewish community, through its CIJA organization, was "complicit" in the "massacre" in Gaza.[124] Even though this violence pales in comparison with anti-Jewish violence in Europe,[125] David

Ouellette of CIJA stated in June 2014 that, for the first time in years, the conflict in the Middle East has led to a rise in anti-Jewish sentiment in Montreal,[126] and thousands marched in Toronto to protest their perception of "a resurgence of global anti-Semitism."[127]

The curricula of Canadian Muslim schools have also come under scrutiny for possible antisemitism. In 2012, the Toronto District School Board (TDSB) reacted to complaints that a Toronto Islamic school, the East End Madrassah, which was housed in TDSB facilities, utilized textbooks referring to Jews as "treacherous" and comparing them to Nazis.[128] Imam Sayed Mohammed Rizvi and the East End Madrassah were criticized for disparaging Jews and Judaism in the school's textbooks, which had been published by Iranian foundations.[129] A subsequent investigation of the Madrassah's syllabus books by the York Region Police hate crimes unit found portions originating in Iran that "challenged some of Canada's core values" and "suggested intolerance." No charges were laid, however.[130]

The BDS Movement

In recent years, the movement to boycott Israel has become a prominent part of the discourse concerning Israel's standing in the world. There are differing opinions on the possible antisemitic nature of the international campaign of boycott, divestment, and sanctions (BDS). Some observers, like Andrew Griffith, argue that it constitutes "legitimate pressure on Israeli policies and activities." It is also evident to Griffith, however, that much of the messaging of BDS campaigns "neither distinguish[es] between Israel itself and the occupied territories, nor is careful about language with anti-Semitic overtones."[131] In May 2006, the Ontario wing of the Canadian Union of Public Employees (CUPE) took an anti-Israel stand and voted unanimously to support BDS against Israel until it recognizes the Palestinian right to self-determination. In doing so, it was following the lead of a 2002 resolution of the Canadian Labour Congress that compared Palestinians in the West Bank and Gaza to Blacks living under apartheid in South Africa.[132] The CUPE National leadership, however, distanced itself from the Ontario resolution and affirmed that it "respects the right of its chartered organizations to take a stand on all issues. As a national union we are governed by policy resolutions adopted at our national conventions. And as such, we will not be issuing a call to our local unions across Canada to boycott Israel."[133]

Israel's military struggle against Hezbollah in South Lebanon in July 2006, as Terry Glavin observes, "further entrenched anti-Zionism and an overt identification with Israel's enemies as a ubiquitous element of left-wing politics in Canada."[134] The war brought thousands of Quebecers, including mainstream politicians like Bloc Québécois leader Gilles Duceppe and Liberal MP (now Montreal mayor) Denis Coderre to a demonstration for peace that was in effect taken over by partisan supporters of Hezbollah.[135] In this Montreal demonstration as well as in another in Toronto, Hezbollah flags and photos of its leader Hassan Nasrallah were carried.[136] The perception of widespread support for Hezbollah in Quebec was strengthened by a September 2006 Léger survey that found a higher proportion of the population in Quebec (38 percent, compared to the Canadian average of 31 percent) attributed the onus for the conflict in Lebanon to "Israel's actions in the Middle East."[137]

Israel's military action in Gaza in 2008–9 also stimulated anti-Israel activity that was interpreted as antisemitic by Jews, and was experienced all over Canada, even in places with small Jewish populations, such as Yellowknife, Northwest Territories.[138] In this connection, numerous organizations renewed their activities aimed at boycotting Israeli people or products. Thus in January 2009, the Canadian Union of Public Employees' Ontario University Workers Coordinating Committee proposed a resolution banning Israeli academics from speaking, teaching, or researching at Ontario universities. In reaction, CUPE's national president, Paul Moist, issued a statement that the resolution "would violate the anti-discrimination standards set out in the CUPE Constitution," adding that "I will be using my influence in any debates on such a resolution to oppose its adoption." CUPE Ontario then retracted its call to boycott individual academics and clarified that "this is not a call to boycott individual Israeli academics. Rather, the boycott call is aimed at academic institutions and the institutional connections that exist between universities here and those in Israel." On February 22, 2009, CUPE's university workers committee passed a version of the original resolution which called for members at Ontario universities to boycott working with Israeli institutions doing research that benefits Israel's army, but not individual academics, while its president, Sid Ryan, "apologized for comparing Israel's bombings of academic institutions in Gaza to actions perpetrated by the Nazis."[139]

The Canadian Parliamentary Coalition to Combat Antisemitism

In this sort of atmosphere, the Canadian Parliamentary Coalition to Combat Antisemitism was established in 2009 and issued its report in July 2011. The coalition, allied with the international Inter-parliamentary Committee for Combating Antisemitism, was chaired by Liberal MP Irwin Cotler, the former attorney general of Canada, and then–citizenship and immigration minister Jason Kenney. It held ten hearings, heard a total of 74 witnesses, and received more than 150 written submissions between November 2009 and February 2010.[140] Its report claims that "Canada is turning into a hotbed of antisemitic activity, especially on university campuses."[141]

The coalition was initially made up of members of all parties represented in the House of Commons. The Bloc Québécois, however, eventually withdrew, contending that the coalition was much too pro-Israel in its approach and was in fact attempting to delegitimize criticism of Israel by calling it antisemitism. The coalition's main conclusions were that while "criticism of Israel is not anti-Semitic … denying its right to exist, or seeking its destruction, could be considered anti-Semitic acts." The report further stated that "in the most vile and clear expressions of the new anti-Semitism, Jewish support for Israel and the notion of Israel as a criminal state is used to further traditional anti-Semitic themes. These manifestations use the discourse of politics but, in fact, constitute masked hatred."[142] The coalition's report was widely reported the media. However the report does not seem to have had a dramatic impact on the Canadian conversation about antisemitism.

Such are the facts and the ambiguities of the Canadian discourse on anti-Zionism and antisemitism. In the next chapter, we will reflect on current perceptions and realities of antisemitism in Canada in the early twenty-first century.

CHAPTER TEN

Perspectives on Antisemitism in Twenty-First-Century Canada

Six million victims have not rooted out anti-Semitism. There are days when the progress of the human race seems dismally slow.
—André Laurendeau[1]

At the beginning of the twenty-first century life has never been better for Canada's Jews. The quotas, barriers, and restrictions of an earlier period of Canadian history are largely gone, though hardly forgotten. In 1983, Irving Abella and Harold Troper wrote their now-classic study, *None Is Too Many*, describing Canada as a country prior to 1948: "with immigration policies that were racist and exclusionary, a country blighted with an oppressive anti-Semitism in which Jews were the pariahs of Canadian society, demeaned, despised, and discriminated against." In contrast, Abella asserted in a newspaper article marking the thirtieth anniversary of the book's publication: "Today's Canada is far different—generous, open, decent, humane."[2]

As Abella has stated elsewhere, Jews now hold prominent positions in many sectors of Canadian society that were practically unattainable a generation or two ago.[3] Yet he also asserts: "There remain significant pockets of discrimination and racism. Nazi war criminals and collaborators, thousands of whom were welcomed into this country immediately after the war, still live freely among us."[4]

Perceptions of Antisemitism

What, then, can be said of antisemitism in Canada today? Any approach to this question leads to ambiguity and paradox. To begin with, the considerable success which Jews have attained in the Canadian community, in almost every field of endeavour, raises the question of whether Jewish perceptions of antisemitism match reality. Levitt and Shaffir, for instance, have argued that in contemporary Canada, the phenomenon of antisemitism is not anywhere near as pervasive as many in the Jewish community believe.[5] This possible discrepancy has to be understood in the context of the lasting psychological scarring that is one of the real legacies of the Holocaust for Canadian Jewry.[6] Even though the many survivors of the Holocaust who came to Canada in the mid-twentieth century are rapidly passing from the scene, Eli Rubenstein states: "children of Holocaust survivors, and the extended Jewish people, still deeply mourn the loss of six million of their ancestors, and they do so in a very personal way."[7]

Perception of antisemitism is likely one of the ways in which this feeling is expressed. In any event, there seems to be a feeling among many Jewish Canadians that antisemitism is on the increase, though they also tend not to feel that their own safety is compromised in any significant way. In a 2013 survey of Jews in Toronto 61.1 percent of the respondents thought antisemitism in Toronto had increased in the previous ten years, whereas only 6.3 percent thought it had decreased.[8] However when the same survey asked "As a member of the Jewish community, how safe do you feel?" there was a nearly unanimous response that they felt either "somewhat safe" or "very safe."[9] This is fairly consistent with earlier data from the United States, where a 1980s survey observed that most non-Jewish respondents who were aware of antisemitic incidents in that country believed that such events were either stable or declining in number, while most Jews believed that the incidence of antisemitism was rising. The Jews' perception of their position in the United States in that survey thus showed itself to be much more pessimistic than the corresponding perception by non-Jews.[10] A 1988 poll similarly found that 57 percent of American Jews believed that "when it comes to the crunch few non-Jews will come to Israel's side in its struggle to survive."[11]

Are the Jews, then, paranoid? Not entirely. According to a 2010 report, law enforcement studies both in the United States and Canada show that "when the motivation behind hate crimes is analyzed by religion, Jews are overwhelmingly and disproportionately targeted compared to other religious minorities,[12] while Statistics Canada calculated in 2011 that there had been a 42 percent increase in hate crimes in Canada and a 71 percent increase in religiously motivated crimes targeting the Jewish community.[13]

Jewish Community Reactions

In precautionary reaction to such reports, there has been a significant increase in recent years in the number and the sophistication of security guards at Jewish offices, schools, and synagogues in Canada.[14] This is a direct consequence of the new globalized antisemitism.[15] In March 2014, for example, the Centre for Israel and Jewish Affairs (CIJA) announced that it is planning to train approximately twenty-five to fifty unarmed volunteers to monitor antisemitic threats and vandalism in heavily Jewish neighbourhoods in Toronto.[16]

Thus, though antisemitism is objectively in decline in Canada from many perspectives, it remains a live factor in the discourse of the Jewish community and of Canadian society as a whole. As Morton Weinfeld points out, antisemitism lives on in the sensibilities of Canadian Jews both individually and organizationally.[17] Thus the memory of iconic antisemitic events like the 1933 Christie Pits riot in Toronto have become part of the collective historical memory of Toronto Jews, and the stories of the riot are now "told and retold at family gatherings with pride of people and place."[18]

With respect to the consciousness of antisemitism on the part of Jews in contemporary Canada, historian Harold Troper has the following observation:

> Jewish students in my classes generally indicate familiarity with the major themes of antisemitism in Canadian history. When it comes to historical detail, however, much of what they "know" is wrong. I sense they feel a strong proprietary right to the history of antisemitism, to the Holocaust, and to the earlier era of overt anti-Jewish discrimination in Canada. It is their proximate history, a basic element in their Jewish identity … That their experience of antisemitism is secondhand or thirdhand, however, does not seem to weaken their deeply-held and often-expressed conviction that antisemitism is a clear and present danger today.[19]

It would not be a bold step to extrapolate the attitudes of Troper's sample of Jewish university students to the Canadian Jewish community at large.

Canadian Jewish Organizations and Antisemitism

As was the case almost a century ago, when Canadian Jewish activists who had established the Canadian Jewish Congress assumed the burden of confronting the phenomenon of antisemitism in Canada, the contemporary Jewish community discourse on antisemitism has been dominated and shaped by Jewish organizations and their leadership.[20] In today's Canada, the fight against antisemitism and anti-Zionism is organizationally addressed by several agencies, whose agendas and messages differ considerably. They include most prominently CIJA, which represents the major Jewish federations of Canada and which sees itself as having taken over the task of fighting antisemitism in contemporary Canada from the now-defunct Canadian Jewish Congress,[21] and B'nai Brith Canada, whose League for Human Rights concentrates on the fight against antisemitism and which has published an annual *Audit of Antisemitic Incidents in Canada* under various titles uninterruptedly since 1982.[22] However these two major agencies do not nearly comprise all the organizational energies of the Canadian Jewish community in its struggle against antisemitism. To round out the list we would need to include such organizations as the Canadian Institute for Jewish Research,[23] the Canadian Institute for the Study of Antisemitism,[24] the Canadian Friends of the Simon Wiesenthal Center,[25] and Honest Reporting Canada.[26]

These groups are organized to detect and attempt to remedy any antisemitic phenomena they are able to detect. They pay close attention to even comparatively small incidents. For example, in 2013, when a Toronto secondary school teacher posted a link to an Iranian website which contained antisemitic material and another to a strongly pro-Palestinian article by Richard Falk, the school itself and the Toronto District School Board were contacted.[27] Another recent incident is an attempt by pro-Palestinian activists to boycott an Israeli brand of hummus at the cafeteria of the University of Ottawa.[28] These incidents are not untypical of those that make up the bulk of B'nai Brith Canada's Audit, the latest of which covers the year 2013. The scope and sophistication of the Audit's reporting have greatly increased in the more than thirty years in which the report has appeared, as have the number of incidents reported.

B'nai Brith Canada has heavily invested its resources in the effort to protect the Canadian Jewish community from antisemitism. As its mission statement emphasizes: "It is Canadian Jewry's most senior human rights advocacy organization … Its team of dedicated volunteers and professional staff is engaged in combating antisemitism, bigotry and racism in Canada and abroad … It is uniquely positioned to rise to today's challenges, which include the emergence in recent years of growing antisemitism and rampant anti-Israel sentiment."[29] In 2011 B'nai Brith Canada expressed these feelings in a full-page advertisement in its journal, the *Jewish Tribune*, which stated: "B'nai Brith operates as a firewall between antisemitism and its victims."[30] Another such advertisement warning against antisemitism in Canada was published in 2014 and was based on the recently published Anti-Defamation League global survey of antisemitic attitudes.[31] Its headline stated: "Almost 4 Million Canadians Are Afflicted by This Disease."[32]

The idea expressed in these advertisements that acts of antisemitism, whether small or large, remain a threat to the Jewish community is certainly widely held within the Jewish community. This sort of stance, however, also has its critics. For example, the French Jewish academics Esther Benbassa and Jean-Christophe Attias have written: "In constantly returning to antisemitism and relentlessly condemning every speech that is not entirely standard, in relentlessly tracking down the smallest indices of hatred, rejection, or mere indifference, one undoubtedly creates a community of fantasied suffering."[33]

B'nai Brith's Audit has also been subject to criticism over the years by those who, like *National Post* editor Jonathan Kay, do not agree with B'nai Brith Canada's policies and who tend to argue that many essentially trifling antisemitic incidents are being blown out of proportion.[34] B'nai Brith and other Jewish agencies are also often criticized by anti-Zionist individuals and groups who receive criticism from these agencies for their anti-Israel views on the grounds that this criticism is an infringement on their right to free speech, as is the case with the anti-Zionist organization Independent Jewish Voices Canada.[35] There are also journalists critical of Israel who, in the face of Jewish institutional criticism of their writings or productions, openly ask the question whether it is possible to criticize Israel in the media.[36]

B'nai Brith Canada is well aware of this criticism of its work and responds in this way:

> There are elements within the Jewish community that concede that there are concerns, but at times take an almost paternalistic approach in response. This says more about the community's inherent need for reassurance, than about the scope of the problem. There are certain entities within the Jewish community that even attempt to undermine the findings of the "Audit" ... The League does not agree with the notion that suppressing or censoring data is an approach that best serves either community interests or serious research on the topic ... Furthermore the attempts by some parties to query the Audit's supporting data, amount to a second guessing of the reliability of those individuals which is condescending in the extreme and borders on further abuse of the victimized.[37]

Elah Feder states the essential problem confronting those who wish to combat antisemitism in contemporary Canada: "It seems the more we talk about anti-Semitism, the more appealing it becomes. If that's true, we have a conundrum. How do you address a problem without letting people know it exists?"[38] For its primary intended victims and those who would protect them, antisemitism is understood to be a real problem that needs to be addressed in one way or another.[39]

Current Statistics

What can we say, then, about the state of antisemitism in Canada today? Whether they are disputed or not, we have to start with the statistics available. In May 2014, the Anti-Defamation League of B'nai Brith published a large survey of antisemitic attitudes in one hundred countries worldwide, including Canada. The Canadian survey, which surveyed 505 Canadians, found that the respondents had an 80 percent favourable attitude toward Jews, as opposed to 8 percent negative. However it also found that 14 percent of Canadians responded "probably true" to a majority of questions designed to elicit antisemitic attitudes.[40]

In the past three years of the B'nai Brith Canada Audit, covering the years 2011–13, antisemitic incidents cited averaged approximately 1,300 (1,297 in 2011, 1,345 in 2012, and 1,274 in 2013). This pattern of more or less 1,300 incidents has remained essentially unchanged since 2009. The incidents recorded range from verbal taunts to vandalism, such as occurred at the Mishkan Ha-Torah Yeshiva in Toronto in 2013,[41] to death threats, though only approximately 1 percent of the incidents were classified in the 'Audit" as "violent" in nature (13 in 2012 and 14 in 2013).[42]

The Nature of Contemporary Canadian Antisemitism

Manifestations of antisemitism and anti-Zionism across Canada today come from a wide variety of sources. A portion of them come from Canadian right-wing racist, antisemitic, and anti-Zionist individuals and groups that have targeted Jews in the past, and whose activities parallel those of similar individuals and groups in other Western countries. An example of this sort of individual is Arthur Topham of Quesnel, British Columbia, who was charged with a hate crime in 2012 for publishing antisemitic remarks on his website, referring to Jews as "snakes and Zionists."[43] He is of the opinion "that Canada's judicial system has been infiltrated and co-opted by foreign Zionist Jew lobby groups operating in Canada since 1919, [and] that Canada's Zionist Jew media cartel is, and always has been, an integral part of their overall plan to formulate and establish Orwellian laws inimical to the rights and freedoms of the people."[44] An example of an antisemitic group is the National Socialist Party of Canada.[45] These individuals and groups are generally not numerous, nor do they seem very influential within Canadian society.

Anti-Zionist incidents, which have been understood by their victims as antisemitic, also emerge from Canadian left-wing political organizations and trade unions as well as on university campuses. It is arguable that this phenomenon can be explained by the anti-Zionist sentiment that resonates within the anti-globalization movement in which Israel is thought of by many as the prime source of international instability.[46] This is the sort of phenomenon Rabbi Jonathan Sacks and others identify as a new antisemitism. For Sacks, this new antisemitism comes from a "left-wing, anti-American cognitive elite with strong representation in the European media." He feels that this "is not, or not as yet, a clearly developed and consciously espoused anti-Semitism ... but rather the floating, impalpable anti-Semitism of a certain climate of opinion."[47] This climate of opinion tends to resist the notion of Jews as victims. Since Jews are, by and large, considered "white"—not just in the sense of pigmentation, but, more broadly, in their class and cultural milieux— they do not fit easily into what has become the dominant academic framework for the study of intergroup antipathy.[48] These leftist groups seem presently more active than the right-wing groups and their activities seem to be relatively of much more consequence to Canadian society as a whole as well as to its Jewish community.

Finally, attitudes toward Jews in Canada encompass people who often belong to intellectual and political elites, but who zealously oppose not only the "Jewish State" but also "the Jews" in Canada, who seemingly almost single-handedly prevent Canada from strongly opposing Israel. As journalist Margaret Wente puts it, these people "seem to believe that Canada's Jews are so numerous, so powerful, and so single-mindedly devoted to Israel that they can significantly influence [Canada's] politics and foreign policy."[49]

A measure of the anti-Israel trend on the Canadian left was the ouster of Paul Estrin from the presidency of the Green Party of Canada in 2014 for having written a blog on the war in Gaza that was deemed to be pro-Israel.[50] Indeed, some of the reactions within the Green Party included one from a person who asserted, among other things, that Israel and not al Qaeda was the power behind the events of 9/11.[51]

We see a similarly strong anti-Israel trend in the small leftist Quebec provincial party Québec Solidaire, which presently has two elected members in the Quebec National Assembly. The party has supported the movement for Boycott, Divest, and Sanctions (BDS) against Israel, its representatives have taken part in anti-Israel demonstrations, and in 2011 its representative in the National Assembly, Amir Khadir, prevented unanimous consent to a motion that condemned the anti-Israel boycott of a Montreal shoe store that was selling shoes made in Israel.[52]

As we have seen in a previous chapter, a significant number of Muslims have immigrated to Canada in recent years from countries where antisemitic and anti-Zionist sentiments are endemic, and where the "enemy" to be opposed and fought is, interchangeably, Israel and "the Jews." The Muslim community in Canada thus includes not only numerous anti-Zionist activists in a cultural milieu that sees no essential difference between "Israel" and "Jews," but also individuals who have committed antisemitic acts.

Consequences of Allegations of Antisemitism

It is clear that accusations of antisemitism in Canadian society have serious consequences for the accused and are strongly resented by them. Accusations of antisemitism caused Winnipeg journalist Lesley Hughes to be dropped as a federal Liberal candidate in 2009. In response, she filed a suit against the Canadian Jewish Congress, B'nai Brith Canada, and others that ended in a settlement wherein the parties acknowledged that she was not an antisemite. As she put it after the settlement: "I really hope that the doors that have been closed for the last four years will open again. These were associations that were very important to me with people that I respected. People don't call you back, they don't answer your emails, they don't see you when they see you in public. It's an exercise in being 'disappeared.'"[53]

The Pierre Lacerte case is another example of a person accused of antisemitism who vehemently denies it. After he was exonerated by the Quebec Court of Appeals from charges of harassing his Hasidic neighbours in Outremont in 2013 by chronicling alleged Hasidic infractions of municipal bylaws and by repeatedly photographing Hasidim coming and going from their synagogue,[54] Lacerte is quoted as saying: "Since the Second World War, there are not many things as damaging to one's reputation as being called anti-Semitic ... Not even pedophilia." If his blog was antisemitic, he added, he would have heard about it from B'nai Brith.[55]

Canadian Politics and the Antisemitism Issue

All mainstream Canadian political parties officially oppose antisemitism in Canadian life and support the existence of the State of Israel. The three major parties, Conservative, NDP, and Liberal, have also opposed the BDS movement. That having been said, there is undoubtedly wider support for Israel and its positions within the Conservative Party. Under the leadership of Prime Minister Stephen Harper it is clear that Canada's policies are among the most supportive of Israel in the Western world. For example, the Canadian government recently agreed to officially recognize Jewish refugees from Arab countries, a significant counterbalance to the "right of return" of the Arab refugees from Palestine.[56] Within the Liberal Party, support for Israel is somewhat moderate compared with that of the Harper Conservatives, though Irwin Cotler, who is to retire from the House of Commons in 2015, remains a strong pro-Israel voice within the Liberal caucus.[57] The New Democratic Party as well as the Bloc Québécois tend to be far more critical of Israel, though within the NDP sharp opposition to Israel has largely been prevented by party leader Thomas Mulcair in his bid to make the NDP more mainstream in preparation for the general election expected in 2015.[58]

Anti-Zionist Discourse on Canadian Campuses

In contemporary Canadian universities there is significant sympathy for the Palestinian cause and there are a number of individual anti-Zionist students and professors as well as numerous pro-Palestinian organizations functioning on campus. At my own university, Concordia, for example, Solidarity for Palestinian Human Rights, which was heavily implicated in creating the atmosphere that led to the Netanyahu riot of 2002, is still active and affiliated with the Concordia Student Union. Groups of Muslim students and separate groups of students coming from such countries as Egypt, Syria, and Lebanon are likewise affiliated with the Concordia Student Union and likely share large portions of the SPHR agenda. Concordia is far from unique among Canadian universities in this respect, though it does have a particularly problematic history that was detailed in the previous chapter. This history continued in the fall of 2014 with a campaign within the Concordia Student Union to support BDS. One of the leaders of the pro-Israel opposition characterized this campaign in the following way: "Jews on and off campus have been constantly insulted, humiliated and harassed."[59] At the University of Calgary, a Jewish professor of Islamic studies was made so uncomfortable by confrontations with militant supporters of Hamas and Islamic jihad in his classes, that he felt he had to leave the university.[60]

Tensions of this nature at Canadian universities have in the past decade been largely focused on anti-Zionist activities such as Israel Apartheid Week (IAW), which originated at the University of Toronto in 2005. Also significant in this regard is the activism surrounding the debate over BDS resolutions against Israel. These resolutions have been introduced, debated, and voted upon in student unions at several Canadian universities in the past decade as part of a coordinated international BDS campaign. In the opinion of student supporters of Israel, this campaign "pose[s] an unacceptable restriction on the right of Jewish students to be openly, expressively Jewish."[61] Over the past decade, according to some observers, IAW has "fundamentally shifted the Israel conversation on campuses" in Canada and around the world.[62]

BDS campaigns tend not to operate solely on the intellectual plane. They often involve demonstrations and other tactics that BDS opponents see as antisemitic. Reports concerning anti-Jewish intimidation on university campuses in the context of BDS campaigns have received extensive media coverage. In March 2014 a student referendum at the University of Windsor on the issue of boycotting Israel, undertaken amid charges of serious irregularities,[63] reportedly caused a number of Jewish students there to feel that their university had become a "hostile environment." In addition, an office in a university building was vandalized by anti-Israel activists in what Windsor police described as a "hate crime."[64] A similar vote taken by the Student Union of Toronto's Ryerson University in April 2014 also caused Jewish students discomfort on campus,[65] while a vote taken in August 2014 by the Ontario branch of the Canadian Federation of Students allegedly was marked by serious irregularities.[66] This wave of anti-Israel activism on Canadian campuses has been characterized by Melanie Phillips as an "academic intifada."[67] At Ryerson, this discomfort led to a concerted effort on the part of its Jewish students to propose a motion committing the Ryerson Student Union "to publicly oppose actions on campus that are antisemitic and work with the Jewish student community to combat antisemitism at

Ryerson."[68] These feelings of discomfort are well expressed by Nora Gold, who has written a novel concerning anti-Israel feeling on Canadian campuses:

> I was so distressed about the anti-Israelism around me that I really couldn't write about anything else. It was like having a fish hook in my stomach. I was pained not only by the most obvious manifestations of anti-Israelism, like Israel Apartheid Week—during which, year after year, I witnessed the emotional and psychological damage wreaked on Jewish students and professors—but also the increasing normalization of Israel-bashing in classes, in faculty meetings, and at conferences. I was appalled that in certain disciplines it was almost de rigueur to trash Israel.[69]

Such feelings about IAW are also captured by Yoni Goldstein, editor of the *Canadian Jewish News*, who wrote: "If [IAW] is not, at the core, really just about Jew-hatred, then it's pretty damn close—and, either way, it's an exercise in intellectual dishonesty."[70]

The University of Windsor incident was the subject of a question in the House of Commons addressed to Canadian Minister of State for Multiculturalism Tim Uppal. Uppal stated in his response that he understood BDS to be a new form of antisemitism: "We stand in solidarity with the Jewish students and others on campuses who are being forced to endure this travesty. We condemn this one-sided resolution that singles out Israel alone with boycott, divestment, and sanctions. As the Prime Minister has said, Israel's right to exist as a Jewish state is absolute and non-negotiable. This new type of anti-Semitism is despicable and does not belong in Canada."[71] Uppal's statement basically confirmed the Conservative government's stance on this issue, connected to its strong support of Israel's position internationally. Prime Minister Harper, in his 2014 speech at the Knesset in Jerusalem, cited at length in the previous chapter, demonstrated that he had absorbed the message that opposition to the policies of the State of Israel, while certainly legitimate in the context of freedom of speech, can and does lead to antisemitic consequences.

The pro-Israel aspect of Canadian government policy has elicited considerable and severe criticism of the Harper government by those who think it panders to the Jewish vote,[72] and by others who would prefer a much more "even-handed" (i.e., less pro-Israel) Middle East policy for Canada.[73] An extreme expression of this sentiment is that of Canadian pianist Anton Kuerti, who reacted to the Cast Lead operation in Gaza in 2008–9 by saying: "Israel's behavior makes me ashamed of being a Jew, and Canada's servile support of the United States position, that it is all Hamas' fault, makes me ashamed of being a Canadian."[74]

In Quebec

Quebec has historically been one of the places in Canada where overt manifestations of antisemitism tended to surface. In contemporary Quebec, religious, ethnic, and linguistic conflicts have manifested themselves in the public square, and thus issues related to antisemitism and anti-Zionism are often aired in the media, particularly in the French language, as was noted in previous chapters. It is in this context that we note the refusal by a Laval, Quebec, recreational centre in the spring of 2014 to accept bookings by Jewish day camps on the grounds that the camps did not pay promptly and their campers had discipline problems. Rabbi Levi Raskin, the Jewish camp director involved in this controversy, stated: "They don't like us … We feel that they always had a problem with us."[75]

With respect to Quebec's coverage of Israel and the controversies surrounding it, Radio-Canada, the Canadian Broadcasting Corporation's (CBC's) French-language network, has come in for special criticism, and the CBC Ombudsman's annual report recently called upon Radio-Canada to address a "systemic bias" in its coverage of Israel.[76] Other French-language media outlets have been called to task for excesses in this area as when, in 2012, Montreal radio talk show host Jacques Fabi received a call from a woman who identified herself as a person of Arab descent who was upset at the deaths of her "brothers and sisters" in Gaza and went on to "compare Israelis to dogs and said the Holocaust was the most beautiful event in world history." Fabi responded that it was her democratic right to speak out but that she should be careful about saying anything "offensive" against the Israelis; making negative comments about the Jewish people always has "consequences," and continued by saying that he found Montreal's Jewish community sometimes "annoying."[77] In August 2014, Gilles Proulx similarly spoke on a Montreal radio program about the power of Jews to bend world governments to their will while provoking the hatred of local populations because they took economic control of the countries in which they lived.[78] Pro-Israel journalist Lise Ravary commented in the midst of the Gaza campaign of summer 2014 that she "won't be writing about Israel for a while. At least not at home in Quebec, where the time-honoured pro-Palestinian, anti-Israel bias in the media is now so strong that columnists like me who strive to offer a more balanced view of the Israeli–Palestinian conflict are symbolically marched out of town. Sometimes with a yellow star on their sleeve."[79] These particular public exchanges are examples of a climate of opinion in which, according to one recent survey, as many as 39 percent of francophones in Quebec were prepared to say that Jews have too much power, or caused the Holocaust, or that six million did not perish in the Holocaust.[80]

With respect to other issues in Quebec, it is of some significance that antisemitism seems not to have entered into public discourse concerning the 2012 appointment of Michael Applebaum as the first Jewish mayor of Montreal or with respect to his resignation under the cloud of an indictment a few months later. As journalist Lysiane Gagnon pointed out, when Applebaum was mayor there were no nasty comments about Jews taking over city hall.[81]

Within the past year the position of Jews among other religious and ethnic minorities in Quebec was the subject of a sometimes-heated debate with respect to a law proposed by the previous Parti Québécois government (Bill 60) that would have outlawed the wearing of overt religious garb (kippot for Jews, hijab and niqab for Muslims, turbans for Sikhs, etc.) in the Quebec public service. All the polling done in the political campaign indicates that a large number of voters in Quebec supported this measure. While the supporters of Bill 60 were concerned about the preservation of religious neutrality and "laïcité" (secularism) in Quebec, it was clear that the preservation of religio-ethnic difference by Muslims, Jews, and others in Quebec was defined by the bill as being opposed to "Quebec values" and hence placed in public question. As Gérard Bouchard, co-chair of the Bouchard-Taylor Commission stated, the campaign on behalf of Bill 60 constituted "a particularly shameful episode" in the political history of Quebec, containing "inflammatory and misleading statements to whip up Quebec's majority against minorities and immigrants."[82] It is important to note, however, that none of the often-vehement criticism directed against this legislation, which went down to defeat along with the Parti Québécois in the April 2014 elections, has overtly characterized it as antisemitic.

However in the 2014 campaign itself, one Parti Québécois candidate, Louise Mailloux, publicly expressed her opinion that kosher food was a sort of scam by the Jewish community, that its proceeds might be funding religious wars, and that ritual circumcision, as practised by Jews and Muslims, was equivalent to rape.[83] Mailloux's opinion on kosher food is quite similar to the "kosher tax" accusation propagated by antisemites.[84] CIJA's allegation that Mailloux's remarks constituted antisemitic rhetoric was vigorously denied by then PQ leader Pauline Marois, who emphasized that "the Parti Québécois is not an anti-Semitic party. We have good relations with the leaders of this community and all the different communities in Quebec."[85]

Mailloux's opinion on ritual circumcision, like her problem with kosher food, goes well beyond the boundaries of Quebec. It is echoed in a complaint against Jewish ritual circumcision brought to the Ontario College of Physicians and Surgeons in 2013 against a Jewish physician and mohel (ritual circumciser) in Toronto. The complainant, an anti-circumcision activist, alleged that the physician in question was no longer fit to practise medicine "due to personal bias surrounding his religious beliefs," adding that "one cannot rule out sexual motive." The accused understood the charges against him, which were dismissed by the College, to have been motivated by antisemitism.[86]

Despite the results of the 2014 Quebec election, the intense and sometimes fractious relationship between Jews and French Canadians in Quebec that has been ongoing for well over a century, and the controversies engendered by this relationship, show no sign of abating in the near future.

Morton Weinfeld has pointed out that "French Quebec has not come to a full societal resolution of its attitude toward the Jews ... during the 1930s and 1940s."[87] This is certainly true, but it must also be understood in the larger context that Quebec has also not yet come to a full societal resolution of its attitude toward itself. What does it to mean to be a part of Quebec society today? Is Quebec to be a society that is inclusive of all its citizens or will it be the sort of society in which, as Gérard Bouchard points out, it is difficult if not impossible for immigrants to Quebec, no matter what their expertise in the French language, to be universally accepted in mainstream Quebec society without completely renouncing their cultural and linguistic past?[88]

In historical context, some specific issues in dispute with respect to Jews in Quebec have indeed changed. One hundred years ago, for instance, issues concerning kosher food were for the most part internal to the Jewish community and involved kosher meat almost exclusively.[89] It is worth noting in this context that Quebec in the 1920s and 1930s never generated a significant, let alone successful, campaign to ban the kosher slaughter of animals, such as occurred in such countries as Germany, Switzerland, Poland, and Norway.[90] That kosher food became an issue that was presented to the Bouchard Taylor Commission of 2006, as described in chapter 7, and that it remains an active topic in 2014 is a significant change.

Another important change involves the nature of the Jewish "irritant" in French Canadian society. In the early twentieth century, Jews were "visible" to the French Canadian community, and the presence of Jews in many areas of Quebec, including the Laurentians, was deemed objectionable.[91] By the early twenty-first century, the presence of Montreal Jews and their summer homes in the Laurentians is fairly widespread and mostly non-controversial. Open conflict and controversy in the Laurentians with respect to Jews seems mostly related to the Hasidic community. The situation has evolved in this way at least partially because Hasidim have become the symbolic "visible" Jews in Quebec society, and male Hasidic garb has been used, in editorial cartoons and elsewhere, as media shorthand for "Jew."[92] Moreover, the Hasidim, who tend to live in close proximity to one another, are visible to the rest of society in a way that most other Jews are not (even though most Jews in Quebec, and not merely Hasidim, also tend to live in "Jewish" neighborhoods).[93]

A final issue of note in this survey is that in the early twentieth century, French Canadians considered themselves economically subordinated to "the English" and expressed their resentment of this situation in campaigns like "achat chez nous" that deeply impacted the Quebec Jewish community psychologically. By the early twenty-first century, the Quiet Revolution has achieved many of its economic goals and has changed both perceptions and facts concerning French Canadian economic power.[94] Nonetheless, the fact that Jews came under criticism at the Bouchard-Taylor Commission for their economic power indicates that this is an area in which "plus ça change, plus c'est la même chose."

Although much has changed in Quebec since the 1950s, it seems that the status of Jews as "others" to most French Canadians has not. The key difference today is that in the early twentieth century the Jewish community was the sole significant non-Christian, non-Aboriginal group in Quebec. It has now been joined by Muslims, Hindus, Sikhs, and a host of others.

Toward a Conclusion

In examining the mass of anecdotal evidence on the state of antisemitism in Canada in the early twenty-first century, it is hard to arrive at any sort of definitive conclusion. Nonetheless the following three anecdotes illustrate both the difficulties and ambiguities of the study of antisemitism in contemporary Canada.

The first anecdote concerns Catherine Chatterly, head of the Winnipeg-based Canadian Institute for the Study of Anti-Semitism. In 2012, it was reported that Chatterley had received two death threats against her and lots of hate mail. She was forced to get an unlisted telephone number and required police security at all of the institute's public events.[95] Chatterly's activism in the fight against antisemitism is obviously taken seriously by at least some who wish to silence her and her cause.

The second involves an April 2013 production by students of a play written by Quebec author Eric Noël, entitled *A Play on the Role of Your Children in the Global Economic Recovery*, whose publicity promised "authentic characters, at once universal and symbolic of today's world." Among these characters is Martha Goldberg, who represents the globalized economy and who does not hesitate to sell her own children, and her two accomplices, Cohen 1 and Cohen 2, Orthodox Jews who are supposed to be Nazi hunters but who willingly renounce their pursuit in exchange for a wad of cash.[96] In a number of ways, this play resembles one written by an adolescent Pierre Elliott Trudeau in the 1930s entitled *On est Canadien français ou on ne l'est pas*, whose main character, a Jew named Ditreau, speaks of how he could sell French Canadians shoddy merchandise and is advised by the French Canadian hero of the play to "take all your things and beat it."[97] Clearly Trudeau's play emerged from the antisemitic climate of opinion of 1930s French Canada. What of Noël's twenty-first century play? The author vehemently denies the antisemitic nature of his play and argues: "How can we not read the play as a caricature when the cliché of the rich Jew (like all others) is shown, emphasized, and explained with such transparency? It goes without saying that to present such a character is part of a satirical approach. It is unthinkable and unfortunate … to pretend here that this is a resurgence of antisemitic theater worthy of the 1930s."[98]

Finally, we have the case of the teenaged girl who had her hair singed by a lighter-wielding classmate in a Winnipeg high school in November 2011. The case attracted media attention and was spoken of as a hate crime due to the offender's antisemitic comment. According to the crown attorney, the offender and his victim crossed paths near his locker and they began talking. He pulled out a lighter and started flicking it near her head, saying, "Let's burn the Jew." The court decided in January 2014 that the girl was not singled out because she was Jewish, but rather because her tormentor was "a jerk and a bully."[99] Was this a hate crime or not?

There are no absolute and final answers to the questions raised by these three incidents and numerous other similar incidents experienced and reported in contemporary Canada. Nonetheless, there are certain conclusions we can make about the *longue durée* of antisemitism in Canada.

The first is that people labelled as antisemites by and large did not and do not wish to self-identify as such, and indeed often strongly resist the accusations levelled at them, though their statements may include many of the most blatant anti-Jewish stereotypes.

Secondly, the many attempts on the part of Jewish Canadians and their supporters to combat and eradicate antisemites and antisemitism have not succeeded in erasing the phenomenon from Canadian society.

In particular the numerous laws put on the books to suppress hate speech against Jews or other groups have not proved adequate when balanced against the right of Canadians to free speech.

The third conclusion is that, in contemporary Canada and elsewhere in the world, issues of antisemitism are closely intertwined with public perceptions of the State of Israel. As we have seen, from the moment that the Zionist project to build a Jewish homeland became more than a utopian hope, it elicited sharp opposition as well as support from Canadians, and this opposition has, in its more extreme forms, utilized, sometimes consciously, the plethora of anti-Jewish accusations and stereotypes that are the intellectual legacy of antisemitism. It seems clear that as long as Israel's conflict with its neighbours remains unresolved, the Jewish community of Canada will remain the target of antisemitic accusations and actions related to Israel.

I would also argue that hatred against Jews persists in contemporary Canada because, as Jewish historian Benzion Netanyahu states in the context of early modern Spain, "What is perhaps of greater importance is the receptive mood of the audience involved ... They create the condition in which every conceivable evil, however absurd, about the object of hate may be readily believed because it satisfies a deep psychological need—to justify the hatred and the desired end."[100]

In the course of my research for this book the truth of Gavin Langmuir's insight has also become evident to me: "There may still be situations in which Jewish existence is much more seriously endangered because real Jews have been converted in the minds of many to a symbol, 'the Jews,' a symbol whose meaning does not depend on the empirical characteristics of Jews yet justifies their total elimination from the earth."[101]

I began this book by dedicating it to my grandson, and expressing the hope that he will grow up in a world in which antisemitism will be of historical interest only. I close it by saying that as long as there are people, in Canada or anywhere else on earth, who have come to the conclusion that standing between them and the fulfillment of their ideal society—whatever that may be—are "the Jews," like Hitler in his time and Hamas in our own, the issues and ideas discussed in this book will persist and retain much more than historical significance.

Notes

NOTES TO PREFACE

1 http://en.wikipedia.org/wiki/William_Norman_Ewer.
2 "The Canadian Jewish Committee," *Canadian Jewish Chronicle*, January 22, 1932, 6. Stanley R. Barrett makes a somewhat similar claim when he says that the amount of actual violence perpetrated by the radical right in Canada is less than that perpetrated by comparable groups in the United States. Stanley R. Barrett, *Is God a Racist? The Right Wing in Canada* (Toronto: University of Toronto Press, 1987), 10.
3 Robert Wistrich, *A Lethal Obsession: Anti-Semitism from Antiquity to the Global Jihad* (New York: Random House, 2010), 1132, 1139–41.
4 The first comprehensive scholarly book on antisemitism in the United States did not appear until the 1990s. See Leonard Dinnerstein, *Antisemitism in America* (New York: Oxford University Press, 1994).
5 Alan Davies, ed., *Antisemitism in Canada: History and Interpretation* (Waterloo, ON: Wilfrid Laurier University Press, 1992).
6 For a survey of this field, see Ira Robinson, "The Field of Canadian Jewish Studies and Its Importance for the Jewish Community of Canada," *Jewish Political Studies Review* 21, nos. 3–4 (Fall 2009): 75–86; David Koffman, "Canadian Jewish Studies since 1999: The State of the Field," in *Canada's Jews in Time, Space, and Spirit*, ed. Ira Robinson (Boston: Academic Studies Press, 2013), 451–67.
7 Jürgen Osterhamel, *The Transformation of the World: A Global History of the Nineteenth Century* (Princeton, NJ: Princeton University Press, 2014), xvii.
8 Cited in Alan Mendelson, *Exiles from Nowhere: The Jews and the Canadian Elite* (Montreal: Robin Brass Studio, 2008), 7.
9 Phyllis Senese, "'La Croix de Montréal': A Link to the French Radical

Right," *Canadian Catholic Historical Association, Historical Studies* 53 (1986): 94n44.

10 André Elbaz, "Antisémitisme: Mythe et images du juif au Québec (essaie d'analyse)," *Voix et Images du Pays* 9 (1975): 87.

NOTES TO CHAPTER ONE

1 Cited in Jonathan Israel, *European Jewry in the Age of Mercantilism, 1550–1750* (Oxford: Clarendon Press, 1985), 15.
2 Anthony Julius, *Trials of the Diaspora: A History of Anti-Semitism in England* (Oxford: Oxford University Press, 2010), xvi.
3 Babylonian Talmud, *Shabbat* 89a.
4 Gotthard Deutsch, "Anti-Semitism," *Jewish Encyclopedia* (New York: Funk and Wagnalls, 1901), 1: 642. For a discussion of this "wider" use of the term and its implications, see Robert Chazan, *Medieval Stereotypes and Modern Antisemitism* (Berkeley: University of California Press, 1997), 126–27.
5 Julius, *Trials of the Diaspora*, xliii.
6 Cited in Shulamit Volkov, "Antisemitism as a Cultural Code: Reflections on the History and Historiography of Antisemitism in Imperial Germany," *Leo Baeck Institute Year Book* 23 (1978), 25.
7 Reinhard Rürup, "Anti-Jewish Prejudices, Antisemitic Ideologies, Open Violence: Antisemitism in European Comparison from the 1870s to the First World War. A Commentary," *Quest. Issues in Contemporary Jewish History. Journal of Fondazione CDEC* 3 (July 2012), www.quest-cdecjournal.it/focus.php?id=305.
8 Cited in David Engel, "Away from a Definition of Antisemitism: An Essay in the Semantics of Historical Description," in *Rethinking European Jewish History*, ed. Jeremy Cohen and Moshe Rosman (Oxford and Portland: Littman Library of Jewish Civilization, 2009), 49.
9 Emil Fackenheim, "Post-Holocaust Anti-Jewishness, Jewish Identity, and the Centrality of Israel," in *World Jewry and the State of Israel*, ed. Moshe Davis (New York: Arno Press, 1977), 11n2.
10 Gavin I. Langmuir, *History, Religion, and Antisemitism* (Berkeley: University of California Press, 1990), 19.
11 David Nirenberg, *Anti-Judaism: The Western Tradition* (New York: W.W. Norton, 2013), 2.
12 Steven Katz, *The Holocaust in Historical Context*, vol. 1: *The Holocaust and Mass Death before the Modern Age* (New York: Oxford University Press,

1994), 227–35. Cf. Robert Chazan, *Medieval Stereotypes and Modern Antisemitism* (Berkeley: University of California Press, 1997), 125ff.

13 Langmuir, *History, Religion, and Antisemitism*, 275. Langmuir has his critics. See Engel, "Away from a Definition of Antisemitism," in Cohen and Rosman, eds., *Rethinking European Jewish History*, 30–53.

14 For a grounding in the early development of Christianity in relation to the sources available for ancient Judaism, see Ellis Rivkin, *What Crucified Jesus? Messianism, Pharasaism, and the Development of Christianity* (New York: UAHC Press, 1997). Cf. J.D.G. Dunn, "Messianic Ideas and Their Influence on the Jesus of History," in *The Messiah: Developments in Earliest Judaism and Christianity*, ed. James H. Charlesworth (Minneapolis: Fortress Press, 1992), 365–81.

15 John G. Gager, *The Origins of Anti-Semitism: Attitudes toward Judaism in Pagan and Christian Antiquity* (New York: Oxford University Press, 1983), 135.

16 Paula Fredrikson, *From Jesus to Christ: The Origins of the New Testament Images of Jesus* (New Haven, CT: Yale University Press, 1988), vii.

17 Cited in ibid., 119.

18 Gavin Langmuir, *Toward a Definition of Antisemitism* (Berkeley: University of California Press, 1990), 7.

19 David Graizbord, "Religion and Ethnicity among 'Men of the Nation': Toward a Realistic Interpretation," *Jewish Social Studies*, n.s., 15, no. 1 (Fall 2008): 37.

20 Matthew 27:25; I Thessalonians 2:14–16; Acts 2:22–3, 36.

21 Elaine Pagels, cited in Robert Chazan, *Medieval Stereotypes and Modern Antisemitism* (Berkeley: University of California Press, 1997), 13.

22 John Connelly, *From Enemy to Brother: The Revolution in Catholic Teaching on the Jews, 1933–1965* (Cambridge, MA: Harvard University Press, 2012), 2.

23 This aspect of Christian doctrine relative to Jews is best expressed by the fourth-century Church Father Augustine. See Paula Fredriksen, *Augustine and the Jews: A Christian Defense of Jews and Judaism* (New Haven, CT: Yale University Press, 2010).

24 Robert Chazan, *Church, State and Jew in the Middle Ages* (New York: Behrman, 1980), 15–51.

25 R. Po-chia Hsia, *The Myth of Ritual Murder: Jews and Magic in Reformation Germany* (New Haven, CT: Yale University Press, 1988), 1–12.

26 Chazan, *Church, State and Jew in the Middle Ages*, 221–38.

27 Ibid., 197–220.

28 Elisheva Carlebach, "The Last Deception: Failed Messiahs and Jewish Conversion in Early Modern German Lands," in *Jewish Messianism in the Early Modern World*, ed. Matt D. Goldish and Richard H. Popkin (Dordrecht: Kluwer, 2001), 126.

29 Langmuir, *Toward a Definition of Antisemitism*, 14. See also Miri Rubin, *Gentile Tales: The Narrative Assault on Late-Medieval Jews* (New Haven, CT: Yale University Press, 1999).

30 Nirenberg, *Anti-Judaism*, 267.

31 Cited in Israel, *European Jewry in the Age of Mercantilism*, 11.

32 Carey C. Newman, "Preface" in *Jesus, Judaism, and Christian Anti-Judaism: Reading the New Testament after the Holocaust*, ed. Paula Fredriksen and Adele Reinharz (Louisville, KY: Westminster John Knox Press, 2002), x.

33 Cf. Bernard Harrison, *The Resurgence of Anti-Semitism: Jews, Israel, and Liberal Opinion* (Lanham, MD: Rowman and Littlefield, 2006), 14.

34 Chazan, *Church, State, and Jew*, 309–22.

35 Nirenberg, *Anti-Judaism*, 218.

36 David Nirenberg, *Communities of Violence: Persecution of Minorities in the Middle Ages* (Princeton, NJ: Princeton University Press, 1996), 4.

NOTES TO CHAPTER TWO

1 William Shakespeare, *The Merchant of Venice*, act 3, scene 1.

2 On medieval French Jewry, see Robert Chazan, *Medieval Jewry in Northern France: A Political and Social History* (Baltimore: Johns Hopkins University Press, 1973); William Jordan, *The French Monarchy and the Jews* (Philadelphia: University of Pennsylvania Press, 1989).

3 On medieval English Jews, see R.B. Dobson, *The Jewish Communities of Medieval England: The Collected Essays of R.B. Dobson*, ed. Helen Birkett, with a new preface by Joe Hillaby (York, UK: Borthwick Institute, University of York, 2010); Robin R. Mundill, *England's Jewish Solution: Experiment and Expulsion, 1262–1290* (New York: Cambridge University Press, 1998).

4 One of these exceptions for France was Avignon, and its surrounding territory, which was called the "Comtat Venaissin" and retained a Jewish community because it was not French but Papal territory.

5 Claudine Fabre-Vessas, *The Singular Beast: Jews, Christians and the Pig* (New York: Columbia University Press, 1997).

6 Cited in Jay Berkovitz, *Rites and Passages: The Beginnings of Modern*

Jewish Culture in France, 1650–1860 (Philadelphia: University of Pennsylvania Press, 2004), 16.

7 Ibid., 17.

8 Stephen Wilson, *Ideology and Experience: Antisemitism in France at the Time of the Dreyfus Affair* (Rutherford, NJ: Farleigh Dickinson University Press, 1982), 298; George L. Mosse, *Toward the Final Solution: A History of European Racism* (London: J.M. Dent and Sons, 1978), 114–15.

9 Julius, *Trials of the Diaspora*, xxxviii.

10 Sheila Delany, ed., *Chaucer and the Jews: Sources, Contexts, Meanings* (New York: Routledge, 2002); Anthony Bale, *The Jew in the Medieval Book: English Antisemitisms 1350–1500* (Cambridge: Cambridge University Press, 2007).

11 James Shapiro, *Shakespeare and the Jews* (New York: Columbia University Press, 1997). An example of the ongoing influence of Shakespeare's image of the "pound of flesh" his Jewish character, Shylock, wished to exact is an incident that occurred in Toronto in 1985 when antisemite Gilles Gervais dumped three pounds of raw liver in the office of B'nai Brith in Montreal and shouted, "Here is your pound of flesh." League for Human Rights of B'nai Brith Canada, *Review of Anti-Semitism in Canada 1985* (Downsview, ON, 1986), 8.

12 Haim Beinart, *The Expulsion of the Jews from Spain*, trans. Jeffrey M. Green (Oxford; Portland, OR: Littman Library of Jewish Civilization, 2002).

13 David L. Graizbord, *Souls in Dispute: Converso Identities in Iberia and the Jewish Diaspora, 1580–1700* (Philadelphia: University of Pennsylvania Press, 2003); Yirmiyahu Yovel, *The Other Within: The Marranos, Split Identity and Emerging Modernity* (Princeton, NJ: Princeton University Press, 2009).

14 On the various scholarly opinions on this issue, see Ira Robinson, "Who Is a Marrano? Reflections on Modern Jewish Identity," in *History, Memory and Jewish Identify*, forthcoming.

15 Arthur Hertzberg, *The French Enlightenment and the Jews* (New York: Columbia University Press, 1968), 16.

16 Miriam Bodian, *Hebrews of the Portuguese Nation: Conversos and Community in Early Modern Amsterdam* (Indianapolis: Indiana University Press, 1997); Daniel Swetschinski, *Reluctant Cosmopolitans: The Portuguese Jews of Seventeenth Century Amsterdam* (London: Littman Library of Jewish Civilization, 2000).

17 Hertzberg, *French Enlightenment*, 15–18.

18 Cecil Roth, *History of the Jews in England* (Oxford: Clarendon Press, 1964).

19 Todd Endelman, *The Jews of Georgian England: 1714–1830* (Philadelphia: Jewish Publication Society, 1979), 87.

20 Harrison, *The Resurgence of Anti-Semitism*, 12–13.

21 Paula Sutter Fichtner, *Terror and Toleration: The Habsburg Empire Confronts Islam, 1526–1850* (London: Reaktion, 2008).

22 "Reasons for Naturalizing the Jews in Great Britain and Ireland" (1714), cited in Paul Mendes-Flohr and Jehuda Reinharz, *The Jew in the Modern World: A Documentary History*, 3rd ed. (New York: Oxford University Press, 2011), 12.

23 Julius, *Trials of the Diaspora*, 492. On Eisenmenger, see Jacob Katz, *From Prejudice to Destruction: Anti-Semitism, 1700–1933* (Cambridge, MA: Harvard University Press, 1980), 13–22.

24 Jonathan Israel, *European Jewry in the Age of Mercantilism, 1550–1750* (Oxford: Clarendon Press, 1985), 249. Cf. David Nirenberg, *Anti-Judaism: The Western Tradition* (New York: W.W. Norton, 2013), 357.

25 Ronald Schechter, *Obstinate Hebrews: Representations of Jews in France, 1715–1815* (Berkeley: University of California Press, 2003), 47.

26 Jerry Z. Muller, *Capitalism and the Jews* (Princeton, NJ: Princeton University Press, 2010), 31.

27 Israel, *European Jewry in the Age of Mercantilism*, 251.

28 Cecil Roth, *A Life of Menasseh Ben Israel: Rabbi, Printer, and Diplomat* (Philadelphia: Jewish Publication Society, 1934), 225–47. Yosef Kaplan, Henry Méchoulan, and Richard H. Popkin, eds., *Menasseh Ben Israel and His World* (Leiden and New York: E.J. Brill, 1989).

29 Gertrude Himmelfarb, *The People of the Book: Philosemitism in England from Cromwell to Churchill* (New York: Encounter Books, 2011), 47–48.

30 Sheldon J. Godfrey and Judith C. Godfrey, *Search Out the Land: The Jews and the Growth of Equality in British Colonial America, 1740–1867* (Montreal and Kingston: McGill-Queen's University Press, 1995), 23–24.

31 Cited in Leonard Dinnerstein, *Antisemitism in America* (New York: Oxford University Press, 1994), 10.

32 Thomas Whipple Perry, *Public Opinion, Propaganda, and Politics in Eighteenth-Century England: A Study of the Jew Bill of 1753* (Cambridge, MA: Harvard University Press, 1962).

33 Godfrey and Godfrey, *Search Out the Land*, 10.

NOTES TO CHAPTER THREE

1 Cited in Arlette Corcos, *Montréal, les Juifs, et l'école* (Sillery: Septentrion, 1997), 21.

2 Michael Dobkowski, *The Tarnished Dream: The Basis of American Anti-Semitism* (Westport, CT: Greenwood, 1979), 13.

3 Pierre Anctil, "Jews and New France," in *Canada's Jews: In Time, Space and Spirit*, ed. Ira Robinson (Boston: Academic Studies Press, 2013), 17.

4 Cited in Gertrude Himmelfarb, *The People of the Book: Philosemitism in England from Cromwell to Churchill* (New York: Encounter Books, 2011), 57.

5 Jacob R. Marcus, *Early American Jewry* (Philadelphia: Jewish Publication Society, 1951), 1: 230.

6 Gerald Tulchinsky, *Canada's Jews: A People's Journey* (Toronto: University of Toronto Press, 2008), 17.

7 Gérard Bouchard, *La nation québécoise au futur et au passé* (Montreal: VLB éditeur, 1999), 87.

8 Tulchinsky, *Canada's Jews*, 21.

9 Denis Vaugeois, *The First Jews in North America: The Extraordinary Story of the Hart Family, 1760–1860*, trans. Käthe Roth (Montreal: Baraka Books, 2012), 278. On Vaugeois's attitudes toward antisemitism in his earlier work, *Les Juifs et la Nouvelle France*, see Richard Menkis, "Historiography, Myth, and Group Relations: Jewish and Non-Jewish Québécois on Jews and New France," *Canadian Ethnic Studies* 23, no. 2 (1991): nn. 72–78. Cf. André Elbaz, "Antisémitisme: Mythe et images du juif au Québec (essaie d'analyse)," *Voix et Images du Pays* 9 (1975): 88.

10 Jeremy Waldron, *The Harm in Hate Speech* (Cambridge, MA: Harvard University Press, 2012), 42.

11 Ibid., 22.

12 Maura Jane Farrelly, *Papist Patriots: The Making of an American Catholic Identity* (New York: Oxford University Press, 2012).

13 Eli Faber, *A Time for Planting: The First Migration, 1654–1820* (Baltimore: Johns Hopkins University Press, 1992), 100–101.

14 Tulchinsky, *Canada's Jews*, 24.

15 Cited in Corcos, *Montréal, les Juifs, et l'école*, 21.

16 Cited in Tulchinsky, *Canada's Jews*, 25.

17 David Rome, "On the Early Harts, part 3," *Canadian Jewish Archives*, n.s. 17 (Montreal: Canadian Jewish Congress, 1980): 226.

18 Tulchinsky, *Canada's Jews*, 28.
19 Irving Abella, *A Coat of Many Colours: Two Centuries of Jewish Life in Canada* (Toronto: Key Porter, 1999), 23–24; Sheldon J. Godfrey and Judith C. Godfrey, *Search Out the Land: The Jews and the Growth of Equality in British Colonial America, 1740–1867* (Montreal and Kingston: McGill-Queen's University Press, 1995), 158.
20 Abella, *A Coat of Many Colours*, 25.
21 Ibid., 28–29.
22 Richard Menkis, "Antisemitism and Anti-Judaism in Pre-Confederation Canada," in Davies, *Antisemitism in Canada*, 16.
23 Abella, *A Coat of Many Colours*, 69–70.
24 Tulchinsky, *Canada's Jews*, 36.
25 B.G. Sack, *History of the Jews of Canada* (Montreal: Harvest House, 1965), 132.
26 Louis Rosenberg, *Canada's Jews: A Social and Economic Study of the Jews of Canada* (Montreal: Canadian Jewish Congress, 1939), 10.
27 Gilles Marcotte, "Le romancier canadien-français et son Juif," in *Juifs et canadiens, deuxième cahier du Cercle juif de langue française*, ed. Naïm Kattan (Montreal: Éditions du Jour, 1967).
28 Ibid., 24. See also Tulchinsky, *Canada's Jews*, 37ff. for more such references to Jewish businessmen and perceptions of their practices.
29 Tulchinsky, *Canada's Jews*, 52.
30 Sheldon and Judith Godfrey, *Burn This Gossip: The True Story of George Benjamin of Belleville, Canada's First Jewish Member of Parliament, 1857–1863* (Toronto: Duke and George Press, 1991), 24–26. Cf. Jonathan Sarna, "The Pork on the Fork: A Nineteenth Century Anti-Jewish Ditty," http://www.brandeis.edu/hornstein/sarna/antisemitism/theporkonthefork.pdf (accessed December 25, 2014).
31 Godfrey and Godfrey, *Burn This Gossip*, 34.
32 Ibid., 84.
33 Abella, *A Coat of Many Colours*, 78.
34 Tulchinsky, *Canada's Jews*, 78.
35 Abella, *A Coat of Many Colours*, 99.
36 Margaret Cannon, *The Invisible Empire: Racism in Canada* (Mississauga, ON: Random House Canada, 1992).
37 On the "Jew Bill" in Maryland and the political debate surrounding it, see Isaac M. Fein, *The Making of an American Jewish Community: The History of Baltimore Jewry from 1773 to 1920* (Philadelphia: Jewish Publication Society, 1971), 25–36.

38 Abella, *A Coat of Many Colours*, 37.
39 Michael Brown, *Jew or Juif? Jews, French Canadians and Anglo-Canadians, 1759–1914* (Philadelphia: Jewish Publication Society, 1987), 124.

NOTES TO CHAPTER FOUR

1 Cited in Julius, *Trials of the Diaspora*, 21.
2 Stanley B. Ryerson, *Unequal Union: Confederation and the Roots of Conflict in the Canadas, 1815–1873* (New York: International Publishers, 1968).
3 Abella, *A Coat of Many Colours*, 103.
4 James W. St.G. Walker, *"Race," Rights and the Law in the Supreme Court of Canada: Historical Case Studies* (Waterloo, ON: Wilfrid Laurier University Press, 1997), 251.
5 Harold B. Troper, *Only Farmers Need Apply: Official Canadian Government Encouragement of Immigration from the United States, 1896–1911* (Toronto: Griffin House, 1972).
6 Ibid., 7.
7 W. Scott, *The History of Canada*, 2nd ed. (Toronto: Grey House, 2010), 330.
8 The vision of the ideal Canadian as a farmer was shared by many nineteenth-century French Canadians. See Paul-André Linteau, René Durocher, and Jean-Claude Robert, *Quebec: A History, 1867–1929* (Toronto: James Lorimer, 1983), 284. On the widely held idea that Jews were essentially foreign to the land and to agriculture, see Stephen Wilson, *Ideology and Experience: Antisemitism in France at the Time of the Dreyfus Affair* (Rutherford, NJ: Fairleigh Dickinson University Press, 1982), 267.
9 Rosenberg, *Canada's Jews*, 10.
10 Cited in Alan Mendelson, *Exiles from Nowhere: The Jews and the Canadian Elite* (Montreal: Robin Brass Studio, 2008), 2.
11 Jean-Pierre Beaud and Jean-Guy Prevost, "Immigration, Eugenics and Statistics: Measuring Racial Origins in Canada (1921–1941)," *Canadian Ethnic Studies* 28, no. 2 (1996): 18.
12 Brown, *Jew or Juif?* 230.
13 Cyril Edel Leonoff, *The Jewish Farmers of Western Canada* (Vancouver: Jewish Historical Society of British Columbia, 1984), 10.
14 Elazar Barkan, *The Retreat of Scientific Racism: Changing Concepts of Race in Britain and the United States between the World Wars* (Cambridge: Cambridge University Press, 1992), 15.

15 Volkov, "Antisemitism as a Cultural Code," 39.

16 George L. Mosse, *Toward the Final Solution: A History of European Racism* (London: J.M. Dent and Sons, 1978), 43.

17 Susannah Heschel, *The Aryan Jesus: Christian Theologians and the Bible in Nazi Germany* (Princeton, NJ: Princeton University Press, 2008), 30.

18 Edward Said, *Orientalism* (London: Penguin, 1987).

19 Volkov, "Antisemitism as a Cultural Code," 38.

20 Julius, *Trials of the Diaspora*, 423.

21 Mendes-Flohr and Reinharz, *The Jew in the Modern World*, 332.

22 Susanne Terwey, "British Discourses on 'the Jew' and 'the Nation' 1899–1919," in *Quest. Issues in Contemporary Jewish History. Journal of Fondazione CDEC* 3 (July 2012), www.quest-cdecjournal.it/focus.php?id=298 (accessed July 20, 2012).

23 Literally, "transmigrated souls of Haman."

24 Adolf Stoecker (1835–1909) was a German antisemitic political figure. *Encyclopedia Judaica* (Ramat Gan: Keter, 1972), cols. 408–9.

25 It is spelled "Ismotsi" in the original. The reference is to Gyözö Istóczy (1842–1915), a Hungarian antisemitic leader who founded an antisemite party which won seventeen seats in parliament in 1884. *Encyclopedia Judaica* (Ramat Gan: Keter, 1972), 9: col. 1099.

26 "Dolgwin" in English characters in the original.

27 On Goldwin Smith, see Gerald Tulchinsky, "Goldwin Smith: Victorian Antisemite," in Alan Davies, ed., *Antisemitism in Canada*, 67–91.

28 Cf. Leviticus 13:51–52.

29 Y.E. Bernstein, *The Jews in Canada (in North America): An Eastern European View of the Montreal Jewish Community in 1884*, trans. Ira Robinson (Montreal: Hungry I Books, 2004), 6–7.

30 Martin Robin, *Shades of Right: Nativist and Fascist Politics in Canada, 1920–1940* (Toronto: University of Toronto Press, 1992), 186.

31 Cited in Tulchinsky, "Goldwin Smith: Victorian Antisemite," 73.

32 Arthur A. Chiel, *The Jews of Manitoba: A Social History* (Toronto: University of Toronto Press, 1961), 49–50.

33 Cited in Mendelson, *Exiles from Nowhere*, 49.

34 Terwey, "British Discourses on 'the Jew' and 'the Nation' 1899–1919."

35 Tulchinsky, "Goldwin Smith: Victorian Antisemite," 83; cf. Abella, *A Coat of Many Colours*, 106.

36 Tulchinsky, "Goldwin Smith: Victorian Antisemite," 84.

37 Lita-Rose Betcherman, "Clara Brett Martin's Anti-Semitism," *Canadian Journal of Women and the Law* 5 (1992): 286.

38 Cited in Tulchinsky, *Canada's Jews*, 128. Cf. Richard Menkis, "Antisemitism in the New Nation: From New France to 1950," in L. Ruth Klein, ed., *Nazi Germany, Canadian Responses: Confronting Antisemitism in the Shadow of War* (Montreal and Kingston: McGill-Queen's University Press, 2012), 40–41.

39 Stephen Speisman, *The Jews of Toronto: A History to* 1937 (Toronto: McClelland and Stewart, 1979), 119.

40 Richard Menkis, "Antisemitism in the New Nation: From New France to 1950," in Ruth Klein, ed., *Nazi Germany, Canadian Responses*, 41.

41 Dennis Wrong, cited in Lita-Rose Betcherman, *The Swastika and the Maple Leaf: Fascist Movements in Canada in the Thirties* (Toronto: Fitzhenry and Whiteside, 1975), 47.

42 Robin, *Shades of Right*, 186.

43 James S. Woodsworth, *Strangers within Our Gates, or Coming Canadians* (Toronto: University of Toronto Press, 1972), 127.

44 Brenda Cossman and Marlee Kline, "'And if not now, when?': Feminism and Anti-Semitism beyond Clara Brett Martin," in *The Canadian Jewish Studies Reader*, ed. Richard Menkis and Norman Ravvin (Calgary: Red Deer Press, 2004), 96.

45 Jürgen Osterhamel, *The Transformation of the World: A Global History of the Nineteenth Century* (Princeton, NJ: Princeton University Press, 2014), 460.

46 Speisman, *The Jews of Toronto*, 121.

47 Abella, *A Coat of Many Colours*, 81.

48 Julius, *Trials of the Diaspora*, 431.

49 Speisman, *The Jews of Toronto*, 120.

50 Stephen Speisman, "Antisemitism in Ontario: The Twentieth Century," in Davies, ed., *Antisemitism in Canada*, 116.

51 Linteau, Durocher, and Robert, *Quebec: A History*, 18–19.

52 Betcherman, *The Swastika and the Maple Leaf*, 23.

53 Richard Menkis, "Antisemitism in the New Nation: From New France to 1950," in *From Immigration to Integration: The Canadian Jewish Experience: A Millennium Edition*, ed. Ruth Klein and Frank Dimant (Toronto: Institute for International Affairs, B'nai Brith Canada, 2001), 42; Hughes Théorêt, *Les chemises bleues: Adrien Arcand, journaliste antisémite canadien-français* (Sillery: Septentrion, 2012), 203.

54 Bernard L. Vigod, *Quebec before Duplessis: The Political Career of Louis-Alexandre Taschereau* (Montreal and Kingston, McGill-Queen's University Press, 1986), 8.

55 Terence J. Fay, *A History of Canadian Catholics: Gallicanism, Romanism, and Canadianism* (Montreal and Kingston: McGill-Queen's University Press, 2002), 69.

56 Ibid., 80.

57 Paul-André Linteau, René Durocher, Jean-Claude Robert, and François Ricard, *Quebec since 1930* (Toronto: James Lorimer, 1991), 74.

58 Julius, *Trials of the Diaspora*, 492; Katz, *From Prejudice to Destruction*, 219–20; David Bercuson and Douglas Wertheimer, *A Trust Betrayed: The Keegstra Affair* (Toronto: Doubleday Canada, 1985), 11–15; Mosse, *Toward the Final Solution*, 139–40.

59 On this theory, see Jacob Katz, *Jews and Freemasons in Europe 1723–1939* (Cambridge, MA: Harvard University Press, 1970).

60 Robert F. Byrnes, *Antisemitism in Modern France* (New Brunswick, NJ: Rutgers University Press, 1950), 1: 91.

61 Linteau, Durocher, and Robert, *Quebec: A History, 1867–1929*, 282.

62 Ibid., 458.

63 Robert S. Wistrich, *Antisemitism: The Longest Hatred* (London: Methuen, 1991), 127.

64 Pierre Birnbaum, *The Anti-Semitic Moment: A Tour of France in 1898* (New York: Hill and Wang, 2003), 334.

65 Julius, *Trials of the Diaspora*, 14.

66 John Connelly, *From Enemy to Brother: The Revolution in Catholic Teaching on the Jews, 1933–1965* (Cambridge: Harvard University Press, 2012), 79.

67 Terwey, "British Discourses on 'the Jew' and 'the Nation' 1899–1919."

68 Ronald Schechter, *Obstinate Hebrews: Representations of Jews in France, 1715–1815* (Berkeley: University of California Press, 2003), 1; Byrnes, *Antisemitism in Modern France*, 153.

69 Cited in Wistrich, *Antisemitism: The Longest Hatred*, xxiv.

70 Tulchinsky, *Canada's Jews*, 104; Brown, *Jew or Juif?* 135.

71 Martin P. Johnson, *The Dreyfus Affair: Honour and Politics in the Belle Époque* (New York: St. Martin's Press, 1999).

72 Fay, *A History of Canadian Catholics*, 236–37.

73 Muller, *Capitalism and the Jews*, 54.

74 Michael Oliver, *The Passionate Debate: The Social and Political Ideas of Quebec Nationalism, 1920–1945* (Montreal: Véhicule Press, 1991), 73, 78.

75 Walker, *"Race," Rights and the Law in the Supreme Court of Canada: Historical Case Studies*, 141.

76 Ibid., 142.

77 Linteau et al., *Quebec since 1930*, 76–77; Everett C. Hughes, *French Canada in Transition* (Chicago: University of Chicago Press, 1963), 217.

78 Oliver, *The Passionate Debate*, 74.

79 Cited in David Rome, Judith Nefsky, and Paule Obermeir, *Les Juifs du Québec: Bibliographie rétrospective annotée* (Quebec: Institut Québécois de Recherche Sur la Culture, 1981), 121, no. 583.

80 Oliver, *The Passionate Debate*, 23.

81 Ibid., 28.

82 Cited in Victor Teboul, *Mythes et images du Juif au Québec: Essai d'analyse critique* (Montreal: Éditions de Lagrave, 1977), 173–74.

83 Michael Brown, "From Stereotype to Scapegoat: Anti-Jewish Sentiment in French Canada from Confederation to World War I," in Davies, ed., *Antisemitism in Canada*, 46.

84 Abella, *A Coat of Many Colours*, 109. Cf. Birnbaum, *The Anti-Semitic Moment*, 43–44.

85 Abella, *A Coat of Many Colours*, 109; William Kernaghan, "Freedom of Religion in the Province of Quebec with Particular Reference to the Jews, Johovah's Witnesses, and Church-State Relations, 1930–1960" (doctoral dissertation, Duke University, 1966), 51.

86 Tulchinsky *Canada's Jews*, 138.

87 Ibid., 107.

88 Abella, *A Coat of Many Colours*, 131–32.

89 Richard Menkis, "Antisemitism in the New Nation: From New France to 1950," in Klein and Dimant, eds., *From Immigration to Integration*, 40.

90 Corcos, *Montréal, les Juifs, et l'école*, 83.

91 Roderick MacLeod and Mary Anne Poutanen, "Little Fists for Social Justice: Anti-Semitism, Community, and Montreal's Aberdeen School Strike, 1913," *Labour/le Travail* 70 (Fall 2012): 21.

92 Ibid.; Israel Medres, *Montreal of Yesterday: Jewish Life in Montreal 1900–1920*, trans. Vivian Felsen (Montreal: Véhicule Press, 2000), 135–36; Pierre Anctil, ed., *Through the Eyes of the Eagle: The Early Montreal Yiddish Press, 1907–1916*, tr. David Rome (Montreal: Véhicule Press, 2001), 78–80.

93 Ruth Frager, "Communities and Conflicts: East European Jewish Immigrants in Ontario and Quebec from the Late 1800s to the 1930s," in Robinson, ed., *Canada's Jews in Time, Space, and Spirit*, 63.

94 Cited in Paul Laverdure, *Sunday in Canada: The Rise and Fall of the Lord's Day* (Yorkton, SK: Gravelbooks, 2004), 31.

95 Pierre Anctil, *Le Devoir, les juifs, et l'immigration* (Quebec: Institut Québécois de Recherche sur la Culture, 1988), 38–39.

96 Cited in Laverdure, *Sunday in Canada*, 32. Laverdure notes that Bourassa soon reversed his position and supported the "Jewish exemption" clause. See p. 49.

97 Leverdure, *Sunday in Canada*, 32; Richard Menkis, "Antisemitism in the New Nation: From New France to 1950," in Klein and Dimant, eds., *From Immigration to Integration*, 39; Lorraine Weinrib, "'Do Justice to Us!': Jews and the Constitution of Canada," in *Not Written in Stone: Jews, Constitutions and Constitutionalism in Canada*, ed. Daniel J. Elazar, Michael Brown, and Ira Robinson (Ottawa: University of Ottawa Press, 2003), 37–42.

98 Tulchinsky, *Canada's Jews*, 132.

99 Abella, *A Coat of Many Colours*, 130.

100 Ira Robinson, *Rabbis and Their Community: Studies in the Eastern European Orthodox Rabbinate in Montreal, 1896–1930* (Calgary: University of Calgary Press, 2007), 47.

101 Brown, *Jew or Juif?* 140–45; Richard Menkis, "Antisemitism in the New Nation: From New France to 1950," in Klein and Dimant, eds., *From Immigration to Integration*, 37.

102 Joshua D. MacFayden, "Nip the Noxious Growth in the Bud: Ortenberg v. Plamondon and the Roots of Canadian Anti-Hate Activism," *Canadian Jewish Studies* 12 (2004): 75.

103 Tulchinsky, *Canada's Jews*, 142.

104 Sylvio Normand, "L'affaire *Plamondon*: un cas d'antisémitisme à Québec au début du XXe siècle," *Cahiers de Droit* 48, no 3 (September 2007): 477–504.

105 Medres, *Montreal of Yesterday*, 125.

106 Ibid., 127–28.

107 Robert Weinberg, *Blood Libel in Late Imperial Russia: The Ritual Murder Trial of Mendel Beilis* (Bloomington: Indiana University Press, 2014). Cf. Abella, *A Coat of Many Colours*, 110–11.

108 Leonard Dinnerstein, *The Leo Frank Case* (New York: Columbia University Press, 1968; paperback, University of Georgia Press, 1987; Notable Trials Library edition, 1991).

109 In British law there is precedent for this reasoning in the eighteenth-century *Osborne* case with respect to a pamphlet defamatory to the Jews which was not considered actionable because the "allegation was so general that no particular persons could pretend to be injured by it." Cited in Waldron, *The Harm in Hate Speech*, 205.

110 Menkis, "Antisemitism in the New Nation: From New France to 1950," in Klein and Dimant, eds., *From Immigration to Integration*, 38.

NOTES TO CHAPTER FIVE

1 A.M. Klein, *The Collected Poems of A.M. Klein* (Toronto: McGraw-Hill Ryerson, 1974), 328.

2 Abella, *A Coat of Many Colours*, v–vi.

3 Franklin Bialystok, *Delayed Impact: The Holocaust and the Canadian Jewish Community* (Montreal and Kingston: McGill-Queen's University Press, 2000), 19.

4 Allan Levine, *Coming of Age: A History of the Jewish People of Manitoba* (Winnipeg: Heartland, 2009), 251.

5 Peter C. Newman, *Izzy: The Passionate Life and Turbulent Times of Izzy Asper, Canada's Media Mogul* (Toronto: HarperCollins, 2008), 40.

6 Gerald Tulchinsky, "The Third Solitude: A.M. Klein's Jewish Montreal, 1900–1950," *Journal of Canadian Studies* 19, no. 2 (Fall 1984): 97–98.

7 Abella, "Anti-Semitism in Canada in the Interwar Years," in Rischin, ed., *The Jews of North America*, 230.

8 Cited in Joe King, *From the Ghetto to the Main: The Story of the Jews of Montreal* (Montreal: Montreal Jewish Publication Company, 2001), 198.

9 Speisman, "Antisemitism in Ontario: The Twentieth Century," in Davies, ed., *Antisemitism in Canada*, 117.

10 Reuben Slonim, *Family Quarrel: The United Church and the Jews* (Toronto and Vancouver: Clarke, Irwin, 1977), 122.

11 Bialystok, *Delayed Impact*, 22.

12 Walker, *"Race," Rights and the Law in the Supreme Court of Canada*, 12–13.

13 Speisman, *The Jews of Toronto*, 320–21.

14 Cf. Zev Eleff, "The Baptism of Four Little Roxbury Girls: Jewish Angst in America's Religious Marketplace during the Interwar Period," *American Jewish Archives Journal* 65 (2013): 77.

15 Cited in Pierre Anctil, "A.M. Klein: The Poet and His Relations with French Quebec," in Menkis and Ravvin, eds., *Canadian Jewish Studies Reader*, 363.

16 Jacques Langlais and David Rome, *Jews and French Quebecers: Two Hundred Years of Shared History* (Waterloo, ON: Wilfrid Laurier University Press, 1991), 170n85.

17 W. Peter Ward, *White Canada Forever: Popular Attitudes and Public Policy Toward Orientals in British Columbia* (Montreal and Kingston: McGill-Queen's University Press, 2002).

18 Speisman, *The Jews of Toronto*, 320.

19 Speisman, "Antisemitism in Ontario," in Davies, ed., *Antisemitism in Canada*, 117.

20 James S. Woodsworth, *Strangers within Our Gates, or Coming Canadians* (Toronto: University of Toronto Press, 1972), 237.

21 Irving Elson Rexford, *Our Educational Problem: The Jewish Population and the Protestant Schools* (Montreal: Renouf, 1924).

22 Kernaghan, "Freedom of Religion in the Province of Quebec," 37.

23 Vigod, *Quebec before Duplessis*, 157.

24 Linteau, Durocher, and Robert, *Quebec: A History*, 466.

25 Corcos, *Montréal, les Juifs, et l'école*, 101–12.

26 Kernaghan, "Freedom of Religion in the Province of Quebec," 39.

27 Ibid., 116.

28 *L'Action Patriotique* (Quebec), December 7, 1933, 2. Cited in Pierre Anctil, "Maurice Pollack: Homme d'affaires et philanthrope," in *Les Juifs de Québec: Quatre siècles d'histoire*, ed. Pierre Anctil (Quebec: Presses de l'Université Laval, 2015), 129. Cf. Richard Jones, *L'idéologie de L'Action Catholique (1917–1939)* (Quebec: Presses de l'Université Laval, 1974), 276.

29 Abella, "Anti-Semitism in Canada in the Interwar Years," in Rischin, ed., *The Jews of North America*, 242.

30 Tulchinsky, *Canada's Jews*, 298–99.

31 Walker, *"Race," Rights and the Law in the Supreme Court of Canada*, 140.

32 Abella, *A Coat of Many Colours*, 166; Harold Troper, "New Horizons in a New Land: Jewish Immigration to Canada," in Klein and Dimant, eds., *From Immigration to Integration*, 12.

33 Speisman, *The Jews of Toronto*, 321.

34 Betcherman, *Ernest Lapointe*, 241, 243, 253.

35 Ibid., 254.

36 Irving Abella and Harold Troper, *None Is Too Many: Canada and the Jews of Europe, 1933–1948* (Toronto: Lester and Orpen Dennys, 1982), 8.

37 Irving Abella and Harold Troper, "'The Line Must Be Drawn Somewhere: Canada and Jewish Refugees, 1933–1939," in *The Canadian Jewish Mosaic*, ed. M. Weinfeld, William Shaffir, and Irwin Cotler (Toronto: John Wiley, 1981), 53–54.

38 Ibid., 52.

39 Cohn, *Warrant for Genocide*.

40 Neil Baldwin, *Henry Ford and the Jews: The Mass Production of Hate* (New York: Public Affairs, 2001).

41 Janine Stingel, *Social Discredit: Anti-Semitism, Social Credit, and the Jewish Response* (Montreal and Kingston, McGill-Queen's University Press, 2000), 17.

42 Jones, *L'idéologie de L'Action Catholique*, 77.

43 Cited in Arthur Goldwag, *The New Hate: A History of Fear and Loathing on the Populist Right* (New York: Pantheon, 2012), 61.

44 Haim Genizi, *The Holocaust, Israel, and Canadian Protestant Churches* (Montreal and Kingston: McGill-Queen's University Press, 2002), 42.

45 Stingel, *Social Discredit*, 4.

46 Howard Palmer, "Politics, Religion, and Antisemitism in Alberta, 1880–1950" in Davies, ed., *Antisemitism in Canada*, 177; Wistrich, *A Lethal Obsession*, 373–74.

47 Norman Fergus Black, *What About the Jews?* (Toronto: Canadian Association for Adult Education, 1944), 9.

48 Howard Palmer, "Politics, Religion, and Antisemitism in Alberta, 1880–1950" in Davies, ed., *Antisemitism in Canada*, 175; David Elliott, "Anti-Semitism and the Social Credit Movement," *Canadian Ethnic Studies* 17 (1985): 84.

49 Alan Davies and Marilyn F. Nefsky, *How Silent Were the Churches? Canadian Protestantism and the Jewish Plight during the Nazi Era* (Waterloo, ON: Wilfrid Laurier University Press, 1997), 11.

50 Stingel, *Social Discredit*, 59–60.

51 Ibid., 69–70.

52 Cited in Alan Mendelson, *Exiles from Nowhere: The Jews and the Canadian Elite* (Montreal: Robin Brass Studio, 2008), 64.

53 Abella and Troper, *None Is Too Many*, 228.

54 Jacob Neusner, *The Way of Torah: An Introduction to Judaism*, 7th ed. (Belmont, CA: Wadsworth/Thomson, 2004), 184.

55 Rosenberg, *Canada's Jews*, 303.

56 Walker, *"Race," Rights and the Law in the Supreme Court of Canada*, 182.

57 Abella, *A Coat of Many Colours*, 181.

58 Speisman, "Antisemitism in Ontario," in Davies, ed., *Antisemitism in Canada*, 121.

59 Speisman, *The Jews of Toronto*, 332; Robin, *Shades of Right*, 187; Benjamin Kayfetz and Stephen Speisman, *Only Yesterday: Collected Pieces on the Jews of Toronto* (Toronto: Now and Then Books, 2013), 115.

60 Michael Oliver, *The Passionate Debate: The Social and Political Ideas of Quebec Nationalism, 1920–1945* (Montreal: Véhicule Press, 1991), 191–92; Théorêt, *Les chemises bleues*, 146.

61 Abella, "Anti-Semitism in Canada in the Interwar Years," in Rischin, ed., *The Jews of North America*, 236.

62 Abella, *A Coat of Many Colours*, 198.

63 Abella, "Anti-Semitism in Canada in the Interwar Years," in Rischin, ed., *The Jews of North America*, 236.

64 Gerald Tulchinsky, *Joe Salsberg: A Life of Commitment* (Toronto: University of Toronto Press, 2013), 73.

65 Abella, *A Coat of Many Colours*, 180.

66 Henry Trachtenberg, "The Winnipeg Jewish Community in the Inter-War Period, 1919–1939: Anti-Semitism and Politics," *Canadian Jewish Historical Society Journal* 4, no. 1 (1980): 50.

67 Charles Herbert Stember, *Jews in the Mind of America* (New York: Basic, 1966), 8.

68 Robin, *Shades of Right*, 186.

69 Menkis, "Antisemitism in the New Nation," in Klein and Dimant, eds., *From Immigration to Integration*, 45.

70 Speisman, "Antisemitism in Ontario," in Davies, ed., *Antisemitism in Canada*, 119.

71 Robin, *Shades of Right*, 158–59.

72 Wallace Clement, "The Canadian Corporate Elite: Ethnicity and Inequality of Access," in Rita M. Bienvenue and Jay E. Goldstein, *Ethnicity and Ethnic Relations in Canada*, 2nd ed. (Toronto: Butterworths, 1985), 148–49.

73 Kayfetz and Speisman, *Only Yesterday*, 110.

74 Slonim, *Family Quarrel*, 85–86; Kayfetz and Speisman, *Only Yesterday*, 113–14.

75 Abella, *A Coat of Many Colours*, 181; Speisman, *The Jews of Toronto*, 120–21; Betcherman, *The Swastika and the Maple Leaf*, 48.

76 Mendelson, *Exiles from Nowhere*, xiv; Slonim, *Family Quarrel*, 86; Kayfetz and Speisman, *Only Yesterday*, 113.

77 Michael Brown, "On Campus in the Thirties: Antipathy, Support, and Indifference," in Klein, ed., *Nazi Germany, Canadian Responses*, 161.

78 Newman, *Izzy*, 53.

79 Nigro and Mauro, "The Jewish Immigrant Experience and the Practice of Law," 1018.

80 J. Bickenbach, "Lawyers, Law Professors, and Racism in Ontario," *Queen's Quarterly* 96, no. 3 (1989): 585–94.

81 Ibid., 594.

82 Ibid., 595.

83 E. Digby Baltzell, *The Protestant Establishment: Aristocracy and Caste in America* (New York: Random House, 1964), 211.

84 Seymour Martin Lipset and David Riesman, *Education and Politics at Harvard* (New York: McGraw-Hill, 1975), 144–47.

85 Tulchinsky, *Canada's Jews*, 132.

86 Pierre Anctil, *Le rendez-vous manqué: Les juifs de Montréal face au Québec de l'entre-deux-guerres* (Quebec: Institut Québécois de Recherche sur la Culture, 1988), 65.

87 Menkis, "Antisemitism in the New Nation," in Klein and Dimant, eds., *From Immigration to Integration*, 47.

88 Pierre Anctil, "Interlude of Hostility: Judeo-Christian Relations in Quebec in the Interwar Period, 1919–1939," in Davies, ed., *Antisemitism in Canada*, 142.

89 Morton Weinfeld, *Like Everyone Else ... But Different: The Paradoxical Success of Canadian Jews* (Toronto: McClelland and Stewart, 2001), 325.

90 Menkis, "Antisemitism in the New Nation," in Klein and Dimant, eds., *From Immigration to Integration*, 47.

91 Betcherman, *The Swastika and the Maple Leaf*, 102.

92 Cited in Nigro and Mauro, "The Jewish Immigrant Experience and the Practice of Law," 1012.

93 Brown, "On Campus in the Thirties," in Klein, ed., *Nazi Germany, Canadian Responses*, 147.

94 Ibid., 159.

95 Pierre Anctil, *Trajectoires juives au Québec* (Quebec: Presses de l'Université Laval, 2010), 56.

96 Anctil, *Le rendez-vous manqué*, 113.

97 Anctil, "Interlude of Hostility," in Davies, ed., *Antisemitism in Canada*, 147; Théorêt, *Les chemises bleues*, 74; Anctil, *Le rendez-vous manqué*, 119.

98 Jean-François Nadeau, *Adrien Arcand: Führer canadien* (Montreal: Lux, 2010), 179.

99 *Le Quartier Latin*, 25 avril, 1941, 5. English translation: http://faculty.marianopolis.edu/c.Belanger/quebechistory/docs/jews/letters.htm (accessed February 14, 2014).

100 This is quite similar to contemporary proposals in the United States for reducing "the crowding of Jewish young men into the medical schools and the law schools" for fear of provoking antisemitism. Joan Friedman, *Guidance, Not Governance: Rabbi Solomon Freehof and Reform Responsa* (Cincinnati, OH: Hebrew Union College Press, 2013), 182.

101 Brown, "On Campus in the Thirties," in Klein, ed., *Nazi Germany, Canadian Responses*, 159.

102 Leonard Dinnerstein, *Uneasy at Home: Antisemitism and the American Jewish Experience* (New York: Columbia University Press, 1987), 183.

103 Saul Hayes, "Report on Anti-Semitism in Canada," Canadian Jewish Congress Charities Committee National Archives (hereafter CJCCCNA) ZA

1949/3/26, 20. Cf. Brown, "On Campus in the Thirties," in Klein, ed., *Nazi Germany, Canadian Responses*, 161; *American Jewish Year Book* (hereafter *AJYB*) (1951): 236, http://www.ajcarchives.org/AJC_DATA/Files/1951 _9_BritishCommon.pdf (accessed January 1, 2014).

104 Paul Axelrod, *Making a Middle Class: Student Life in English Canada during the Thirties* (Montreal and Kingston: McGill-Queen's Univeristy Press, 1990), 32.

105 *AJYB* 51 (1950): 232, http://www.ajcarchives.org/AJC_DATA/Files/1951 _9_BritishCommon.pdf (accessed January 1, 2014).

106 Speisman, "Antisemitism in Ontario," in Davies, ed., *Antisemitism in Canada*, 117.

107 Menkis, "Antisemitism in the New Nation," in Klein and Dimant, eds., *From Immigration to Integration*, 46; Kayfetz and Speisman, *Only Yesterday*, 112.

108 Jewish Telegraphic Agency (hereafter JTA), http://www.jta.org/1927/07/29/ archive/anti-semitism-in-toronto-hospitals-charged-by-rabbi-isserman (accessed December 30, 2013).

109 Brown, "On Campus in the Thirties," in Klein, ed., *Nazi Germany, Canadian Responses*, 159.

110 Stephen Scheinberg, "From Self-Help to National Advocacy: The Emergence of Community Activism" in Klein, ed., *Nazi Germany, Canadian Responses*, 59.

111 Arnold Ages, "Antisemitism: The Uneasy Calm," in Weinfeld et al., eds., *The Canadian Jewish Mosaic*, 387.

112 Walker, *"Race," Rights and the Law in the Supreme Court of Canada*, 185.

113 Abella, *A Coat of Many Colours*, 180.

114 Betcherman, *The Swastika and the Maple Leaf*, 40; Davies and Nefsky, *How Silent Were the Churches?* 10; Walker, *"Race," Rights and the Law in the Supreme Court of Canada*, 185.

115 Abella, "Anti-Semitism in Canada in the Interwar Years" in Rischin, ed., *The Jews of North America*, 235.

116 Abella, *A Coat of Many Colours*, 179–80.

117 Tulchinsky, *Canada's Jews*, 313.

118 Israel Medres, "Dr. Sam Rabinovitch Explains Why He Resigned" [Yiddish], *Keneder Adler*, June 19, 1934, 5.

119 "Re: Sam Rabinovitch Case 1934 copied from Notre Dame Hospital and McGill Archives by researcher Harold Toulch, May 1997," CJCCCNA.

120 Betcherman, *Ernest Lapointe*, 221.

121 Ibid., 231.

122 Ibid., 304.
123 Hughes, *French Canada in Transition*, 76.
124 Byrnes, *Antisemitism in Modern France*, 269.
125 Hughes, *French Canada in Transition*, 217–18.
126 Abella, *A Coat of Many Colours*, 182.
127 Théorêt, *Les chemises bleues*, 226.
128 A.M. Klein, "The Tactics of Race Hatred" (29 December, 1944), in *Beyond Sambatyon: Selected Essays and Editorials, 1928–1955*, ed. M.W. Steinberg and Usher Caplan (Toronto: University of Toronto Press, 1982), 230.
129 Library and Archives Canada (hereafter LAC), PA-107943, "Jews Are Not Wanted Here in Ste. Agathe."
130 Abella, "Anti-Semitism in Canada in the Interwar Years," in Rischin, ed., *The Jews of North America*, 230; Anctil, *Le rendez-vous manqué*, 248.
131 *AJYB* 42 (1940–41): 326, http://www.ajcarchives.org/AJC_DATA/Files/1940_1941_5_YRForeign.pdf (accessed January 1, 2014); Betcherman, *The Swastika and the Maple Leaf*, 142–43. Cf. Tulchinsky, *Canada's Jews*, 315.
132 JTA, http://www.jta.org/1942/08/07/archive/anti-semites-riot-in-canadian-resort-town-vandals-invade-jewish-shops (accessed December 30, 2013).
133 JTA, http://www.jta.org/1943/08/06/archive/son-of-canadian-chief-of-police-sought-in-connection-with-anti-jewish-riots (accessed December 30, 2013).
134 Cited in Stingel, *Social Discredit*, 27.
135 Anctil, "A.M. Klein: The Poet and His Relations with French Quebec," in Menkis and Ravvin, *Canadian Jewish Studies Reader*, 364.
136 JTA, http://www.jta.org/1931/12/22/archive/rontreal-archbishop-promises-rabbi-his-help-in-stopping-anti-jewish-agitation-in-canada (accessed December 30, 2013).
137 Jean-Marie-Rodrigue Villeneuve to Nicola Canali, February 15, 1936, Archives de l'archdiocèse de Québec 119, 10cm, Rome.
138 Jack Jedwab, "The Politics of Dialogue: Rapprochement Efforts between Jews and French Canadians: 1939–1960," in *Renewing Our Days: Montreal Jews in the Twentieth Century*, ed. Ira Robinson and Mervin Butovsky (Montreal, Véhicule Press, 1995), 47; Medres, *Between the Wars*, 102.
139 David Rome, "Canada," *AJYB* (1944–45): 200, http://www.ajcarchives.org/AJC_DATA/Files/1944_1945_6_BritCommonwealth.pdf (accessed January 1, 2014).
140 Medres, *Between the Wars*, 70–71.
141 Connelly, *From Enemy to Brother*, 82.
142 Ibid., 100.

143 Pierre Anctil, "Les rapports entre francophones et juifs dans le contexte montréalais," in *Les Communautés juives de Montréal: Histoire et enjeux contemporains*, ed. Pierre Anctil and Ira Robinson (Sillery: Septentrion, 2010), 56; Robin, *Shades of Right*, 128.

144 Stuart Rosenberg, *The Jewish Community in Canada* (Toronto: McClelland and Stewart, 1970), 1: 225.

145 For other assertions of Jewish control of the press, see Jones, *L'Idéologie de L'Action Catholique*, 10.

146 Anctil, *Le Devoir, les juifs, et l'immigration*, 52–53.

147 Betcherman, *Ernest Lapointe*, 277; Mendelson, *Exiles from Nowhere*, 63.

148 Jedwab, "The Politics of Dialogue," in Robinson and Butovsky, eds., *Renewing Our Days*, 50.

149 Hughes, *French Canada in Transition*, 135.

150 Julius, *Trials of the Diaspora*, 478–79.

151 Abella, *A Coat of Many Colours*, 183.

152 Cited in Anctil, *Le rendez-vous manqué*, 273. Cf. Jean-Pierre Gaboury, *Le nationalism de Lionel Groulx* (Ottawa: Éditions de l'Université d'Ottawa, 1970), 35.

153 Marsha Rozenblit, "Note on Galician Jewish Immigration to Vienna," *Austrian History Yearbook* 19 (1983): 150; Dermot Keogh and Andrew McCarthy, *Limerick Boycott 1904: Anti-Semitism in Ireland* (Cork, Ireland: Mercier Press, 2005).

154 Robin, *Shades of Right*, 108–9; Kernaghan, "Freedom of Religion in the Province of Quebec," 87.

155 Théorêt, *Les chemises bleues*, 247.

156 Walker, *"Race," Rights and the Law in the Supreme Court of Canada*, 141.

157 Tulchinsky, *Canada's Jews*, 302.

158 Abella, "Anti-Semitism in Canada in the Interwar Years," in Rischin, ed., *The Jews of North America*, 239.

159 Kernaghan, "Freedom of Religion in the Province of Quebec," 86.

160 Cited in Pierre Anctil, "Bâtir une synagogue à la haute ville de Québec, 1931–1952," Concordia Institute for Canadian Jewish Studies Working Papers in Canadian Jewish Studies No. 4 (March 8, 2013), http://cjs.concordia.ca/publications/working-papers-in-canadian-jewish-studies/ (accessed March 15, 2013).

161 Anctil, "Maurice Pollack," 10.

162 A.M. Klein, "*Le Canada* and 'This Hatred'" (November 16, 1945), in *Beyond Sambatyon: Selected Essays and Editorials, 1928-1955*, ed. M.W. Steinberg and Usher Caplan (Toronto: University of Toronto Press, 1982), 251–52.

163 Tulchinsky, *Canada's Jews*, 323–24.

164 Cited in Harold Troper and Morton Weinfeld, *Old Wounds: Jews, Ukrainians and the Hunt for Nazi War Criminals in Canada* (Markham, ON: Viking, 1988), 26.

165 Leverdure, *Sunday in Canada*, 114–15.

166 Harold B. Troper, *The Defining Decade: Identity, Politics, and the Canadian Jewish Community in the 1960s* (Toronto: University of Toronto Press, 2010), 57.

167 Cited in Anctil, "Bâtir une synagogue à la haute ville de Québec."

168 A.M. Klein, "Quebec City Gets Another Park" (18 June, 1943), in Steinberg and Caplan, eds., *Beyond Sambatyon*, 191.

169 Kernaghan, "Freedom of Religion in the Province of Quebec," 138.

170 Rachel Smiley, "Historic Sketch of the Quebec Jewish Community and Synagogue," *Dedication of the Beth Israel-Ohev Sholom Synagogue and Community Centre* (Quebec City, 1944), 9.

171 A.M. Klein, "Incendiary Antisemitism" (26 May, 1944), in Steinberg and Caplan, eds., *Beyond Sambatyon*, 219.

172 Isidore Goldstick, "Where Jews Can't Pray," *Contemporary Jewish Record* 6 (1943): 587–97. For documents on this case from the perspective of the Quebec municipality, see Ville de Québec, Service du greffe et des archives, file QP 1-4/194–98.

173 On housing restrictions in Toronto, see Kayfetz and Speisman, *Only Yesterday*, 115–16.

174 Jack Lipinsky, *Imposing Their Will: An Organizational History of Jewish Toronto, 1933–1948* (Montreal and Kingston: McGill-Queen's University Press, 2011), 123.

NOTES TO CHAPTER SIX

1 Cited in Goldwag, *The New Hate*, 266.

2 Lucy S. Davidowicz, *The War against the Jews, 1933–1945* (New York: Holt, Rinehart and Winston, 1975).

3 Karl Marx, "On the Jewish Question," http://www.marxists.org/archive/marx/works/1844/jewish-question/ (accessed February 20, 2013).

4 On Communism, Jews, and Jewish culture in the Soviet Union prior to the Second World War, see Anna Shternshis, *Soviet and Kosher: Jewish Popular Culture in the Soviet Union, 1923–1939* (Bloomington: Indiana University Press, 2006).

5 Jonathan Frankel, *Revolution and Russian Jews* (Cambridge: Cambridge University Press, 2009), 219.

6 William J. Fishman, *Jewish Radicals: From Czarist Stetl to London Ghetto* (New York: Pantheon Books, 1975).

7 Editors of Fortune, *Jews in America* (New York: Random House, 1936), 72.

8 M.M. Silver, *Louis Marshall and the Rise of Jewish Ethnicity in America* (Syracuse, NY: Syracuse University Press, 2013), 460.

9 Muller, *Capitalism and the Jews*, 163; Genizi, *The Holocaust, Israel, and Canadian Protestant Churches*, 191.

10 Richard Frankel, "One Crisis Behind? Rethinking Antisemitic Exceptionalism in the United States and Germany" *American Jewish History* 97, no. 3 (2013): 243.

11 Genizi, *The Holocaust, Israel, and Canadian Protestant Churches*, 61; Wistrich, *A Lethal Obsession*, 159, 370.

12 Winston Churchill, "Zionism versus Bolshevism," *Illustrated Sunday Herald*, February 8, 1920. On Churchill and the Jews, see Martin Gilbert, *Churchill and the Jews: A Lifelong Friendship* (New York: Holt, 2007).

13 Cited in Zvi Gitelman, "Comparative and Competitive Victimization in the Post-Communist Sphere," in *Resurgent Antisemitism: Global Perspectives*, ed. Alvin Rosenfeld (Bloomington: Indiana University Press, 2013), 218.

14 Muller, *Capitalism and the Jews*, 139.

15 Henry Felix Srebrnik, *Creating the Chupah: The Zionist Movement and the Drive for Jewish Communal Unity in Canada, 1898–1921* (Boston: Academic Studies Press, 2011), 239.

16 Robin, *Shades of Right*, 186.

17 Jones, *L'Idéologie de L'Action Catholique*, 9, cf. 52.

18 Robin, *Shades of Right*, 198, 201. Cf. Davies and Nefsky, *How Silent Were the Churches?* 110.

19 Cohn, *Warrant for Genocide*.

20 Goldwag, *The New Hate*, 122.

21 Speisman, "Antisemitism in Ontario," in Davies, ed., *Antisemitism in Canada*, 117.

22 Tulchinsky, *Canada's Jews*, 187; Srebrnik, *Creating the Chupah*, 239.

23 Cited in Trachtenberg, "The Winnipeg Jewish Community," 49.

24 Robin, *Shades of Right*, 198.

25 Betcherman, *Ernest Lapointe*, 213–14.

26 Merrily Weisbord, *The Strangest Dream: Canadian Communists, the Spy Trials, and the Cold War* (Montreal: Véhicule Press, 1994); Anctil, *Le rendez-vous manqué*, 223.

27 Speisman, "Antisemitism in Ontario," in Davies, ed., *Antisemitism in Canada*, 124; Betcherman, *The Swastika and the Maple Leaf*, 103.

28 Speisman, *The Jews of Toronto*, 320; Cyril H. Levitt and William Shaffir, *The Riot at Christie Pits* (Toronto: Lester and Orpen Dennys, 1987), 24.

29 Kernaghan, "Freedom of Religion in the Province of Quebec," 50; Tulchinsky, *Canada's Jews*, 301, 313.

30 Stingel, *Social Discredit*, 105.

31 Palmer, "Politics, Religion, and Antisemitism in Alberta," in Davies, ed., *Antisemitism in Canada*, 180.

32 Stingel, *Social Discredit*, 66.

33 Linteau et al., *Quebec since 1930*, 465.

34 Gitelman, "Comparative and Competitive Victimization in the Post-Communist Sphere," in Rosenfeld, ed., *Resurgent Antisemitism*, 218.

35 Théorêt, *Les chemises bleues*, 58.

36 Cited in Brown, "On Campus in the Thirties," in Klein, ed., *Nazi Germany, Canadian Responses*, 149.

37 Cited in Kernaghan, "Freedom of Religion in the Province of Quebec," 82.

38 Hughes, *French Canada in Transition*, 214.

39 Linteau, *Quebec: A History, 1867–1929*, 540.

40 Bernard Figler and David Rome, *Hannaniah Meir Caiserman: A Biography* (Montreal: Northern Printing and Lithographing, 1962), 249.

41 Weisbord, *The Strangest Dream*, 27–28, 49.

42 Betcherman, *Ernest Lapointe*, 228.

43 Mercedes Stedman, *Angels of the Workplace: Women and the Construction of Gender Relations in the Canadian Clothing Industry, 1890–1940* (Toronto: Oxford University Press, 1997), 241.

44 Weisbord, *The Strangest Dream*, 80.

45 Tulchinsky, *Canada's Jews*, 257.

46 Robin, *Shades of Right*, 112.

47 Betcherman, *The Swastika and the Maple Leaf*, 8–9.

48 Filippo Salvatore, *Fascism and the Italians of Montreal: An Oral History, 1922–1945* (Toronto: Guernica, 1998).

49 Betcherman, *The Swastika and the Maple Leaf*, 8.

50 Muller, *Capitalism and the Jews*, 133–34.

51 Théorêt, *Les chemises bleues*, 96.

52 John Herd Thompson and Allen Seager, *Canada 1922–1939: Decades of Discord* (Toronto: McClelland and Stewart, 1985), 323.

53 Anctil, *Trajectoires juives au Québec*, 60.

54 Betcherman, *The Swastika and the Maple Leaf*, 11.

55 JTA, http://www.jta.org/1931/08/29/archive/ritual-murder-allegation-in
    -canadian-general-election-talmud-teaches-jews-to-kill-christian
    -children (accessed January 1, 2014).

56 Jean-François Nadeau, *Adrien Arcand: Führer canadien* (Montreal: Lux,
    2010), 66.

57 Ibid., 97.

58 Cited in Abella, "Anti-Semitism in Canada in the Interwar Years," in
    Rischin, ed., *The Jews of North America*, 241.

59 Théorêt, *Les chemises bleues*, 105.

60 Robin, *Shades of Right*, 112–13.

61 Betcherman, *Ernest Lapointe*, 256.

62 Théorêt, *Les chemises bleues*, 27.

63 Ages, "Antisemitism: The Uneasy Calm," in Weinfeld, Shaffir, and Cotler,
    eds., *The Canadian Jewish Mosaic*, 386–87.

64 Abella, *A Coat of Many Colours*, 191–92.

65 JTA, http://www.jta.org/1933/10/20/archive/toronto-deluged-with-friends
    -of-new-germany-anti-semitic-leaflets (accessed December 30, 2013).

66 Rosenberg, *Canada's Jews*, 302.

67 Menkis, "Antisemitism in the Evolving Nation," in Klein and Dimant, eds.,
    From Immigration to Integration, 48.

68 Genizi, *The Holocaust, Israel, and Canadian Protestant Churches*, 232.

69 Ibid., 219.

70 Davies and Nefsky, *How Silent Were the Churches?* 76–77.

71 "Anti-Semitism and Its Causes" *Canadian Jewish Chronicle* (hereafter
    CJC), October 12, 1934, 3.

72 Abella and Troper, "'The Line Must Be Drawn Somewhere,'" in Weinfeld,
    Shaffir, and Cotler, eds., *The Canadian Jewish Mosaic*, 51.

73 Cited in Geoffrey G. Field. "Anti-Semitism with the Boots Off," in *Hostages
    of Modernization: Studies on Modern Antisemitism, 1870–1933/9, Ger-
    many—Great Britain—France*, ed. Herbert A. Strauss (Berlin: de Gruyter,
    1993), 318.

74 Cyril H. Levitt and William Shaffir, *The Riot at Christie Pits* (Toronto:
    Lester and Orpen Dennys, 1987), 4, 227.

75 Menkis, "Antisemitism in the New Nation," in Klein and Dimant, eds.,
    From Immigration to Integration, 305.

76 Cited in Nadeau, *Adrien Arcand*, 99.

77 Anctil, *Le Devoir, les juifs, et l'immigration*, 113.

78 Byrnes, *Antisemitism in Modern France*, 270.

79 Nadeau, *Adrien Arcand*, 104.

80 Tulchinsky, *Canada's Jews*, 314–15; Axelrod, *Making a Middle Class*, 142.
81 André Laurendeau, *Witness for Quebec* (Toronto: Macmillan of Canada, 1973), 70.
82 Ibid., 70–72.
83 "Jean-Louis Roux, Actor and Co-founder of TNM, Dies at 90," *Montreal Gazette*, November 29, 1942. http://www.montrealgazette.com/enter tainment/Actor+Jean+Louis+Roux+founder+dies/9228245/story.html (accessed January 26, 2014).
84 Esther Delisle, *The Traitor and the Jew: Anti-Semitism and the Delirium of Extremist Right-wing Nationalism in French Canada from 1929–1939* (Toronto: Robert Davies, 1993), 33.
85 Laurendeau, *Witness for Quebec*, 278.
86 Cited in Stingel, *Social Discredit*, 27. Cf. Anctil, *Le rendez-vous manqué*, 221.
87 Abella, *A Coat of Many Colours*, 182.
88 Editors of Fortune, *Jews in America*, 9–10.
89 Cited in Cyril H. Levitt and William Shaffir, *The Riot at Christie Pits* (Toronto: Lester and Orpen Dennys, 1987), 9.
90 Elazar Barkan, *The Retreat of Scientific Racism: Changing Concepts of Race in Britain and the United States Between the World Wars* (Cambridge: Cambridge University Press, 1992), 9.
91 "Si les juifs n'exaggèrent pas ces chiffres à la façon orientale ou talmudique," in Pierre Anctil, ed., *À chacun ses juifs: 60 éditoriaux pour comprendre la position du Devoir à l'égard des juifs (1910–1947)* (Sillery: Septentrion, 2014), 237.
92 Cited in Pierre Anctil, *Jacob Isaac Segal 1896–1954: Un poète Yiddish de Montréal et son milieu* (Quebec: Presses de l'Université Laval, 2012), 262–63.
93 Davies and Nefsky, *How Silent Were the Churches?* 45.
94 Stingel, *Social Discredit*, 89.
95 Davies and Nefsky, *How Silent Were the Churches?* 86.
96 James Walker, "Claiming Equality for Canadian Jewry: The Struggle for Inclusion 1930–1945," in Klein, ed., *Nazi Germany, Canadian Responses*, 237.
97 Walker, *"Race," Rights and the Law in the Supreme Court of Canada*, 189.
98 Cited in Esther Delisle, *Myths, Memories and Lies: Quebec's Intelligentsia and the Fascist Temptation 1939-1960* (Westmount, QC: Robert Davies Multimedia, 1998), 198–99.
99 Robin, *Shades of Right*, 133–34.

100 Betcherman, *The Swastika and the Maple Leaf*, 13–19.
101 Kernaghan, "Freedom of Religion in the Province of Quebec," 101; Robin, *Shades of Right*, 136–37.
102 Vigod, *Quebec before Duplessis*, 160.
103 Speisman, "Antisemitism in Ontario," in Davies, ed., *Antisemitism in Canada*, 122–23.
104 Betcherman, *The Swastika and the Maple Leaf*, 50; Walker, *"Race," Rights and the Law in the Supreme Court of Canada*, 193.
105 Walker, *"Race," Rights and the Law in the Supreme Court of Canada*, 195.
106 Speisman, "Antisemitism in Ontario," in Davies, ed., *Antisemitism in Canada*, 128.
107 Robin, *Shades of Right*, 204.
108 Abraham J. Arnold, "The Mystique of Western Jewry" in Weinfeld, Shaffir, and Cotler, eds., *The Canadian Jewish Mosaic*, 70–71.
109 Walker, *"Race," Rights and the Law in the Supreme Court of Canada*, 195.
110 Bialystok, *Delayed Impact*, 21.
111 Abella and Troper, *None Is Too Many*.

NOTES TO CHAPTER SEVEN

1 Tulchinsky, *Joe Salsberg*, 128.
2 Abella and Troper, *None Is Too Many*.
3 Morton Weinfeld, "The Jews of Quebec: An Overview," in Robert J. Brym, William Shaffir, and Morton Weinfeld, eds., *The Jews in Canada* (Toronto: Oxford University Press, 1993), 186.
4 From 1951 to 1960, some 28,000 immigrated to Canada. Anctil, *Le rendez-vous manqué*, 314.
5 Abella, *A Coat of Many Colours*, 210.
6 Troper, "New Horizons in a New Land" in Klein and Dimant, eds., *From Immigration to Integration*, 14.
7 Stember, *Jews in the Mind of America*, 127.
8 Frankel, "One Crisis Behind?" 256.
9 Dinnerstein, *Uneasy at Home*, 179.
10 Cited in Engel, "Away from a Definition of Antisemitism," in Cohen and Rosman, eds., *Rethinking European Jewish History*, 51.
11 Weinfeld, *Like Everyone Else*, 319; Troper, *The Defining Decade*, 32.
12 Michael Keefer, *Antisemitism, Real and Imagined: Responses to the Canadian Parliamentary Coalition to Combat Antisemitism* (Waterloo, ON: Canadian Charger, 2010), 33.

13 Bernie Farber, "Christmas by Any Other Name," http://www.huffingtonpost
    .ca/bernie-farber/christmas-by-any-other-name_b_4508174.html (accessed
    January 1, 2014)
14 Abella and Troper, *None Is Too Many*.
15 Peter Herrndorf, "Ellen Ripstein," *Globe and Mail*, September 12, 2013,
    S8.
16 Bernie M. Farber, "Who Is Ladislaus Csizsik-Csatary?" *National Post*,
    July 19, 2012, A10. For parallel developments in the United States immi-
    gration situation, see Dinnerstein, *Uneasy at Home*, 186–87.
17 Tulchinsky, *Canada's Jews*, 411; Troper and Weinfeld, *Old Wounds*, 304–5.
18 Harold M. Waller, "Canada," *AJYB* 96 (1996): 199, http://www.ajcarchives
    .org/AJC_DATA/Files/1996_7_Canada.pdf (accessed January 2, 2014).
19 Walker, *"Race," Rights and the Law in the Supreme Court of Canada*, 315.
20 Dinnerstein, *Uneasy at Home*, 188.
21 Pierre Berton, "No Jews Need Apply," *Macleans*, November 1, 1948, 7.
22 Stember, *Jews in the Mind of America*, 331.
23 Cited in Martin Sable, "George Drew and the Rabbis: Religious Education
    in Ontario's Public Schools," *Canadian Jewish Studies* 6 (1998): 32.
24 Walker, *"Race," Rights and the Law in the Supreme Court of Canada*, 199.
25 "The State of Antisemitism in French Canada," *Congress Bulletin*, May 30,
    1947, 24–25.
26 Hayes, "Report on Anti-Semitism in Canada," 4.
27 Weisbord, *The Strangest Dream*, 217.
28 Barrett, *Is God a Racist?* 42, 64.
29 David Rome, "Canada," *AJYB* (1947–48): 293. http://www.ajcarchives
    .org/AJC_DATA/Files/1947_1948_8_BritCommonwealth.pdf (accessed
    January 1, 2014).
30 Nigro and Mauro, "The Jewish Immigrant Experience and the Practice of
    Law," 1015–16.
31 Saul Hayes, "Report on Anti-Semitism in Canada," Cited in Bialystok,
    Delayed Impact, 70.
32 Baltzell, *The Protestant Establishment*, 369–70.
33 Cited in King, *From the Ghetto to the Main*, 192.
34 Kenneth McRoberts, *Quebec: Social Change and Political Crisis*, 3rd ed.
    (Oxford: Oxford University Press, 1993), 84.
35 Troper, *The Defining Decade*, 7.
36 JTA, http://www.jta.org/1949/08/07/archive/anti-semitism-is-declining-in
    -canada-survey-shows-no-longer-a-cause-for-concern (accessed Decem-
    ber 30, 2013). Cf. Walker, *"Race," Rights and the Law in the Supreme Court
    of Canada*, 190.

37 Louis Rosenberg, "Canada," *AJYB* (1953): 224–25, http://www.ajcarchives .org/AJC_DATA/Files/1953_8_Canada.pdf (accessed January 1, 2014).

38 Troper, *The Defining Decade*, 62–66.

39 John R. Seeley, R. Alexander Sim, and Elizabeth W. Loosley, *Crestwood Heights* (Toronto: University of Toronto Press, 1956), 307.

40 Ibid., 328.

41 Rachel Gordan, "The Precursor to 'Gentleman's Agreement'" *Moment*, http://www.momentmag.com/precursor-gentlemans-agreement/ (accessed December 29, 2014); Anctil, *Le rendez-vous manqué*, 90ff.

42 David Rome, "Canada," *AJYB* (1945–46): 278, http://www.ajcarchives.org/ AJC_DATA/Files/1946_1947_7_BritCommonwealth.pdf (accessed January 1, 2014). Cf. *AJYB* 51 (1950): 235, http://www.ajcarchives.org/AJC _DATA/Files/1951_9_BritishCommon.pdf (accessed January 1, 2014).

43 Lipinsky, *Imposing Their Will*, 273–74; Walker, *"Race," Rights and the Law in the Supreme Court of Canada*, 190ff.

44 *AJYB* (1951): 236, http://www.ajcarchives.org/AJC_DATA/Files/1951_9 _BritishCommon.pdf (accessed January 1, 2014).

45 Troper, *The Defining Decade*, 90.

46 Newman, *Izzy*, 243–44.

47 Abella, *A Coat of Many Colours*, 216–17.

48 Anctil, *Le rendez-vous manqué*, 101.

49 Tulchinsky, *Canada's Jews*, 415; Avi Weinryb, "The University of Toronto— The Institution Where Israel Apartheid Week Was Born," n. 36, http:// jcpa.org/article/the-university-of-toronto-the-institution-where-israel -apartheid-week-was-born/ (accessed July 31, 2014).

50 David Rome, "Canada," *AJYB* (1947–48): 291. http://www.ajcarchives.org/ AJC_DATA/Files/1947_1948_8_BritCommonwealth.pdf (accessed January 1, 2014).

51 David Rome, "Canada," *AJYB* (1948–49): 294. http://www.ajcarchives .org/AJC_DATA/Files/1948_1949_8_BritCommonwealth.pdf (accessed January 1, 2014).

52 Janice Arnold, "Politicians Denounce 'Hateful' Val Morin Vandalism," *Canadian Jewish News* (hereafter *CJN*), April 26, 2012, 3, 20, http://www .cija.ca/antisemitism/minister-kenney-issues-statement-condemning -anti-semitic-vandalism-in-val-morin-quebec/?utm_source=rss&utm _medium=rss&utm_campaign=minister-kenney-issues-statement -condemning-anti-semitic-vandalism-in-val-morin-quebec&utm_sou rce=The+Centre+for+Israel+and+Jewish+Affairs+Mailing+List&utm _campaign=785746dd1d-RSS_EMAIL_CAMPAIGN&utm _medium=email (accessed December 30, 2013).

53 JTA, http://www.jta.org/1949/02/27/archive/two-u-s-jews-bring-suit-for
-expulsion-from-montreal-hotel-allegedly-on-racial-grounds (accessed
December 30, 2013).
54 JTA, http://www.jta.org/1960/08/31/archive/thirty-summer-resorts-in
-canada-indicate-anti-jewish-discrimination (accessed December 30, 2013).
55 David Rome, "Canada," *AJYB* (1946–47): 279, http://www.ajcarchives
.org/AJC_DATA/Files/1946_1947_7_BritCommonwealth.pdf (accessed
January 1, 2014). Cf. http://www.jta.org/1946/05/23/archive/canadian
-government-is-asked-by-jewish-deputy-to-curb-increasing-anti
-semitism (accessed December 30, 2013).
56 CJCCCNA ZA 1945 15/237.
57 Hayes, "Report on Anti-Semitism in Canada," 16, 19.
58 Linteau et al., *Quebec since 1930*, 211. For parallel developments in the
United States, see Stember, *Jews in the Mind of America*, 93.
59 JTA, http://www.jta.org/1961/01/10/archive/canadian-banks-charged-with
-bias-against-jews-in-employment (accessed December 30, 2013).
60 Troper, *The Defining Decade*, 92.
61 *AJYB* 72 (1971): 279, http://www.ajcarchives.org/AJC_DATA/Files/1971_6
_Canada.pdf (accessed January 2, 2014). Cf. Baltzell, *The Protestant Estab-
lishment*, 321.
62 Baltzell, *The Protestant Establishment*, 36.
63 Yaacov Glickman, "Anti-Semitism and Jewish Social Cohesion in Canada"
in Bienvenue and Goldstein, eds., *Ethnicity and Ethnic Relations in Canada*, 271–72.
64 *AJYB* (1953): 223, http://www.ajcarchives.org/AJC_DATA/Files/1953_8_
Canada.pdf (accessed January 1, 2014).
65 Troper, *The Defining Decade*, 251–52.
66 Ibid., 253–63.
67 Ibid., 262.
68 Newman, *Izzy*, 244ff.
69 Barrett, *Is God a Racist?* 306.
70 Weinfeld, *Like Everyone Else*, 107.
71 Newman, *Izzy*, 144.
72 Troper, *The Defining Decade*, 4.
73 Laurendeau, *Witness for Quebec*, 276.
74 http://www.cbc.ca/archives/categories/politics/prime-ministers/john
-diefenbaker-dief-the-chief/the-canadian-bill-of-rights.html (accessed
July 6, 2014).
75 Allan Levine, "The Defining Canadian Political Blockbuster, 50 Years
Later," *National Post*, October 2, 2013, A12.

76 Eugene Korn, "Rethinking Christianity: Rabbinic Positions and Possibilities" in *Jewish Theology and World Religions*, ed. Alon Goshen-Gottstein and Eugene Korn (Oxford: Littman Library of Jewish Civilization, 2012), 205.

77 Ibid., 205.

78 Claude Ryan, "A French Canadian Looks at the Jews" *Viewpoints* 4 (1969): 7.

79 Ibid. Cf. Brown, *Jew or Juif?* 261–62; Tulchinsky, *Canada's Jews*, 413. On the sociological reality behind Ryan's remarks, see Weinfeld, *Like Everyone Else*, 319; Troper, *The Defining Decade*, 32.

80 *AJYB* 73 (1972): 414, http://www.ajcarchives.org/AJC_DATA/Files/1972_7 _Canada.pdf (accessed January 2, 2014).

81 Bouchard, *La nation québécoise au futur et au passé*, 57–58.

82 Menkis, "Historiography, Myth and Group Relations," n. 78.

83 Stember, *Jews in the Mind of America*, 4.

84 Evelyn Kallen, *Spanning the Generations: A Study in Jewish Identity* (Don Mills, ON: Longman Canada, 1977), 139.

85 Slonim, *Family Quarrel*, 87.

86 Ibid., 87.

87 JTA, http://www.jta.org/1995/03/07/archive/focus-on-issues-abortion -flap-erupts-in-canada-with-jewish-group-a-key-player (accessed April 3, 2014).

88 *AJYB* 96 (1996): 198, http://www.ajcarchives.org/AJC_DATA/Files/1996 _7_Canada.pdf (accessed January 2, 2014).

89 League for Human Rights of B'nai Brith Canada, *Review of Anti-Semitism in Canada 1985* (Downsview, ON, 1986), 10.

90 League for Human Rights of B'nai Brith Canada, *Review of Anti-Semitism in Canada 1982* (Downsview, ON, 1983), 3.

91 JTA (November 4, 1986), http://www.jta.org/1986/11/04/archive/anti-semitic -sentiments-are-rife-in-the-province-of-quebec (accessed July 7, 2014).

92 Irving Abella, "Antisemitism in Canada: New Approaches on an Old Problem" in *Approaches to Antisemitism: Context and Curriculum*, ed. Michael Brown (New York: American Jewish Committee, 1994), 52.

93 Robert J. Brym and Rhonda L. Lenton, "The Distribution of Anti-Semitism in Canada in 1984," in Brym et al., eds., *The Jews in Canada*, 115.

94 Weinfeld, *Like Everyone Else*, 342.

95 Paul M. Sniderman, David A. Northrup, Joseph F. Fletcher, Peter H. Russel, and Philip E. Tetlock, *Working Paper on Antisemitism in Quebec* (Institute for Social Research, York University, 1992), 1, 13, 24–25.

96 David Wimhurst, "Anti-Semitism Still Strongest in Quebec, Study Finds" *Montreal Gazette*, October 28, 1986, http://news.google.com/newspapers?nid =1946&dat=19861028&id=m1kiAAAAIBAJ&sjid=S6gFAAAAIBAJ &pg=881,4750277 (accessed July 7, 2014).

97 Sniderman et al., *Working Paper on Antisemitism in Quebec*, 2.

98 *AJYB* 88 (1988), 248, http://www.ajcarchives.org/AJC_DATA/Files/1988 _7_Canada.pdf (accessed January 2, 2014).

99 Charles Liebman and Stephen Cohen, *Two Worlds of Judaism: The Israeli and American Experience* (New Haven, CT: Yale University Press, 1990), 42.

100 Tulchinsky, *Canada's Jews*, 471.

101 *AJYB* 90 (1990), 313–14, http://www.ajcarchives.org/AJC_DATA/Files/1990 _7_Canada.pdf (accessed January 2, 2014). On this controversy, see Dana Herman, "'An Affair to Remember': The Outremont Dispute of 1988" *Canadian Jewish Studies* 16–17 (2008–9): 139–66.

102 *AJYB* 92 (1992), 290, http://www.ajcarchives.org/AJC_DATA/Files/1992 _7_Canada.pdf (accessed January 2, 2014).

103 Valerie Stoker, "Drawing the Line: Hasidic Jews, Eruvim, and the Public Space of Outremont, Quebec," *History of Religions* 43 (2003): 23–24. Cf. Sol Littman, *Quebec's Jews: Vital Citizens or Eternal Strangers: Analysis of Key Newspaper Coverage of Three Pertinent Incidents* (Simon Wiesenthal Center, 1991), 20.

104 http://www.jta.org/2013/01/17/news-opinion/world/montreal-chasidic -leaders-take-blogger-to-court-alleging-libelous-anti-semitism (accessed December 30, 2013).

105 Janice Arnold, "Holiday noise ban legal: Hampstead Mayor," *CJN*, Octo-ber 12, 2011, 19.

106 *CJN*, 3 December 1971, cited in Pierre Anctil, *Trajectoires Juives au Québec* (Quebec: Presses de l'Université Laval, 2010), 191.

107 *AJYB* 73 (1972): 409, http://www.ajcarchives.org/AJC_DATA/Files/1972 _7_Canada.pdf (accessed January 2, 2014).

108 Brym and Lenton, "The Distribution of Anti-Semitism in Canada in 1984," in Brym et al., eds., *The Jews in Canada*, 114–15.

109 Gilles Cournoyer, letter to the editor of *Le Devoir*, October 1, 1969, cited in *AJYB* 71 (1970): 356, http://www.ajcarchives.org/AJC_DATA/Files/1970 _7_Canada.pdf (accessed January 2, 2014).

110 *AJYB* 72 (1971): 275, http://www.ajcarchives.org/AJC_DATA/Files/1971 _6_Canada.pdf (accessed January 2, 2014).

111 *AJYB* 98 (1998): 196, http://www.ajcarchives.org/AJC_DATA/Files/1998 _7_Canada.pdf (accessed January 2, 2014).

112 Littman, *Quebec's Jews*, 20. Cf. Tulchinsky, *Canada's Jews*, 469.

113 Littman, *Quebec's Jews*, 4; Nadeau, *Adrien Arcand*, 317.

114 Tulchinsky, *Canada's Jews*, 470.

115 Weinfeld, "The Jews of Quebec: An Overview," in Brym et al., eds., *The Jews in Canada*, 187.

116 *AJYB* 97 (1997): 241–42, http://www.ajcarchives.org/AJC_DATA/Files/1997 _7_Canada.pdf (accessed January 2, 2014).

117 http://www.jta.org/2013/10/08/news-opinion/world/rising-nationalism -bleeds-montreals-jewish-community?utm_source=Newsletter+subscrib ers&utm_campaign=9717900c2b-JTA_Daily_Briefing_6_18_2013&utm _medium=email&utm_term=0_2dce5bc6f8-9717900c2b-25348069. Cf. Morton Weinfeld, "La question juive au Québec," *Midstream* 23 (1977): 20–29.

118 Delisle, *The Traitor and the Jew*.

119 Mordecai Richler, *Oh Canada! Oh Québec! Requiem for a Divided Country* (New York: Knopf, 1992).

120 Mathieu Pontbriand, "L'affaire Delisle: Champ universitaire et scoop médiatique," in Amélie Bolduc and Martin Paquet, *Faute et réparation au Canada et au Québec contemporains* (Quebec: Éditions Nota Bene, 2006).

121 Tulchinsky, *Canada's Jews*, 470.

122 *CJN*, October 10, 1991, cited in *AJYB* 93 (1993), 226–27, http://www .ajcarchives.org/AJC_DATA/Files/1993_7_Canada.pdf (accessed January 2, 2014).

123 Cited in Ira Robinson, "Vers des échanges plus fructueux dans le domaine des sciences humaines," in Pierre Anctil, Ira Robinson, and Gérard Bouchard, *Juifs et canadiens français dans la société Québécois* (Sillery: Septentrion, 2000), 178.

124 Tulchinsky, *Canada's Jews*, 472.

125 *AJYB* 91 (1991), 232, http://www.ajcarchives.org/AJC_DATA/Files/1991 _7_Canada.pdf (accessed January 2, 2014).

126 John Marttila, *Highlights from an Anti-Defamation League Survey on Anti-Semitism and Prejudice in America* (New York: Anti-Defamation League, 1992), 2, 14.

127 League for Human Rights of Bnai Brith Canada, *1998 Audit of Anti-Semitic Incidents* (Downsview, ON, 1999), 39–44. It is to be noted in this connection that in the United States, at least through the 1960s, Christian missionary work among Jews was not officially classified as antisemitism by the Anti-Defamation League. See Zev Eleff, "The Baptism of Four Little Roxbury Girls: Jewish Angst in America's Religious Marketplace

during the Interwar Period," *American Jewish Archives Journal* 65, nos. 1–2 (2013), 87–88.

128 League for Human Rights of B'nai Brith Canada, *The Heritage Front Report: 1994* (Toronto: 1994), 20–21.

129 Howard Adelman, "Blacks and Jews: Racism, Anti-Semitism, and *Showboat*," in Richard Menkis and Norman Ravvin, eds., *Canadian Jewish Studies Reader* (Calgary: Red Deer Press, 2004), 443.

130 *AJYB* 102 (2002): 285, http://www.ajcarchives.org/AJC_DATA/Files/2002 _7_Canada.pdf (accessed January 2, 2014).

131 League for Human Rights of Bnai Brith Canada, *2004 Audit of Anti-Semitic Incidents* (Downsview, ON, 2005), 77n12.

132 *AJYB* 105 (2005): 301, http://www.ajcarchives.org/AJC_DATA/Files/2005 _8_Canada.pdf (accessed January 3, 2014).

133 *AJYB* 103 (2003): 313, http://www.ajcarchives.org/AJC_DATA/Files/2003 _8_Canada.pdf (accessed January 2, 2104]; Timothy Appleby, "Slaying Not Hate Crime, Judge Says," *Globe and Mail*, February 17, 2005, http:// www.theglobeandmail.com/news/national/slaying-not-hate-crime -judge-says/article975708/ (accessed August 4, 2014)

134 League for Human Rights of Bnai Brith Canada, *2003 Audit of Anti-Semitic Incidents* (Downsview, ON, 2004), 4.

135 *AJYB* 105 (2005): 305, http://www.ajcarchives.org/AJC_DATA/Files/2005 _8_Canada.pdf (accessed January 3, 2014).

136 *AJYB* 106 (2006): 293, http://www.ajcarchives.org/AJC_DATA/Files/ AJYB607.CV.pdf (accessed January 3, 2014).

137 *AJYB* 106 (2006): 306–7, http://www.ajcarchives.org/AJC_DATA/Files/ AJYB607.CV.pdf (accessed January 3, 2014).

138 Gil Troy, "Innuendo and Invective Demonized Montreal's Jewish Community," https://groups.yahoo.com/neo/groups/MediainMontreal/conversations/ topics/10278 (accessed August 4, 2014).

139 League for Human Rights of Bnai Brith Canada, *2005 Audit of Anti-Semitic Incidents* (Downsview, ON, 2006), 17–18.

140 Jim Coggins, canadianchristianity.com (accessed 18 March 2008).

141 Bill Curry, "Forum Dredges Up Quebeckers' Ire toward Minorities," *Globe and Mail*, September 11, 2007, A4.

142 David Lazarus, "Fear of Islam Fuels Accommodation Debate, Trudeau Says," *Canadian Jewish News*, December 20, 2007, 6.

143 Morton Weinfeld, "Quebec Anti-Semitism and Anti-Semitism in Quebec" (2008), 2, 5, http://jcpa.org/article/quebec-anti-semitism-and-anti -semitism-in-quebec/ (accessed October 31, 2103).

144 David Lazarus, "Quebecers' View of Jews Sets Them Apart, Poll Finds," *Canadian Jewish News* February 28, 2008, 3.

145 Elias Levy, "Un débat sur l'avenir de la société québécoise," *Canadian Jewish News*, 20 December 2007. The disquiet felt in English Canada is expressed in the title of an article appearing in *Maclean's* magazine of October 22, 2007, written by Martin Patriquin, "Canada: A Nation of Bigots?" http://www.macleans.ca/canada/features/article.jsp?content=20071022 _110249_110249&page=2 (accessed 14 May 2008).

146 *National Post*, October 9, 2007, A1, 9.

147 "Kosher Tax," http://en.wikipedia.org/wiki/Kosher_tax (accessed 18 May 2008).

148 These accusations were ultimately denounced by Gérard Bouchard as antisemitic. Caroline Touzin and Laura-Julie Perreault, "Bouchard-Taylor: Mythes et réalités," *La Presse*, November 26, 2007, www.cyberpresse .ca/apps/pbcs.dll/article?AID/20071126/ (accessed 19 March 2007); Janice Arnold, "Chassidim Dismiss Complaints against Them at Hearings," *CJN*, December 6, 2007, 3; December 20, 2007, 3.

149 Janice Arnold, "Police Investigate Anti-kashrut Campaign," *CJN*, August 14, 2014, 20.

150 Janice Arnold, *CJN*, December 6, 2007, 3; Jeff Heinrich, "Hasidim Anger Residents," *Montreal Gazette*, September 26, 2007.

151 Janice Arnold, "Accommodation Hearings Raising Concerns," *CJN*, October 18, 2007, 3, 24.

152 Janice Arnold, "Chassidim Dismiss Complaints against Them at Hearings," *CJN*, December 6, 2007, 3, 30.

153 One presenter in St. Jerome stated that "Les juifs sont le tremplin de l'argent national." Stephane Baillargeon, "La commission Bouchard Taylor s'arrêt à St. Jérôme—Les plus vieux se défoulent," *Le Devoir*, September 25, 2007, http://www.ledevoir.com/2007/09/25/158183.html (accessed 16 May 2008). This was slightly mistranslated in the anglophone press as "Jews are ... the most powerful ... the trampoline of money in the world." Jeff Heinrich, "Accommodation Panel Fully Operational," *Montreal Gazette*, September 24, 2007, A8.

154 "The Future of Reasonable Accommodation," *Montreal Gazette*, December 15, 2007, www.cjc.ca/template.php?action=oped&Rec=217.

155 Jewish General Hospital of Montreal, *Care for All: A Brief to the Consultation Commission on Accommodation Practices Related to Cultural Differences*, October 2007, 1.

156 Leaked copies were circulated shortly before the release date of May 23, 2006, and generated press coverage. Jeff Heinrich, "Findings Hailed as Road Map for Integration," *Montreal Gazette*, May 17, 2008, http://www .canada.com:80/montrealgazette/news/story.html?id=e4bdfdff-bfe5 -4356-a408-16edf6e9f652 (accessed 19 May 2008).

157 Margaret Wente, "Ms. Marois Lays an Egg," *Globe and Mail*, September 17, 2013, http://www.theglobeandmail.com/globe-debate/ms-marois-lays -an-egg/article14349530/ (accessed August 21, 2014); "Quebec's Proposed Charter of Values Fails the Decency Test," *Toronto Star*, September 12, 2013, http://www.thestar.com/opinion/editorials/2013/09/12/quebecs _proposed_charter_of_values_fails_the_decency_test_editorial.html (accessed August 21, 2014).

158 Rebeca Kuropatwa, *Jewish Tribune* (hereafter *JT*), September 27, 2012, 7; idem., "Disturbing Antisemitic Posters Surface Again," *JT*, October 25, 2012, 3.

159 Rhonda Spivak, "Question for Bartley Kives, re Antisemitic Posters: How Many Antisemitic Emails Did You Get?" *Winnipeg Jewish Review*, September 16, 2012, http://www.winnipegjewishreview.com/article _detail.cfm?id=2877&sec=1&title=Question_for_Bartley_Kives,_re _Antisemitic_Posters_:_How_many_antisemitic_emails_did_you_get (accessed December 29, 2013).

160 Rhonda J. Prepes, "Shindlemans File Defamation Law Suit," *JT*, March 14, 2013, 2.

NOTES TO CHAPTER EIGHT

1 Steve Mertl and John Ward, *Keegstra: The Trial, the Issues, the Conse-quences* (Saskatoon: Western Producer Prairie Books, 1985), 100.

2 Weinfeld, "The Jews of Quebec: An Overview," in Brym et al., eds., *The Jews in Canada*, 186.

3 Kallen, *Spanning the Generations*, 2.

4 JTA, http://www.jta.org/1953/08/19/archive/vandals-desecrate-winnipeg -synagogue-destroy-ancient-scrolls (accessed December 30, 2013).

5 Simon Epstein, "Cyclical Patterns in Antisemitism: The Dynamics of Anti-Jewish Violence in Western Countries since the 1950s," *Acta No. 2*, Jerusalem: Sicsa, Vidal Sassoon International Center for the Study of Antisemitism—Hebrew University of Jerusalem, 1993, http://sicsa.huji .ac.il/2cycles.htm (accessed July 30, 2014).

6 Barrett, *Is God a Racist?* 306.

7 Joe O'Connor, "The Typewriter in the Kitchen," *National Post*, April 24, 2013, A3.

8 Louis Rosenberg, "Canada," *AJYB* 65 (1964): 170, http://www.ajcarchives .org/AJC_DATA/Files/1964_6_Canada.pdf (accessed January 2, 2014).

9 JTA, http://www.jta.org/1963/07/22/archive/anti-jewish-incidents-in-winnipeg -cause-concern-jews-seek-protection (accessed December 30, 2013).

10 Arnold, "The Mystique of Western Jewry" in Weinfeld, Shaffir, and Cotler, eds., *Canadian Jewish Mosaic*, 268–69.

11 Cited in Bialystok, *Delayed Impact*, 133.

12 Ibid., 97, 110, 120.

13 Ibid., 124–25.

14 Ages, "Antisemitism: The Uneasy Calm," in Weinfeld et al., eds., *The Canadian Jewish Mosaic*, 390.

15 Bialystok, *Delayed Impact*, 148. Cf. Raphael Cohen-Almagor, *The Scope of Tolerance: Studies on the Costs of Free Expression and Freedom of the Press* (London: Routledge, 2006), 157; Brian Platt, "Former Canadian Nazi Runs for Office in Ontario's Cottage Country," *Toronto Star*, September 1, 2014, http://www.thestar.com/news/gta/2014/09/01/former_canadian_nazi _runs_for_office_in_ontarios_cottage_country.html?app=noRedirect (accessed December 29, 2014).

16 Troper, *The Defining Decade*, 107.

17 Philip Rosen, "Hate Propaganda," Library of Parliament 85-6E, http:// www.parl.gc.ca/Content/LOP/researchpublications/856-e.htm (accessed July 9, 2014). Cf. Mertl and Ward, *Keegstra*, 35.

18 Troper, *The Defining Decade*, 289.

19 Sol Littman, *Holocaust Denial: Bigotry in the Guise of Scholarship* (Toronto: Simon Wiesenthal Center, 1994).

20 Barrett, *Is God a Racist?* 94, 99.

21 Mertl and Ward, *Keegstra*, 48.

22 Elliott, "Anti-Semitism and the Social Credit Movement," 81; Stingel, *Social Discredit*, 21.

23 Stingel, *Social Discredit*, 4.

24 Bercuson and Wertheimer, *A Trust Betrayed*, 138–43.

25 Théorêt, *Les chemises bleues*, 325.

26 Ibid., 330.

27 Louis Rosenberg, "Canada," *AJYB* 67 (1966): 279, http://www.ajcarchives .org/AJC_DATA/Files/1966_7_Canada.pdf (accessed January 2, 2014).

28 Barrett, *Is God a Racist?* 14.

29 Ibid., 303.

30 Franklin Bialystok, "Were Things That Bad: The Holocaust Enters Community Memory," in Richard Menkis and Norman Ravvin, eds., *Canadian Jewish Studies Reader* (Calgary: Red Deer Press, 2004), 302.
31 http://www.friendsofsimonwiesenthalcenter.com/war_criminals.aspx (accessed July 13, 2014).
32 Tulchinsky, *Canada's Jews*, 465.
33 Troper and Weinfeld, *Old Wounds*, 115–16.
34 Sol Littman, *War Criminal on Trial: The Rauca Case* (Toronto: Lester and Orpen Dennys, 1983).
35 Troper and Weinfeld, *Old Wounds*, 129.
36 Ibid., 130.
37 Ibid., 255.
38 http://www.parl.gc.ca/Content/LOP/researchpublications/873-e.htm (accessed July 13, 2014).
39 David Matas, with Susan Charendoff, *Justice Delayed: Nazi War Criminals in Canada* (Toronto: Summerhill Press, 1987); David Matas, *Nazi War Criminals in Canada: Five Years After* (Toronto: Institute for International Affairs of B'nai Brith Canada, 1992).
40 Matas, *Nazi War Criminals in Canada*, 3, 6–8.
41 Mertl and Ward, *Keegstra*, 4.
42 Palmer, "Politics, Religion, and Antisemitism in Alberta," in Davies, ed., *Antisemitism in Canada*, 242; Waldron, *The Harm in Hate Speech*, 57.
43 Palmer, "Politics, Religion, and Antisemitism in Alberta," in Davies, ed., *Antisemitism in Canada*, 243.
44 Mertl and Ward, *Keegstra*, 12.
45 http://www.cbc.ca/news/canada/when-is-it-hate-speech-7-significant-canadian-cases-1.1036731.
46 Gabriel Weiman and Conrad Winn, *Hate on Trial: The Zundel Affair, the Media, and Public Opinion in Canada* (Oakville, ON: Mosaic Press, 1986), 13.
47 Bialystok, *Delayed Impact*, 231.
48 Barrett, *Is God a Racist?* 159.
49 Ibid., 159–60.
50 Manuel Prutschi, "The Zundel Affair," in Davies, ed., *Antisemitism in Canada*, 267.
51 Weiman and Winn, *Hate on Trial*, 17.
52 Mertl and Ward, *Keegstra*, 34; Tulchinsky, *Canada's Jews*, 468.
53 Cited in Prutschi, "The Zundel Affair," in Davies, *ed.*, *Antisemitism in Canada*, 259.
54 Barrett, *Is God a Racist?* 161.

55 Weiman and Winn, *Hate on Trial*, 17–18.

56 http://scc-csc.lexum.com/scc-csc/scc-csc/en/item/904/index.do (accessed August 21, 2014).

57 Tylor Orton, "B.C. Blogger Charged with Hate Crime for Promoting Hatred against Jews," *Toronto Sun*, November 6, 2012, http://www.torontosun.com/2012/11/06/bc-blogger-charged-with-hate-crime-for-promoting-hatred-against-jews (accessed August 1, 2014).

58 Atara Beck, "Anti-racism Activist Says You Have to 'Stand Up': Warman Wins Latest Rights Complaint," *JT*, October 23, 2008, 1, 6.

59 Paul Lungen, "CIJA to Consult Community on Hate Law Stand," *CJN*, December 1, 2011, 26.

60 http://www.cbc.ca/news/canada/when-is-it-hate-speech-7-significant-canadian-cases-1.1036731.

61 Weiman and Winn, *Hate on Trial*, 35–37.

62 Troper and Weinfeld, *Old Wounds*, 256.

63 League for Human Rights of B'nai Brith Canada, *Review of Anti-Semitism in Canada 1985* (Downsview, ON, 1986), 38, 42; Cohen-Almagor, *Scope of Tolerance*, 163.

64 Weinfeld, *Like Everyone Else*, 333. Cf. Weiman and Winn, *Hate on Trial*, 147.

65 Weiman and Winn, *Hate on Trial*, 39.

66 *AJYB* 87 (1987): 197, http://www.ajcarchives.org/AJC_DATA/Files/1987_6_Canada.pdf (accessed January 2, 2014).

67 League for Human Rights of Bnai Brith Canada, *Audit of Anti-Semitic Incidents 1990* (Downsview, ON, 1991), 4, 6, 14. Cf. also League for Human Rights of Bnai Brith Canada, *1995 Audit of Anti-Semitic Incidents* (Downsview, ON, 1996), 10.

68 League for Human Rights of Bnai Brith Canada, *Audit of Anti-Semitic Incidents 1988* (Downsview, ON, 1989), 6.

69 Sheva Medjuck and Morty M. Lazar, "Existence on the Fringe: The Jews in Atlantic Canada," in Weinfeld, Shaffir, and Cotler, eds., *Canadian Jewish Mosaic*, 247.

70 Warren Kinsella, *Web of Hate: Inside Canada's Far Right Network* (Toronto: HarperCollins, 1994), 313.

71 *AJYB* 96 (1996): 198, http://www.ajcarchives.org/AJC_DATA/Files/1996_7_Canada.pdf (accessed January 2, 2014).

72 *AJYB* 80 (1980): 177, http://www.ajcarchives.org/AJC_DATA/Files/1980_7_Canada.pdf (accessed January 2, 2014). Cf. Bernard Vigod, "When the System Fails: The Malcolm Ross Case in New Brunswick," in League for Human Rights of B'nai Brith Canada, *Review of Anti-Semitism in Canada 1987* (Downsview, ON, 1987), 28–34.

73 http://scc-csc.lexum.com/scc-csc/scc-csc/en/item/1367/index.do
    (accessed July 11, 2014).

74 *AJYB* 1998 (1998): 198, http://www.ajcarchives.org/AJC_DATA/Files/1998
    _7_Canada.pdf (accessed January 2, 2014).

75 League for Human Rights of Bnai Brith Canada, *1997 Audit of Anti-
    Semitic Incidents* (Downsview, ON, 1998), 20; Robert Fulford, *National
    Post*, November 3, 2001, http://www.robertfulford.com/DougCollins
    .html (accessed July 14, 2014).

76 Alex Roslin, "Speak No Evil," *This Magazine*, July-August, 2003, http://
    www.thismagazine.ca/issues/2003/07/speaknoevil.php (accessed Decem-
    ber 1, 2013).

77 "Once It's Gone, It's Gone," CBC News (January 14, 2008), http://www.cbc
    .ca/news2/canada/politicalbytes/2008/01/ (accessed December 1, 2013).

78 "Canada Native Leader Cleared in Second Hate Trial," Reuters Canada,
    February 23, 2009, http://ca.reuters.com/article/domesticNews/idCATRE
    51M5NZ20090223 (accessed December 1, 2013).

79 Myron Love, "Former Native Leader Seeks Iran's Support," *Canadian Jew-
    ish News*, October 22, 2012, http://www.cjnews.com/news/former-native
    -leader-seeks-iran%E2%80%99s-support (accessed December 1, 2013).

80 Handing Hatred a Microphone," *National Post*, July 5, 2012, A10.

81 Alain Goldschläger, "The Canadian Campus Scene," in *Academics against
    Israel and the Jews*, ed. Manfred Gerstenfeld (Jerusalem: Jerusalem Center
    for Public Affairs, 2007), 154, 159.

82 Deborah E. Lipstadt, "The Iranian President, the Canadian Professor, the
    Literary Journal, and the Holocaust Denial Conference That Never Was:
    The Strange Reality of Shiraz Dossa," in *Global Antisemitism: A Crisis Of
    Modernity*, vol. 5: *Reflections*, ed. Charles Asher Small (New York: Insti-
    tute for the Study of Global Antisemitism and Policy), 71–82, http://isgap
    .org/wp-content/uploads/2013/12/05_ISGAP_Vol.-V_120114_Web.pdf
    (accessed March 13, 2014).

83 Letter to the editor, *Prince Albert Daily Herald*, August 14, 2014, http://
    www.honestreporting.ca/hrc-letter-in-prince-albert-daily-herald-today
    -holocaust-was-no-allegation/14385 (accessed August 24, 2014).

NOTES TO CHAPTER NINE

1 Benjamin Weinthal, "'Zorba the Greek' Composer: I'm Anti-Semitic,"
   Jerusalem Post, February 15, 2011, http://www.jpost.com/JewishWorld/
   JewishNews/Article.aspx?id=208291 (accessed July 31, 2011).

2 Stember, *Jews in the Mind of America*, 4.

3 Michael Marrus, "Is There a New Antisemitism?" in *Antisemitism in the Contemporary World*, ed. Michael Curtis (Boulder, CO: Westview Press, 1986), 178; Cf. Michael Marrus, "Is Anti-Semitism Sweeping Canada?" *National Post*, January 2, 2002, http://www.jewishtoronto.com/page .aspx?id=37867 (accessed July 16, 2014).

4 Marrus, "Is Anti-Semitism Sweeping Canada?"

5 Gil Troy, "Another Take on Controversial Cartoon," *CJN*, February 6, 2014, 8.

6 Harrison, *The Resurgence of Anti-Semitism*, 3.

7 Ages, "Antisemitism: The Uneasy Calm," in Weinfeld, Shaffir, and Cotler, eds., *The Canadian Jewish Mosaic*, 391.

8 Keefer, *Antisemitism, Real and Imagined*, 7.

9 Jonathan Sas, "Breaking the Taboo against Criticizing the Jewish State," *National Post*, October 30, 2012, A13.

10 Nathalie Collard, "Peut-on critiquer Israël?" *La Presse*, February 2, 2014, http://plus.lapresse.ca/screens/45de-7d90-52ebd03d-af60-746aac1c606d%7c _0.html (accessed February 9, 2014).

11 Wistrich, *A Lethal Obsession*, 34.

12 Ibid., 38. Cf. Benjamin Ginsberg, who states that "anti-Zionism and antisemitism are not one and the same thing … is true in principle, but not often in practice." Cited in Eunice G. Pollack, ed., *Antisemitism on the Campus: Past and Present* (Boston: Academic Studies Press, 2011), viii.

13 Abella, "Antisemitism in Canada," in Brown, ed., *Approaches to Anti-semitism*, 53.

14 League for Human Rights of Bnai Brith Canada, *2001 Audit of Anti-Semitic Incidents* (Downsview, 2002), 61–62.

15 United With Israel, "'Through Fire and Water, Canada Will Stand with You': Canadian Prime Minister Stephen Harper," http://unitedwithisrael .org/through-fire-and-water-canada-will-stand-with-you-canadian -prime-minister-stephen-harper/?inf_contact_key=861d749ac4ffd5 7fdcba034de3e2ea50bcc7c07d0e271d990e3ebd6d6afa2b1f (accessed January 24, 2014).

16 Yehuda Bauer, "In Search of a Definition of Antisemitism," in *Approaches to Antisemitism: Context and Curriculum*, ed. Michael Brown (New York: American Jewish Committee, 1994), 20.

17 Janice Arnold, "Criticism of Israel Not Necessarily Antisemitic: Mul-roney," *CJN*, May 23, 2013, 3.

18 JTA, http://www.jta.org/2014/04/01/news-opinion/united-states/adl-audit -anti-semitic-incidents-down-in-u-s-assaults-up?utm_source=Newsletter

+subscribers&utm_campaign=2422f72b23-JTA_Daily_Briefing_4_2
_2014&utm_medium=email&utm_term=0_2dce5bc6f8-2422f72b23
-25348069 (accessed April 3, 2014).

19 Morton Weinfeld, "The Changing Dimensions of Contemporary Cana-
dian Antisemitism," in *Contemporary Antisemitism: Canada and the
World*, ed. Derek J. Penslar, Michael R. Marrus, and Janice Gross Stein
(Toronto: University of Toronto Press, 2005).

20 Tulchinsky, "Goldwin Smith: Victorian Antisemite," in Davies, ed.,
Antisemitism in Canada, 83.

21 JTA, http://www.jta.org/1930/11/18/archive/montreal-mayor-openly-anti
-semitic-at-discussion-of-jewish-school-question (accessed December 30,
2013).

22 Genizi, *The Holocaust, Israel, and Canadian Protestant Churches*, 3–4.

23 Korn, "Rethinking Christianity," 206.

24 Abella and Troper, *None Is Too Many*, 57-58.

25 Cited in David Bercuson, *Canada and the Birth of Israel: A Study in Canadian Foreign Policy* (Toronto: University of Toronto Press, 1985), 46.

26 Genizi, *The Holocaust, Israel, and Canadian Protestant Churches*, 52.

27 Ibid., 63.

28 Stingel, *Social Discredit*, 91.

29 Palmer, "Politics, Religion, and Antisemitism in Alberta," in Davies, ed.,
Antisemitism in Canada, 181.

30 Cited in Bialystok, *Delayed Impact*, 75–76.

31 Ages, "Antisemitism: The Uneasy Calm," in Weinfeld, Shaffir, and Cotler,
eds., *The Canadian Jewish Mosaic*, 386–89.

32 *AJYB* (1959): 131, http://www.ajcarchives.org/AJC_DATA/Files/1959_7
_Canada.pdf (accessed January 1, 2014).

33 Glickman, "Anti-Semitism and Jewish Social Cohesion in Canada," in
Bienvenue and Goldstein, eds., *Ethnicity and Ethnic Relations in Canada*,
277–78.

34 Tulchinsky, *Canada's Jews*, 435–37.

35 Slonim, *Family Quarrel*, 33–34.

36 Genizi, *The Holocaust, Israel, and Canadian Protestant Churches*, 110.

37 Slonim, *Family Quarrel*, 31.

38 Genizi, *The Holocaust, Israel, and Canadian Protestant Churches*, 120.

39 Ibid., 130.

40 Ibid., 126.

41 Ibid., 139.

42 Slonim, *Family Quarrel*, 52–53.

43 http://www.united-church.ca/beliefs/policies/2002/s715 (accessed August 8, 2014).

44 http://www.united-church.ca/getinvolved/unsettling-goods (accessed August 8, 2014); Ron Csillag, "United Church of Canada Approves Boycott of Settlement Goods," JTA, August 19, 2012, http://www.jta.org/2012/08/19/news-opinion/world/united-church-of-canada-approves-boycott-of-settlement-goods#ixzz3A689wqaP (accessed August 11, 2014).

45 Les Whittington, "Fury Grows over Anti-Semitism Charge," *Toronto Star*, December 19, 2009, http://www.thestar.com/news/canada/2009/12/19/fury_grows_over_antisemitism_charge.html (accessed August 8, 2014).

46 Wistrich, *A Lethal Obsession*, 272. Cf. Barrett, *Is God a Racist?* 349.

47 Teboul, *Mythes et images du Juif au Québec*, 212–23.

48 Pierre-André Taguieff, *La nouvelle judéophobie* (Paris: Mille et une nuits, 2002), 12–13, cited in Harrison, *The Resurgence of Anti-Semitism*, 23; Harold M. Waller and Morton Weinfeld, "The Jews of Quebec and 'Le Fait Français,'" in Weinfeld, Shaffir, and Cotler, eds., *The Canadian Jewish Mosaic*, 423.

49 Teboul, *Mythes et images du Juif au Québec*, 212–23.

50 René Lévesque, "Être ou ne pas être," *Dimanche-Matin*, 25 juin 1967, cited in Jean-François Beaudet, "René Lévesque et la communauté juive du Québec (1960–1976): La fragilité d'un dialogue" (MA thesis, Université du Québec à Montréal, 2014), 33–34.

51 *AJYB* 73 (1972): 418, http://www.ajcarchives.org/AJC_DATA/Files/1972_7_Canada.pdf (accessed January 2, 2104).

52 Beaudet, "René Lévesque et la communauté juive du Québec," 34–36.

53 On the 1975 United Nations vote, see Gil Troy, *Moynihan's Moment: America's Fight against Zionism as Racism* (Oxford: Oxford University Press, 2013).

54 Tulchinsky, *Canada's Jews*, 445.

55 *AJYB* 86 (1986): 239, http://www.ajcarchives.org/AJC_DATA/Files/1986_7_Canada.pdf (accessed January 2, 2014); http://www.jta.org/1983/06/03/archive/pro-israel-anti-israel-groups-greet-sharon-in-montreal (accessed July 31, 2014).

56 Waller and Weinfeld, "The Jews of Quebec and 'Le Fait Français,'" in Weinfeld, Shaffir, and Cotler, eds., *The Canadian Jewish Mosaic*, 423.

57 Ages, "Antisemitism: The Uneasy Calm," in Weinfeld, Shaffir, and Cotler, eds., *The Canadian Jewish Mosaic*, 393.

58 Weinfeld, "La question juive au Québec," 25.

59 Tulchinsky, *Canada's Jews*, 445.

60 *AJYB* 80 (1980): 177, http://www.ajcarchives.org/AJC_DATA/Files/1980 _7_Canada.pdf (accessed January 2, 2014]; http://www.jta.org/1979/02/06/ archive/quebec-press-council-condemns-magazine-for-anti-semitic -stance (accessed July 30, 2014).

61 Beaudet, "René Lévesque et la communauté juive du Québec," 87, 95.

62 Weinfeld, "La question juive au Québec," 28; Barrett, *Is God a Racist?* 307.

63 Lorraine E. Weinrib, "Ensuring Equality: The Role of the Community," in Klein and Dimant, eds., *From Immigration to Integration*, 90.

64 League for Human Rights of Bnai Brith Canada, *2000 Audit of Anti-Semitic Incidents* (Downsview, ON, 2001), 21.

65 Weinrib, "Ensuring Equality: The Role of the Community," in Klein and Dimant, eds., *From Immigration to Integration*, 90; http://faculty .marianopolis.edu/c.belanger/quebechistory/docs/michaud/20.htm (accessed October 22, 2013).

66 *AJYB* 103 (2003): 306, http://www.ajcarchives.org/AJC_DATA/Files/2003 _8_Canada.pdf (accessed January 2, 2014]; JTA, "News Brief," http:// www.jta.org/2003/02/13/archive/the-publisher-of-a-canadian-jewish -magazine-called (accessed August 1, 2014).

67 Phyllis Chesler, *The New Anti-Semitism: The Current Crisis and What We Must Do about It* (San Francisco: Jossey-Bass, 2003), 107.

68 League for Human Rights of B'nai Brith Canada, *Review of Anti-Semitism in Canada 1982* (Downsview, ON, 1983), 43. Michael Marrus was skeptical of this and other B'nai Brith claims regarding the strength of antisemitism in Canada. Marrus, "Is There a New Antisemitism?" in Curtis, ed., *Antisemitism in the Contemporary World*, 181n16.

69 Brym and Lenton, "The Distribution of Anti-Semitism in Canada in 1984," in Brym et al., eds., *The Jews in Canada*, 115.

70 *AJYB* 86 (1986): 239, http://www.ajcarchives.org/AJC_DATA/Files/1986 _7_Canada.pdf (accessed January 2, 2014); http://www.jta.org/1983/06/03/ archive/pro-israel-anti-israel-groups-greet-sharon-in-montreal (accessed July 31, 2014).

71 Harrison, *The Resurgence of Anti-Semitism*, 6–7.

72 Pierre-André Taguieff, cited in ibid., 23.

73 Cited in Adelman, "Blacks and Jews," in Menkis and Ravvin, eds., *Canadian Jewish Studies Reader*, 444.

74 Cited in Edward Alexander, "Blushing Professors: Jews Who Hate Israel," in Pollack, ed., *Antisemitism on the Campus*, 244. Cf. Bernard Harrison, "Anti-Zionism, Antisemitism, and the Rhetorical Manipulation of Reality," in Rosenfeld, ed., *Resurgent Antisemitism*, 38.

75 Jonathan Sacks, "Europe's New Anti-Semitism," *Huffington Post*, http://
   www.huffingtonpost.com/chief-rabbi-lord-sacks/europe-new-anti
   -semitism_b_1663157.html (accessed July 15, 2012).
76 Weinfeld, "The Changing Dimensions of Contemporary Canadian
   Antisemitism," in Penslar, Marrus, and Stein, eds., *Contemporary
   Antisemitism*, 42.
77 League for Human Rights of Bnai Brith Canada, *2003 Audit of Anti-
   Semitic Incidents* (Downsview, ON, 2004), 33–35.
78 Barrett, *Is God a Racist?* 209.
79 Centre for Israel and Jewish Affairs (CIJA), http://www.cija.ca/
   antisemitism/swastikas-at-rally-denounced/?utm_source=rss&utm
   _medium=rss&utm_campaign=swastikas-at-rally-denounced&utm_sou
   rce=The+Centre+for+Israel+and+Jewish+Affairs+Mailing+List&utm
   _campaign=e75fbd87a1-RSS_EMAIL_CAMPAIGN&utm
   _medium=email (accessed December 30, 2013).
80 League for Human Rights of Bnai Brith Canada, *2003 Audit of Anti-
   Semitic Incidents* (Downsview, ON, 2004), 24.
81 Emma Jo Aiken-Klar, "The Fear Factor: Assimilation, Antisemitism and
   the Relationship between Zionism and Jewish Diasporic Identity," *vis-à-
   vis: Explorations in Anthropology* 9, no. 1 (2009): 106–14.
82 Brent Sasley, "Who Calls the Shots? An Inquiry into the Effect of Jewish
   and Arab Lobbies on Canadian Middle East Policy," *Literary Review of
   Canada*, http://reviewcanada.ca/magazine/2011/05/who-calls-the-shots/
   (accessed July 30, 2014).
83 David H. Goldberg, "The Post-Statehood Relationship: A Growing
   Friendship," in Klein and Dimant, eds., *From Immigration to Integration*,
   144.
84 *AJYB* 90 (1990): 304, http://www.ajcarchives.org/AJC_DATA/Files/1990
   _7_Canada.pdf (accessed January 2, 2014); League for Human Rights of
   Bnai Brith Canada, *Audit of Anti-Semitic Incidents 1988*, 5. On the dual-
   loyalty accusation and its impact on Canadian Jews, see Morton Weinfeld,
   "If Canada and Israel Are at War, Who Gets My Support? Challenges of
   Competing Diaspora Loyalties: Marshall Sklare Award Lecture," *Contemporary Jewry* 34 (2014): 167–87.
85 Gregory Martire and Ruth Clark, *Anti-Semitism in the United States: A
   Study of Prejudice in the 1980s* (New York: Praeger, 1982), 86–87. This
   finding, however, has been subject to criticism. See Tom W. Smith, *Anti-
   Semitism in Contemporary America* (New York: American Jewish Committee, 1994), 9.

86 *AJYB* 81 (1981): 185, http://www.ajcarchives.org/AJC_DATA/Files/1981 _7_Canada.pdfhttp://www.ajcarchives.org/AJC_DATA/Files/1981_7 _Canada.pdf (accessed January 2, 2014).

87 Ages, "Antisemitism: The Uneasy Calm," in Weinfeld, Shaffir, and Cotler, eds., *The Canadian Jewish Mosaic*, 392.

88 Jonathan Chait, "Nixon Disallowed Jewish Advisors from Discussing Israel Policy," *New Republic*, December 10, 2010, http://www.newrepublic .com/blog/jonathan-chait/79829/nixon-disallowed-jewish-advisors -discussing-israel-policy (accessed August 8, 2014).

89 Weinfeld, "If Canada and Israel Are at War," 177–78.

90 *AJYB* 91 (1991): 232, http://www.ajcarchives.org/AJC_DATA/Files/1991 _7_Canada.pdf (accessed January 2, 2014).

91 Abella, "Antisemitism in Canada," in Brown, ed., *Approaches to Anti- semitism*, 54.

92 Harrison, "Anti-Zionism, Antisemitism, and the Rhetorical Manipulation of Reality," in Rosenfeld, ed., *Resurgent Antisemitism*, 68.

93 Paul Berman, *Terror and Liberalism* (New York: Norton, 2003), 135–36.

94 Patrick Healy, "Summers Hits 'Anti-Semitic' Actions," *Boston Globe*, Sep- tember 20, 2002, http://www.campus-watch.org/article/id/126 (accessed July 31, 2014).

95 http://sphr.concordia.ca/mlist/ (accessed August 8, 2014).

96 *AJYB* 102 (2002): 293, http://www.ajcarchives.org/AJC_DATA/Files/2002 _7_Canada.pdf (accessed January 2, 2014).

97 Concordia University Archives, D/Benjamin Netanyahu's Visit (Septem- ber 9, 2002).

98 *AJYB* 103 (2003): 310–11, http://www.ajcarchives.org/AJC_DATAFiles/ 2003_8_Canada.pdf (accessed January 2, 2014).

99 Corinne Berzon, "Anti-Israeli Activity at Concordia University, 2000– 2003," in Manfred Gerstenfeld, ed., *Academics against Israel and the Jews* (Jerusalem: Jerusalem Center for Public Affairs, 2007), 169–71.

100 Joanne Hill, "Campus Atmosphere Poisoned by Propaganda, Students Say," *JT*, March 14, 2013, 4, 13.

101 Avi Weinryb, "The University of Toronto—The Institution Where Israel Apartheid Week Was Born," http://jcpa.org/article/the-university -of-toronto-the-institution-where-israel-apartheid-week-was-born/ (accessed July 31, 2014).

102 Sheri Shefa, "More anti-Israel Campus Sentiment", *CJN*, December 6, 2007, 34; Ron Csillag, "Cops Quell Anti-Israel Attack at Toronto College," JTA, February 13, 2009, http://www.jta.org/2009/02/13/news-opinion/

world/cops-quell-anti-israel-attack-at-toronto-college (accessed August 8, 2014).

103 CIJA, http://www.cija.ca/campus/carleton-praised-for-tackling-jews-unease/ ?utm_source=rss&utm_medium=rss&utm_campaign=carleton-praised -for-tackling-jews-unease&utm_source=The+Centre+for+Israel+and+ Jewish+Affairs+Mailing+List&utm_campaign=e510aa6d82-RSS_EMAIL _CAMPAIGN&utm_medium=email (accessed December 30, 2013).

104 Jonathan Kay, "On Fake Anti-Semitism at York University and the Credulous Bubbie Net," *National Post*, September 14, 2011, http://fullcomment .nationalpost.com/2011/09/14/jonathan-kay-on-fake-anti-semitism -at-york-u-and-the-credulous-bubbie-net/ (accessed August 8, 2014). Michael Brown, who teaches Jewish Studies at York University, fully concurs. Michael Brown, "Steps Forward and Steps Backward: Toronto Jewry at the Beginning of the Second Decade of the Twenty-First Century," in Robinson, ed., *Canada's Jews*, 204–13.

105 Statistics Canada, "Immigration and Ethnocultural Diversity in Canada," http://www12.statcan.gc.ca/nhs-enm/2011/as-sa/99-010-x/99-010-x 2011001-eng.cfm (accessed July 31, 2014).

106 Derek J. Penslar, "Antisemitism and Anti-Zionism: A Historical Approach," in Penslar, Marrus, and Stein, eds., *Contemporary Antisemitism*, 88.

107 Wistrich, *A Lethal Obsession*, 225.

108 Ezra Levant, "A Muslim Leader Worth Ignoring," *National Post*, June 16, 2006, http://www.nationalpost.com/news/story.html?id=12573ab0-13ce -48c4-9e8e-5765b1a654d9 (accessed July 31, 2014).

109 Stewart Bell, "Arab Group Loses Funding Ruling" *National Post*, January 8, 2014, A4.

110 *AJYB* 105 (2005): 299, http://www.ajcarchives.org/AJC_DATA/Files/2005 _8_Canada.pdf (accessed January 2, 2014); "Man Admits to Firebombing Montreal Jewish School" December 16, 2004 http://www.cbc.ca/news/ canada/man-admits-to-firebombing-montreal-jewish-school-1.490700 (accessed August 1, 2014).

111 *AJYB* 107 (2007): 291, http://www.ajcarchives.org/AJC_DATA/Files/AJYB 711.CV.pdf (accessed January 3, 2014).

112 Paul Cherry, "Montreal Jewish School Firebomber Fit to Stand Trial," *Montreal Gazette*, January 3, 2013, http://www.montrealgazette.com/health/ Montreal+Jewish+school+firebomber+stand+trial/7470099/story.html (accessed August 4, 2014); *AJYB* 108 (2008): 317, http://www.ajcarchives .org/AJC_DATA/Files/*AJYB*808_Canada.pdf (accessed January 3, 2014).

113 *AJYB* 108 (2008): 317 http://www.ajcarchives.org/AJC_DATA/Files/ AJYB808_Canada.pdf (accessed January 3, 2014).

114 League for Human Rights of B'nai Brith Canada, *2012 Audit of Anti-Semitic Incidents* (Downsview, ON, 2013), 8.

115 *AJYB* 105 (2005): 300, http://www.ajcarchives.org/AJC_DATA/Files/2005 _8_Canada.pdf (accessed January 2, 2014).

116 Robert Matas, "Muslim Group Denounces Sheik at Centre of Hate-Crime Probe," *Globe and Mail*, July 21 2005, http://www.theglobeandmail .com/news/national/muslim-group-denounces-sheik-at-centre-of-hate -crime-probe/article1214763/ (accessed August 1, 2014).

117 *AJYB* 106 (2006): 297, http://www.ajcarchives.org/AJC_DATA/Files/ AJYB607.CV.pdf (accessed January 3, 2014).

118 "SUCCESS! Egyptian-Canadian Newspaper Removes Anti-Semitic Cartoons," *HonestReportingCanada*, May 6, 2014, http://www.honest reporting.ca/success-egyptian-canadian-newspaper-removes-anti -semitic-cartoons/13946 (accessed August 18, 2014).

119 "Toronto Arab Newspaper Meshwar Denies the Holocaust ... Again," *HonestReportingCanada*, May 6, 2014, http://www.honestreporting.ca/ toronto-arab-newspaper-meshwar-denies-the-holocaust-again/13935 (accessed August 18, 2014).

120 Joseph Brean, "Section 13's Legal Saga," *National Post*, February 3, 2014, A4.

121 Rob Ferguson and Tonda MacCharles, "Premier Defends Al Quds Rally at Queen's Park," *Toronto Star*, August 17, 2012, http://www.thestar.com/ news/canada/2012/08/17/premier_defends_al_quds_rally_at_queens _park.html (accessed August 8, 2014); Paul Lungem, "Police Investigat-ing Comments at Al-Quds Day Rally, *CJN*, August 7, 2013, http://www .cjnews.com/news/police-investigating-comments-al-quds-day-rally (accessed August 8, 2014).

122 "Call It What It Is: Vile Anti-Semitism in Toronto," http://www.friends ofsimonwiesenthalcenter.com/downloads/news_072914.pdf (accessed August 18, 2014).

123 Sheri Shefa, "Canadians Rally for Israel, Combat anti-Semitism," *CJN*, July 31, 2014, 8–9; David Busheikin, "Two Reasons for the Violence in Calgary," *CJN*, July 31, 2014, 11; "4 Charged after Violence at Anti-Israel Protest," *JT*, August 21, 2014, 5; "Four Anti-Israel Protesters Charged with Assault in Calgary," *CJN*, August 21, 2014, 32.

124 "CJA Building in Montreal Threatened by Protesters," *JT*, August 14, 2014, 2.

125 Deborah Lipstadt, "Why Jews Are Worried," *New York Times*, August 20, 2014, http://www.nytimes.com/2014/08/21/opinion/deborah-e-lipstadt-on-the -rising-anti-semitism-in-europe.html?emc=edit_th_20140821&nl=

todaysheadlines&nlid=66157663&assetType=opinion&_r=2&utm_source=
Newsletter+subscribers&utm_campaign=de9c5bfeb5-JTA_Daily
_Briefing_8_21_2014&utm_medium=email&utm_term=0_2dce5bc6f8
-de9c5bfeb5-25348069 (accessed August 24, 2014).

126 "JDL Looks to Establish Montreal Chapter after Increase in Attacks on
Jews," *JTA*, July 29, 2104, http://www.jta.org/2014/07/29/news-opinion/
israel-middle-east/jdl-looks-to-establish-montreal-chapter-after
-increase-in-attacks-on-jews?utm_source=Newsletter+subscribers&
utm_campaign=7e5060b69b-JTA_Daily_Briefing_7_29_2014&utm
_medium=email&utm_term=0_2dce5bc6f8-7e5060b69b-25348069
(accessed August 18, 2014).

127 Jodie Shupac, "Thousands March Up Bathurst against Anti-Semitism,"
CJN, August 21, 2014, http://www.cjnews.com/node/129671 (accessed
August 24, 2014).

128 Louise Brown, "Islamic School Apologizes for Anti-Jewish Teachings
on Website," *Toronto Star*, May 8, 2012, http://www.thestar.com/news/
gta/2012/05/08/islamic_school_apologizes_for_antijewish_teachings_
on_website.html (accessed December 30, 2013).

129 Carolyn Turgeon, "Hate-Crimes Probe Targeted Muslim Cleric" *National
Post*, February 6, 2014, A5.

130 Stewart Bell, "'Our Teachings Embrace and Celebrate Canadian Values':
Toronto Mosque Condemns Criticism of Islamic School," *National Post*,
November 9, 2012 http://news.nationalpost.com/2012/11/09/east-end
-madrassah-mosque/ (accessed August 1, 2014)

131 Andrew Griffith, "Is Criticism of Israel Anti-Semitic?" *CJN*, March 20,
2104, 7.

132 "CUPE Joins Boycott of Israel," *National Post*, May 29, 2006, http://www
.canada.com/nationalpost/news/story.html?id=8ab8ed08-42c0-4150
-99db-14df1dff31b1 (accessed July 31, 2014)

133 http://archive.today/TCZxK (accessed July 31, 2014).

134 Terry Glavin, "The Cairo Clique: Anti-Zionism and the Canadian Left,"
http://www.ict.org.il/Article.aspx?ID=1028 (accessed August 19, 2014).

135 "Duceppe Rejects Ambassador's Criticism over Anti-War Rally," *National
Post*, August 17, 2006, http://www.canada.com/nationalpost/news/story
.html?id=6a0967c4-64a4-4720-ac65-7ddb4a9edef7 (accessed August 1,
2014).

136 Glavin, "The Cairo Clique."

137 Morton Weinfeld, "Jewish Life in Montreal," in Robinson, ed., *Canada's
Jews*, 160.

138 Ron Csillag, "Is Antisemitism Rising in Canada's North?" *CJN*, July 7, 2011, 20.

139 http://www.jta.org/2009/02/23/news-opinion/world/canadian-union -adopts-israel-boycott-resolution#ixzz3950V2hwH (accessed July 31, 2014).

140 Beatrice Fantoni, "Anti-Semitism Growing Threat on Campuses: Inquiry," *National Post*, July 8, 2011, A5.

141 Ibid., A8.

142 *Report of the Inquiry Panel Canadian Parliamentary Coalition to Combat Antisemitism*, https://www.jewishvirtuallibrary.org/jsource/anti-semitism/ canadareport2011.pdf (accessed July 31, 2014).

NOTES TO CHAPTER TEN

1 Laurendeau, *Witness for Quebec*, 278.

2 Irving Abella, "Never Again May Be None Too Many," *Globe and Mail*, February 26, 2013.

3 Abella, *A Coat of Many Colours*.

4 Abella, "Never Again May Be None Too Many."

5 Levitt and Shaffir, *Riot at Christie Pits*, 286n1.

6 Ibid., 48–49, 200.

7 Eli Rubenstein, "Is the Holocaust Unique?" *CJN*, September 28, 2011, 33.

8 Ronald Rotenberg and Sam Moses, "What Do You Think about Antisemitism in the GTA?" *JT*, August 15, 2013, 12.

9 Ronald Rotenberg and Sam Moses, "Most Feel Safe at Shul, Work or Home," *JT*, September 12, 2013, 7.

10 Martire and Clark, *Anti-Semitism in the United States*, 107–8.

11 Liebman and Cohen, *Two Worlds of Judaism*, 42.

12 League for Human Rights of Bnai Brith Canada, *2009 Audit of Anti-Semitic Incidents* (Downsview, ON, 2010), 3.

13 Mario Silva, "Standing Up against Antisemitism," *JT*, July 7, 2011, 22.

14 Mike Cohen, "Jewish Day Schools Get Increased Security Presence," *JT*, August 28, 2014, 10. Cf. Jodie Shupac, "No Increased Threat to Day Schools, CIJA says," *CJN*, September 4, 2014, 8.

15 Weinfeld, "The Changing Dimensions of Contemporary Canadian Anti-semitism," in Penslar, Marrus, and Stein, eds., *Contemporary Antisemitism*, 43.

16 CIJA, http://www.cija.ca/community-partners/community-security -network-to-launch-pilot-program-in-toronto/ (accessed August 12, 2104).

17 Weinfeld, *Like Everyone Else*, 319.

18 Bernie Farber, "Remembering the Christie Pits Riot," *CJN*, August 5, 2013, 7.

19 Harold Troper, "Ethnic Studies and the Classroom Discussion of Antisemitism: Personal Observations," in *Approaches to Antisemitism: Context and Curriculum*, ed. Michael Brown (New York: American Jewish Committee, 1994), 202.

20 Penslar, Marrus, and Stein, eds., *Contemporary Antisemitism*, 6.

21 CIJA, http://www.cija.ca/ (accessed May 11, 2014).

22 The latest audit, covering the year 2013 is available online: http://bnaibrith .ca/wp-content/uploads/2014/04/Audit-2013-English.pdf (accessed May 11, 2014). Cf. Joel Goldenberg, "Reported Anti-Semitic Incidents Down in Quebec: B'nai Brith Canada Audit," *Suburban*, April 16, 2014, 9, 12.

23 http://www.isranet.org/ (accessed May 11, 2014).

24 http://canisa.org/ (accessed May 11, 2014).

25 http://www.friendsofsimonwiesenthalcenter.com/ (accessed May 11, 2014).

26 http://www.honestreporting.ca/ (accessed May 11, 2014).

27 Brian Henry, "Toronto High School Teacher Links to Antisemitic Website," *JT*, October 3, 2013, 13.

28 "No, Canada! Ottawa Students Group Wants to Ban Israeli Hummus from Campus," *JP*, March 10, 2014, http://www.jpost.com/Diplomacy -and-Politics/No-Canada-Ottawa-students-group-wants-to-ban-Israeli -hummus-from-campus-344845 (accessed March 13, 2014).

29 http://bnaibrith.ca/about-us/ (accessed August 12, 2014).

30 *JT*, September 29, 2011, 24.

31 http://global100.adl.org/#country/canada (accessed August 18, 2014); Katrina Clarke, "Canadians More Likely to Be Anti-Semitic than Americans, Poll Finds," *National Post*, May 13, 2014, http://news.nationalpost.com/ 2014/05/13/canadians-more-likely-to-be-anti-semitic-than-americans -poll-finds/ (accessed August 18, 2014).

32 *JT*, June 5, 2014, 11.

33 Cited in Wistrich, *A Lethal Obsession*, 322.

34 Jonathan Kay, "Jonathan Kay on B'nai Brith's Latest Attempt to Conjure Anti-Semitism out of Thin Air," *National Post*, September 22, 2010, http://fullcomment.nationalpost.com/2010/09/22/jonathan-kay-on -bnai-briths-latest-attempt-to-conjure-anti-semitism-out-of-thin-air/; idem., "Jonathan Kay: B'nai B'rith Report on Anti-Semitism Debunked," *National Post*, December 5, 2010, http://fullcomment.nationalpost .com/2010/05/12/jonathan-kay-bnai-brith-report-on-anti-semitism -debunked/ (accessed May 11, 2014).

35 http://ijvcanada.org/2013/defend-free-speech/ (accessed August 1, 2014).

36 Nathalie Collard, "Peut-on critiquer Israël?" *La Presse*, February 2, 2014, http://plus.lapresse.ca/screens/45de-7d90-52ebd03d-af60-746aac1c606d %7c_0.html (accessed March 13, 2014).

37 League for Human Rights of Bnai Brith Canada, *2002 Audit of Anti-Semitic Incidents* (Downsview, ON, 2003), 17–18.

38 Elah Feder, "The Problem with Fighting Anti-Semitism," *Huffington Post*, http://www.huffingtonpost.ca/elah-feder/anti-semitism_b_989668.html (accessed January 1, 2014).

39 Penslar, Marrus, and Stein, eds., *Contemporary Antisemitism*, viii.

40 http://global100.adl.org/#country/canada (accessed August 18, 2014).

41 http://www.cija.ca/antisemitism/statement-ministers-kenney-and-oliver -issue-statement-condemning-anti-semitic-vandalism-in-toronto/?utm _source=rss&utm_medium=rss&utm_campaign=statement-ministers -kenney-and-oliver-issue-statement-condemning-anti-semitic -vandalism-in-toronto&utm_source=The+Centre+for+Israel+and+Je wish+Affairs+Mailing+List&utm_campaign=83e4eac4fb-RSS_EMAIL _CAMPAIGN&utm_medium=email (accessed December 30, 2013).

42 http://bnaibrith.ca/wp-content/uploads/2014/04/Audit-2013-English.pdf (accessed August 11, 2014); Sharon Chisvin, "Course Explores History of Anti-Semitism," *Winnipeg Free Press*, October 12, 2013, http://www .winnipegfreepress.com/arts-and-life/life/faith/course-explores-history -of-anti-semitism-227489951.html?story=Course%20explores%20 history%20of%20anti-Semitism (accessed December 29, 2013).

43 Stewart Bell, "B.C. Man Facing Hate Charges," *National Post*, November 7, 2012.

44 Arthur Topham, "Bad Moon Rising: How the Jewish Lobbies Created Canada's 'Hate Propaganda' Laws," http://www.radicalpress.com/?p=4589 (accessed August 18, 2014).

45 http://nspcanada.nfshost.com/ (accessed August 1, 2014).

46 Penslar, Marrus, and Stein, eds., *Contemporary Antisemitism*, 10.

47 Jonathan Sacks, "A New Anti-Semitism," in *A New Anti-Semitism? Debating Judeophobia in the 21st Century*, ed. Paul Iganski and Barry Kosmin (London: Profile Books, 2003), 38–53, cited in Harrison, *The Resurgence of Anti-Semitism*, 6.

48 Penslar, Marrus, and Stein, eds., *Contemporary Antisemitism*, 5.

49 Margaret Wente, "Harper and the Jewish Vote," *Globe and Mail*, January 28, 2014, 15.

50 Paul Estrin, "Why I'm No Longer President of the Green Party of Canada,"

CJN, http://www.cjnews.com/news/why-im-no-longer-president-green -party-canada#s (accessed August 12, 2014); "Green Party Forces Out Its President over Pro-Israel Blog," *JT*, August 14, 2014, 4.

51 "A Call for Paul Estrin to Resign from the Presidency of the Green Party of Canada," http://unpublishedottawa.com/letter/1065/call-paul-estrin -resign-presidency-green-party-canada#sthash.QKBAjg4L.Rq4tAUfl .dpuf (accessed August 20, 2014).

52 Janice Arnold, "Khadir Blocks Debate on Anti-Israel Boycott Motion," *CJN*, February 17, 2011, http://www.cjnews.com/node/87238 (accessed August 11, 2014).

53 http://www.winnipegfreepress.com/local/Hughes-cleared-of-anti -Semitic-allegations-in-settlement-189045281.html (accessed December 31, 2013). Cf. "Former Liberal Candidate Settles Lawsuit," *CJN*, February 7, 2013, 2.

54 "Appeals Court Rejects Suit against Blogger," *CJN*, March 27, 2014, 2.

55 Graeme Hamilton, "Unneighbourly Behavior, Prominent Hasidic leaders Take Montreal Blogger to Court over Libel Claims," *National Post*, January 17, 2013, A3.

56 Dean Allison, Chair, Standing Committee on Foreign Affairs and International Development, Canadian House of Commons, *Recognizing Jewish Refugees from the Middle East and North Africa: Report of the Standing Committee on Foreign Affairs and International Development*, http://www .parl.gc.ca/content/hoc/Committee/412/FAAE/Reports/RP6294835/ faaerp01/faaerp01-e.pdf (accessed August 12, 2014).

57 Daniel Leblanc, "Veteran Liberal MP Irwin Cotler to Retire from Politics," *Globe and Mail*, February 5, 2014, http://www.theglobeandmail.com/ news/politics/veteran-liberal-mp-irwin-cotler-to-retire-from-politics/ article16706618/ (accessed August 12, 2014).

58 Konrad Yakabuski, "What Gaza Tells Us about Canadian Politics," *Globe and Mail*, August 7, 2014, http://www.theglobeandmail.com/globe-debate/ what-gaza-tells-us-about-canadian-politics/article19946283/ (accessed August 12, 2014).

59 Jonathan Mamane, "The Concordia BDS Experience," *Suburban*, December 17, 2014, 17; Karen Seidman, "Question of Israel Boycott Divides Concordia Campus," *Montreal Gazette*, November 28, 2014, http:// montrealgazette.com/news/local-news/question-of-israel-boycott -divides-concordia-campus (accessed December 29, 2014); "Concordia Undergrad Students Vote in Favour of Israel Boycott," *Montreal Gazette*, December 5, 2014, http://montrealgazette.com/news/

local-news/concordia-undergrad-students-vote-in-favour-of-israel -boycott (accessed December 29, 2014).

60 Reid Southwick, "University of Calgary Refused to Remove Student Spreading Pro-Jihad Messages from Jewish Professor's Class," *National Post*, June 26, 2014, http://news.nationalpost.com/2014/06/26/university -of-calgary-refused-to-remove-student-spreading-pro-jihad-messages -from-jewish-professors-class/?recipient_id=14mcWCVNaKzrliFfLhM_ Qwfe9eh5cMbE5r (accessed August 18, 2014).

61 Marc Newburgh and Raphael Szajnfarber, "Why We Must Fight BDS on Campus," *CJN*, April 10, 2014, 7.

62 Yoni Goldstein, "The Bottom Line on IAW," *CJN*, March 6, 2014, 6.

63 "BDS Vote Criticized," *CJN*, April 3, 2014, 2.

64 Rebecca Wright, "U of W Students Pass Controversial Referendum to Boycott Israel," *Windsor Star*, March 2, 2014, http://blogs.windsorstar.com/ 2014/03/02/u-of-w-students-pass-controversial-referendum-to-boycott -israel/?recipient_id=14mcWCVNaKzrn6Yb8t-_n-Zu9eh5cMbE5r (accessed March 13, 2014).

65 Jen Gerson, "Anti-Israel Campaign Growing: Student Union Vote," *National Post*, April 5, 2014, A4; "Pro-Israel Students Walk Out of Ryer-son BDS Vote," *CJN*, April 4, 2014, http://www.cjnews.com/campus/pro -israel-students-walk-out-ryerson-bds-vote (accessed August 18, 2014).

66 CIJA, "Statement on CFS-Ontario BDS Motion," http://www.cija.ca/ centre-publications/media/cfs-ontario-bds-motion/?utm_source= rss&utm_medium=rss&utm_campaign=cfs-ontario-bds-motion&utm_ source=Daily+Blog+Updates&utm_campaign=816135e3c9 -RSS_EMAIL_CAMPAIGN&utm_medium=email&utm _term=0_646375c4e9-816135e3c9-37905201 (accessed August 24, 2014); "Ontario Students' Organization Passes BDS Resolution," JTA, August 22, 2014, http://www.jta.org/2014/08/22/news-opinion/world/ontario -students-organization-votes-for-bds?utm_source=Newsletter+subscrib ers&utm_campaign=1ebd1d9ab9-JTA_Daily_Briefing_8_22_2014&utm _medium=email&utm_term=0_2dce5bc6f8-1ebd1d9ab9-25348069 (accessed August 24, 2014).

67 Melanie Phillips, "As I See It: The Academic Intifada," *Jerusalem Post*, October 30, 2014, http://www.jpost.com/Opinion/As-I-See-It-The -academic-intifada-380377 (accessed December 29, 2014). For a somewhat less pessimistic view, see Marc Newburgh and Baily Fox, "Ask Us First," CIJA, November 3, 2014, http://www.cija.ca/antisemitism/ ask-us-first/?utm_source=rss&utm_medium=rss&utm_campaign

=ask-us-first&utm_source=Daily+Blog+Updates&utm_campaign
=0030b1e0b7-RSS_EMAIL_CAMPAIGN&utm_medium=email&utm
_term=0_646375c4e9-0030b1e0b7-37905201 (accessed December 29,
2013).

68 http://www.cija.ca/antisemitism/hillel-against-antisemitism/ (accessed
December 29, 2014).

69 "Israel Hate Up Close and Personal," *JP*, June 30, 2014, http://blogs.jpost
.com/content/israel-hate-close-and-personal (accessed August 18, 2014).

70 Yoni Goldstein, "The Bottom Line on IAW," *CJN*, March 6, 2014, 6.

71 CIJA, http://salsa4.salsalabs.com/o/50830/t/0/blastContent.jsp?email
_blast_KEY=1237364 (accessed March 13, 2104).

72 "Tristin Hopper, "Harper's Foreign Policies Pander to Voters: Trudeau,"
National Post, April 5, 2014, A4. Cf. Troy, "Another Take on Controversial
Cartoon," 8.

73 Gerald Caplan, "It Is, in Fact, Possible to Criticize Israel without Being Anti-
Semitic," *Globe and Mail*, January 24, 2014, http://www.theglobeandmail
.com/news/politics/it-is-in-fact-possible-to-criticize-israel-without-being
-anti-semitic/article16501029/ (accessed August 11, 2014).

74 Emanuele Ottolenghi, "Present Day Antisemitism and the Centrality of
the Jewish Alibi," in *Resurgent Antisemitism: Global Perspectives*, ed. Alvin
Rosenfeld (Bloomington: Indiana University Press, 2013), 439.

75 Janice Arnold, "Trampoline Club Defends Rejection of Jewish Camps,"
CJN, May 29, 2104, 12.

76 "A Word from Our Chair—Radio-Canada, CIJA Statement on Iran Agreement, Community Engagement," CIJA, December 3, 2013, http://www
.cija.ca/middle-east/iran/a-word-from-our-chair-radio-canada-cija-state
ment-on-iran-agreement-community-engagement/ (accessed August 11,
2014).

77 Bertrand Marotte, "Quebec Radio Host Blasted for Comments about
Jewish Community," *Globe and Mail*, November 25, 2012, http://www
.theglobeandmail.com/news/national/quebec-radio-host-blasted-for
-comments-about-jewish-community/article5656854/ (accessed August 12,
2014).

78 Katrina Clarke and Graeme Hamilton, "Jews Pull the Strings: Quebec
Media Star," *National Post*, August 14, 2104, A1, A5; Janice Arnold, "Gilles
Proulx's 'Anti-Semitic' Views Not Retracted," *CJN*, August 21, 2014, 20.

79 Lise Ravary, "Lise Ravary: In Quebec's Media, Israel Is Always the
Aggressor," *National Post*, July 30, 2014, http://fullcomment.nationalpost
.com/2014/07/30/lise-ravary-in-quebecs-media-israel-is-always-the
-aggressor/ (accessed August 18, 2014). On the parallel situation in

Toronto, see Brian Henry, "Is It Time to Boycott the Toronto Star Again?" *JT*, August 14, 2014, 21.

80 "L'affaire Fabi: The Need to Hold to a Higher Standard," *Suburban*, November 28, 2012, 12; Janice Arnold, "Radio Host Suspended for Handling of Antisemitic Call," *CJN*, December 6, 2012, 6; Karen Seidman, "Holocaust Education Lacking in Quebec School Textbooks, Study Shows," *Montreal Gazette*, April 2, 2014, http://www.montrealgazette.com/news/Holocaust +education+lacking+Quebec+school+textbooks+study+shows/9687763/ story.html (accessed April 3, 2014).

81 Lysiane Gagnon, "A Breath of Fresh Air in Montreal," *Globe and Mail*, November 21, 2012, A15.

82 "Drainville's Political Future Is in Serious Doubt" *Montreal Gazette*, May 7, 2014, A20.

83 Janice Arnold, "Pressure Continues on PQ to Drop Mailloux," *CJN*, March 27, 2014, 10.

84 Chaim Steinmetz, "Something Is Not Quite Kosher with the PQ Election Strategy," *Montreal Gazette*, March 29, 2014, B7.

85 Janice Arnold, "Marois Stands by 'Kosher Tax' Candidate," *CJN*, March 20, 2014, 10.

86 Lila Sarick, "Mohel Blames anti-Semitism for Circumcision Complaint," *CJN*, July 24, 2014, 19; Tristin Hopper, "Doctor Cleared AFTER Complaint over Orthodox Jewish Practice of Sucking Blood from Baby's Penis after Circumcision," *National Post*, July 9, 2014, http://news.nationalpost .com/2014/07/09/doctor-cleared-after-complaint-over-orthodox -jewish-practice-of-sucking-blood-from-babys-penis-after-circumci- sion/ (accessed August 8, 2014).

87 Morton Weinfeld, "Quebec Anti-Semitism and Anti-Semitism in Quebec," http://jcpa.org/article/quebec-anti-semitism-and-anti-semitism-in -quebec/ (accessed August 24, 2014), 7.

88 Gérard Bouchard, *La nation québécois au futur et au passé* (Montreal: VLB éditeur, 1999), 57–58.

89 Ira Robinson, *Rabbis and Their Community* (Calgary: University of Calgary Press, 2007).

90 For an interesting early-twentieth-century document relevant to the banning of shehita, see Ira Robinson, ed., *Cyrus Adler: Selected Letters* (Philadelphia: Jewish Publication Society, 1985), 2:143–45.

91 Tulchinsky, *Canada's Jews*, 315.

92 Ira Robinson, "A Letter from the Sabbath Queen: Rabbi Rosenberg Addresses Montreal Jewry," *An Everyday Miracle: Yiddish Culture in Montreal* (Montreal: Véhicule Press, 1990), 101.

93 Weinfeld, "Quebec Anti-Semitism and Anti-Semitism in Quebec."

94 http://bnaibrith.ca/files/brief-final-eng.pdf (accessed 19 May 2008), 6, 8.

95 Bob Hepburn, "Canadian Anti-Semitism Institute Aims to Fill World-wide Void," *Toronto Star*, May 9, 2012, http://www.thestar.com/opinion/editorialopinion/2012/05/09/canadian_antisemitism_institute_aims_to_fill_worldwide_void.html (accessed August 11, 2014).

96 Elie Barnavi, "Is France Becoming anti-Semitic?" http://mosaicmagazine.com/picks/2014/01/reflections-on-the-jewish-question/?utm_source=Mosaic+Daily+Email&utm_campaign=ebf34ec867-2014_1_30&utm_medium=email&utm_term=0_0b0517b2ab-ebf34ec867-41162645 (accessed February 9, 2014).

97 Jonathan Kay, "From PET's childhood, Lessons for Fighting PQ Intolerance," *National Post*, April 3, 2014, A13.

98 https://sites.google.com/site/soutientheatreetudiant/lettre-ouverte-d-eric-noeel (accessed February 9, 2014).

99 James Turner, "Hair-Burning Incident No Hate Crime," *Winnipeg Free Press*, January 3, 2014, http://www.winnipegfreepress.com/local/hairburning-incident-no-hate-crime-crown-238556751.html (accessed January 7, 2014).

100 Benzion Netanyahu, *Toward the Inquisition* (Ithaca, NY: Cornell University Press, 1997), 198.

101 Langmuir, *Toward a Definition of Antisemitism*, 352.

Bibliography

Archives

Archives de l'archdiocèse de Québec
    119, 10cm, Rome. Jean-Marie-Rodrigue Villeneuve to Nicola Canali,
        February 15, 1936
Canadian Jewish Congress Charities Committee National Archives
        (CJCCCNA)
    ZA 1945 15/237
    ZA 1949/3/26: "Report on Anti-Semitism in Canada"
    "Re: Sam Rabinovitch Case 1934 copied from Notre Dame Hospital and
        McGill Archives by researcher Harold Toulch, May 1997"
Concordia University Archives
    D/Benjamin Netanyahu's Visit (September 9, 2002)

Newspapers, Periodicals, and Websites

American Jewish Year Book (*AJYB*)
Boston Globe
Canadian Broadcasting Corporation (CBC)
Canadian Jewish Chronicle (Montreal) (*CJC*)
Canadian Jewish News (Toronto) (*CJN*)
Centre for Israel and Jewish Affairs (CIJA)
Congress Bulletin (Montreal)
Montreal Gazette (Montreal)
Globe and Mail (Toronto)
Huffington Post, http://www.huffingtonpost.ca/
Jerusalem Post
Jewish Telegraphic Agency (JTA), http://www.jta.org/jta-archive/archive-page
Jewish Tribune (Toronto) (*JT*)

Keneder Adler (Montreal)
National Post (Toronto)
New Republic
New York Times
La Presse (Montreal)
Toronto Star (Toronto)
The Suburban (Montreal)
Winnipeg Free Press (Winnipeg)
Windsor Star (Windsor)

Books and Articles

Abella, Irving. "Anti-Semitism in Canada in the Interwar Years." In *The Jews of North America*. Edited by Moses Rischin. Detroit: Wayne State University Press, 1987.

———. "Antisemitism in Canada: New Approaches on an Old Problem." In Michael Brown, ed., *Approaches to Antisemitism: Context and Curriculum*. New York: American Jewish Committee, 1994.

———. *A Coat of Many Colours: Two Centuries of Jewish Life in Canada*. Toronto: Key Porter, 1999.

Abella, Irving, and Harold Troper. "'The Line Must Be Drawn Somewhere: Canada and Jewish Refugees, 1933–1939." In *The Canadian Jewish Mosaic*. Edited by M. Weinfeld, William Shaffir, and Irwin Cotler. Toronto: John Wiley, 1981.

———. *None Is Too Many: Canada and the Jews of Europe, 1933–1948*. Toronto: Lester and Orpen Dennys, 1982.

Adelman, Howard. "Blacks and Jews: Racism, Anti-Semitism, and *Showboat*." In *Canadian Jewish Studies Reader*. Edited by Richard Menkis and Norman Ravvin. Calgary: Red Deer Press, 2004.

Ages, Arnold. "Antisemitism: The Uneasy Calm." In *The Canadian Jewish Mosaic*. Edited by M. Weinfeld, William Shaffir, and Irwin Cotler. Toronto: John Wiley, 1981.

Aiken-Klar, Emma Jo. "The Fear Factor: Assimilation, Antisemitism and the Relationship between Zionism and Jewish Diasporic Identity." *vis-à-vis: Explorations in Anthropology* 9, no. 1 (2009): 106–14.

Anctil, Pierre. *Le Devoir, les juifs, et l'immigration*. Quebec: Institut Québécois de Recherche sur la Culture, 1988.

———. *Le rendez-vous manqué: Les juifs de Montréal face au Québec de l'entre-deux-guerres*. Quebec: Institut Québécois de Recherche sur la Culture, 1988.

———. "Interlude of Hostility: Judeo-Christian Relations in Quebec in the Interwar Period, 1919–1939." In *Antisemitism in Canada: History and Interpretation*. Edited by Alan Davies. Waterloo, ON: Wilfrid Laurier University Press, 1992.

———, ed. *Through the Eyes of the Eagle: The Early Montreal Yiddish Press, 1907–1916*. Translated by David Rome. Montreal: Véhicule Press, 2001.

———. "A.M. Klein: The Poet and His Relations with French Quebec." In *Canadian Jewish Studies Reader*. Edited by Richard Menkis and Norman Ravvin, 350–72. Calgary: Red Deer Press, 2004.

———. "Les Rapports entre francophones et Juifs dans le contexte montréalais." In *Les communautés juives de Montréal: Histoire et enjeux contemporains*. Edited by Pierre Anctil and Ira Robinson. Sillery: Septentrion, 2010.

———. *Trajectoires juives au Québec*. Quebec: Presses de l'Université Laval, 2010.

———. *Jacob Isaac Segal 1896–1954: Un poète Yiddish de Montréal et son milieu*. Quebec: Presses de l'Université Laval, 2012.

———. "Bâtir une synagogue à la haute ville de Québec, 1931–1952." Concordia Institute for Canadian Jewish Studies Working Papers in Canadian Jewish Studies no. 4, March 8, 2013. http://cjs.concordia.ca/publications/working-papers-in-canadian-jewish-studies/. Accessed March 15, 2013.

———. "Jews and New France." In *Canada's Jews: In Time, Space and Spirit*. Edited by Ira Robinson, 13–20. Boston: Academic Studies Press, 2013.

———. *À chacun ses Juifs: 60 éditoriaux pour comprendre la position du Devoir à l'égard des Juifs (1910–1947)*. Sillery: Septentrion, 2014.

———. "Maurice Pollack: Homme d'affaires et philanthrope." In *Les Juifs de Québec: Quatre siècles d'histoire*. Edited by Pierre Anctil. Quebec: Presses de l'Université Laval, forthcoming.

Arnold, Abraham J. "The Mystique of Western Jewry." In *The Canadian Jewish Mosaic*. Edited by M. Weinfeld, William Shaffir, and Irwin Cotler. Toronto: John Wiley, 1981.

Asselin, Olivar. "The Jews in Montreal." *Canadian Century* 4, no. 11 (September 16, 1911): 14–15, 18–19. http://news.google.com/newspapers?nid=oldoQiaHq2UC&dat=19110909&printsec=frontpage&hl=en. Accessed October 21, 2013.

Axelrod, Paul. *Making a Middle Class: Student Life in English Canada during the Thirties*. Montreal and Kingston: McGill-Queen's University Press, 1990.

Baldwin, Neil. *Henry Ford and the Jews: The Mass Production of Hate*. New York: Public Affairs, 2001.

Bale, Anthony. *The Jew in the Medieval Book: English Antisemitisms 1350–1500*. Cambridge: Cambridge University Press, 2007.

Baltzell, E. Digby. *The Protestant Establishment: Aristocracy and Caste in America*. New York: Random House, 1964.

Barkan, Elazar. *The Retreat of Scientific Racism: Changing Concepts of Race in Britain and the United States between the World Wars*. Cambridge: Cambridge University Press, 1992.

Barrett, Stanley R. *Is God a Racist? The Right Wing in Canada*. Toronto: University of Toronto Press, 1987.

Bauer, Yehuda. "In Search of a Definition of Antisemitism." In *Approaches to Antisemitism: Context and Curriculum*. Edited by Michael Brown. New York: American Jewish Committee, 1994.

Beaud, Jean-Pierre, and Jean-Guy Prevost. "Immigration, Eugenics and Statistics: Measuring Racial Origins in Canada (1921–1941)." *Canadian Ethnic Studies* 28, no. 2 (1996): 1–24.

Beaudet, Jean-François. "René Lévesque et la communauté juive du Québec (1960–1976): La fragilité d'un dialogue." MA thesis, Université du Québec à Montréal, 2014.

Beinart, Haim. *The Expulsion of the Jews from Spain*. Translated by Jeffrey M. Green. Oxford and Portland, OR: Littman Library of Jewish Civilization, 2002.

Bercuson, David. *Canada and the Birth of Israel: A Study in Canadian Foreign Policy*. Toronto: University of Toronto Press, 1985.

Bercuson, David, and Douglas Wertheimer. *A Trust Betrayed: The Keegstra Affair*. Toronto: Doubleday Canada, 1985.

Berkovitz, Jay. *Rites and Passages: The Beginnings of Modern Jewish Culture in France, 1650–1860*. Philadelphia: University of Pennsylvania Press, 2004.

Berman, Paul. *Terror and Liberalism*. New York: Norton, 2003.

Bernstein, Y.E. *The Jews in Canada (In North America): An Eastern European View of the Montreal Jewish Community in 1884*. Translated by Ira Robinson. Montreal: Hungry I Books, 2004.

Berton, Pierre. "No Jews Need Apply." *Maclean's*, November 1, 1948, 52–57.

Berzon, Corinne. "Anti-Israeli Activity at Concordia University, 2000–2003." In *Academics against Israel and the Jews*. Edited by Manfred Gerstenfeld, 163–73. Jerusalem: Jerusalem Center for Public Affairs, 2007.

Betcherman, Lita-Rose. *The Swastika and the Maple Leaf: Fascist Movements in Canada in the Thirties*. Toronto: Fitzhenry and Whiteside, 1975.

———. "Clara Brett Martin's Anti-Semitism." *Canadian Journal of Women and the Law* 5 (1992): 280–97.

————. *Ernest Lapointe: Mackenzie King's Great Quebec Lieutenant.* Toronto: University of Toronto Press, 2001.

Bialystok, Franklin. *Delayed Impact: The Holocaust and the Canadian Jewish Communty.* Montreal and Kingston: McGill-Queen's University Press, 2000.

————. "Were Things That Bad: the Holocaust Enters Community Memory." In *Canadian Jewish Studies Reader.* Edited by Richard Menkis and Norman Ravvin. Calgary: Red Deer Press, 2004.

Bickenbach, Jerome. "Lawyers, Law Professors, and Racism in Ontario." *Queen's Quarterly* 96, no. 3 (1989): 585–98.

Birnbaum, Pierre. *The Anti-Semitic Moment: A Tour of France in 1898.* New York: Hill and Wang, 2003.

————. *A Tale of Ritual Murder in the Age of Louis XIV: The Trial of Raphaël Lévy, 1669.* Stanford, CA: Stanford University Press, 2012.

Black, Norman Fergus. *What About the Jews?* Toronto: Canadian Association for Adult Education, 1944.

Bodian, Miriam. *Hebrews of the Portuguese Nation: Conversos and Community in Early Modern Amsterdam.* Indianapolis: Indiana University Press, 1997.

Bouchard, Gérard. *La nation québécoise au futur et au passé.* Montreal: VLB éditeur, 1999.

Brown, Michael. *Jew or Juif? Jews, French Canadians and Anglo–Canadians, 1759–1914.* Philadelphia: Jewish Publication Society, 1987.

————. "From Stereotype to Scapegoat: Anti-Jewish Sentiment in French Canada from Confederation to World War I." In *Antisemitism in Canada: History and Interpretation.* Edited by Alan Davies. Waterloo, ON: Wilfrid Laurier University Press, 1992.

————. "On Campus in the Thirties: Antipathy, Support, and Indifference." In *Nazi Germany, Canadian Responses: Confronting Antisemitism in the Shadow of War.* Edited by L. Ruth Klein. Montreal and Kingston: McGill-Queen's University Press, 2012.

————. "Steps Forward and Steps Backward: Toronto Jewry at the Beginning of the Second Decade of the Twenty-First Century." In *Canada's Jews: In Time, Space and Spirit.* Edited by Ira Robinson, 184–214. Boston: Academic Studies Press, 2013.

Brym, Robert J., and Rhonda L. Lenton. "The Distribution of Anti-Semitism in Canada in 1984." In *The Jews in Canada.* Edited by Robert J. Brym, William Shaffir, and Morton Weinfeld. Toronto: Oxford University Press, 1993.

Byrnes, Robert F. *Antisemitism in Modern France*. New Brunswick: Rutgers University Press, 1950.

Carlebach, Elisheva. "The Last Deception: Failed Messiahs and Jewish Conversion in Early Modern German Lands." In *Jewish Messianism in the Early Modern World*. Edited by Matt D. Goldish and Richard H. Popkin, 125–38. Dordrecht: Kluwer, 2001.

Chazan, Robert. *Medieval Jewry in Northern France: A Political and Social History*. Baltimore: Johns Hopkins University Press, 1973.

———. *Church, State and Jew in the Middle Ages*. New York: Behrman, 1980.

———. *Medieval Stereotypes and Modern Antisemitism*. Berkeley: University of California Press, 1997.

Chesler, Phyllis. *The New Anti–Semitism: The Current Crisis and What We Must Do about It*. San Francisco: Jossey-Bass, 2003.

Chiel, Arthur A. *The Jews of Manitoba: A Social History*. Toronto: University of Toronto Press, 1961.

Clement, Wallace. "The Canadian Corporate Elite: Ethnicity and Inequality of Access." In *Ethnicity and Ethnic Relations in Canada*. Edited by Rita M. Bienvenue and Jay E. Goldstein. 2nd ed. Toronto: Butterworths, 1985.

Cohen-Almagor, Raphael. *The Scope of Tolerance: Studies on the Costs of Free Expression and Freedom of the Press*. London: Routledge, 2006.

Cohn, Norman. *Warrant for Genocide: The Myth of the Jewish World Conspiracy and the Protocols of the Elders of Zion*, 2nd ed. London: Serif, 1996.

Connelly, John. *From Enemy to Brother: The Revolution in Catholic Teaching on the Jews, 1933–1965*. Cambridge, MA: Harvard University Press, 2012.

Corcos, Arlette. *Montréal, les Juifs, et l'école*. Sillery: Septenrion, 1997.

Cossman, Brenda, and Marlee Kline, "'And if not now, when?': Feminism and Anti-Semitism beyond Clara Brett Martin." In *The Canadian Jewish Studies Reader*. Edited by Richard Menkis and Norman Ravvin. Calgary: Red Deer Press, 2004.

Davidowicz, Lucy S. *The War against the Jews, 1933–1945*. New York: Holt, Rinehart and Winston, 1975.

Davies, Alan, ed. *Antisemitism in Canada: History and Interpretation*. Waterloo, ON: Wilfrid Laurier University Press, 1992.

Davies, Alan, and Marilyn F. Nefsky. *How Silent Were the Churches? Canadian Protestantism and the Jewish Plight during the Nazi Era*. Waterloo, ON: Wilfrid Laurier University Press, 1997.

Delany, Sheila, ed. *Chaucer and the Jews: Sources, Contexts, Meanings*. New York: Routledge, 2002.

Delisle, Esther. *The Traitor and the Jew: Anti-Semitism and the Delrium of Extremist Right-wing Nationalism in French Canada from 1929-1939.* Toronto: Robert Davies, 1993.

Delisle, Esther. *Myths, Memories and Lies: Quebec's Intelligentsia and the Fascist Temptation 1939-1960.* Westmount, QC: Robert Davies, 1998.

Deutsch, Gotthard. "Anti-Semitism." *Jewish Encyclopedia*, 1: 641-49. New York: Funk and Wagnalls, 1901.

Dinnerstein, Leonard. *Uneasy at Home: Antisemitism and the American Jewish Experience.* New York: Columbia University Press, 1987.

————. *Antisemitism in America.* New York: Oxford University Press, 1994.

Dobkowski, Michael. *The Tarnished Dream: The Basis of American Anti-Semitism.* Westport, CT: Greenwood Press, 1979.

Dobson, R.B. *The Jewish Communities of Medieval England: The Collected Essays of R.B. Dobson.* Edited by Helen Birkett with a new preface by Joe Hillaby. York, UK: Borthwick Institute, University of York, 2010.

Dunn, J.D.G. "Messianic Ideas and Their Influence on the Jesus of History." In *The Messiah: Developments in Earliest Judaism and Christianity.* Edited by James H. Charlesworth, 365-81. Minneapolis: Fortress Press, 1992.

Editors of Fortune. *Jews in America.* New York: Random House, 1936.

Elbaz, André. "Antisémitisme: Mythe et images du juif au Québec (essaie d'analyse)." *Voix et Images du pays* 9 (1975): 87-112.

Eleff, Zev. "The Baptism of Four Little Roxbury Girls: Jewish Angst in America's Religious Marketplace during the Interwar Period." *American Jewish Archives Journal* 65 (2013): 73-94.

Elliott, David. "Anti-Semitism and the Social Credit Movement." *Canadian Ethnic Studies* 17 (1985): 78-89.

Endelman, Todd. *The Jews of Georgian England: 1714-1830.* Philadelphia: Jewish Publication Society, 1979.

Engel, David. "Away from a Definition of Antisemitism: An Essay in the Semantics of Historical Description." In *Rethinking European Jewish History.* Edited by Jeremy Cohen and Moshe Rosman, 30-53. Oxford and Portland, OR: Littman Library of Jewish Civilization, 2009.

Epstein, Simon. "Cyclical Patterns in Antisemitism: The Dynamics of Anti-Jewish Violence in Western Countries since the 1950s." *Acta No. 2*, Jerusalem: Sicsa, The Vidal Sassoon International Center for the Study of Antisemitism – The Hebrew University of Jerusalem, 1993. http://sicsa.huji.ac.il/2cycles.htm. Accessed July 30, 2014.

Faber, Eli. *A Time for Planting: The First Migration, 1654-1820.* Baltimore: Johns Hopkins University Press, 1992.

Fabre-Vessas, Claudine. *The Singular Beast: Jews, Christians and the Pig*. New York: Columbia University Press, 1997.

Fackenheim, Emil. "Post-Holocaust Anti-Jewishness, Jewish Identity, and the Centrality of Israel." In *World Jewry and the State of Israel*. Edited by Moshe Davis. New York: Arno Press, 1977.

Farrelly, Maura Jane. *Papist Patriots: The Making of an American Catholic Identity*. New York: Oxford University Press, 2012.

Fay, Terence J. *A History of Canadian Catholics: Gallicanism, Romanism, and Canadianism*. Montreal and Kingston: McGill-Queen's University Press, 2002.

Fein, Isaac M. *The Making of an American Jewish Community: The History of Baltimore Jewry from 1773 to 1920*. Philadelphia: Jewish Publication Society, 1971.

Fichtner, Paula Sutter. *Terror and Toleration: The Habsburg Empire Confronts Islam, 1526–1850*. London: Reaktion, 2008.

Field, Geoffrey G. "Anti-Semitism with the Boots Off." In *Hostages of Modernization: Studies on Modern Antisemitism, 1870–1933/9, Germany—Great Britain—France*. Edited by Herbert A. Strauss. Berlin: de Gruyter, 1993.

Figler, Bernard, and David Rome. *Hannaniah Meir Caiserman: A Biography*. Montreal: Northern Printing and Lithographing, 1962.

Fishman, William J. *Jewish Radicals: From Czarist Stetl to London Ghetto*. New York: Pantheon, 1975.

Frager, Ruth. "Communities and Conflicts: East European Jewish Immigrants in Ontario and Quebec from the Late 1800s to the 1930s." In *Canada's Jews in Time, Space, and Spirit*. Edited by Ira Robinson, 52–74. Boston: Academic Studies Press, 2013.

Frankel, Jonathan. *Revolution and Russian Jews*. Cambridge: Cambridge University Press, 2009.

Frankel, Richard. "One Crisis Behind? Rethinking Antisemitic Exceptionalism in the United States and Germany," *American Jewish History* 97, no. 3 (2013): 235–58.

Fredriksen, Paula. *From Jesus to Christ: The Origins of the New Testament Images of Jesus*. New Haven, CT: Yale University Press, 1988.

———. *Augustine and the Jews: A Christian Defense of Jews and Judaism*. New Haven, CT: Yale University Press, 2010.

Fredriksen, Paula, and Adele Reinharz, eds. *Jesus, Judaism, and Christian Anti-Judaism: Reading the New Testament after the Holocaust*. Louisville, KY: Westminster John Knox Press, 2002.

Friedman, Joan. *Guidance, Not Governance: Rabbi Solomon Freehof and Reform Responsa*. Cincinnati, OH: Hebrew Union College Press, 2013.

Gaboury, Jean-Pierre. *Le nationalisme de Lionel Groulx*. Ottawa: Éditions de l'Université d'Ottawa, 1970.

Gager, John G. *The Origins of Anti-Semitism: Attitudes toward Judaism in Pagan and Christian Antiquity*. New York: Oxford University Press, 1983.

Gilbert, Martin. *Churchill and the Jews: A Lifelong Friendship*. New York: Holt, 2007.

Gitelman, Zvi. "Comparative and Competitive Victimization in the Post-Communist Sphere." In *Resurgent Antisemitism: Global Perspectives*. Edited by Alvin Rosenfeld. Bloomington: Indiana University Press, 2013.

Glavin, Terry. "The Cairo Clique: Anti-Zionism and the Canadian Left." http://www.ict.org.il/Article.aspx?ID=1028. Accessed August 19, 2014.

Glickman, Yaacov. "Anti-Semitism and Jewish Social Cohesion in Canada." In *Ethnicity and Ethnic Relations in Canada*. Edited by Rita M. Bienvenue and Jay E. Goldstein. 2nd ed. Toronto: Butterworths, 1985.

Godfrey, Sheldon J., and Judith Godfrey. *Burn This Gossip: The True Story of George Benjamin of Belleville, Canada's First Jewish Member of Parliament, 1857–1863*. Toronto: Duke & George Press, 1991.

———. *Search Out the Land: The Jews and the Growth of Equality in British Colonial America, 1740–1867*. Montreal and Kingston: McGill-Queen's University Press, 1995.

Goldberg, David H. "The Post-Statehood Relationship: A Growing Friendship." In *From Immigration to Integration: The Canadian Jewish Experience, a Millenium Edition*. Edited by Ruth Klein and Frank Dimant. Toronto: Lester, 2001.

Goldschläger, Alain. "The Canadian Campus Scene." In *Academics against Israel and the Jews*. Edited by Manfred Gerstenfeld, 154–62. Jerusalem: Jerusalem Center for Public Affairs, 2007.

Goldwag, Arthur. *The New Hate: A History of Fear and Loathing on the Populist Right*. New York: Pantheon, 2012.

Gordan, Rachel. "The Precursor to 'Gentleman's Agreement.'" *Moment*. http://www.momentmag.com/precursor-gentlemans-agreement/. Accessed December 29, 2014.

Graizbord, David. "Religion and Ethnicity Among 'Men of the Nation': Toward a Realistic Interpretation," *Jewish Social Studies*, n.s., 15, no. 1 (Fall 2008): 32–65.

——— *Souls in Dispute: Converso Identities in Iberia and the Jewish Diaspora, 1580–1700*. Philadelphia: University of Pennsylvania Press, 2003.

Harrison, Bernard. *The Resurgence of Anti-Semitism: Jews, Israel, and Liberal Opinion*. Lanham, MD: Rowan and Littlefield, 2006.

———— "Anti-Zionism, Antisemitism, and the Rhetorical Manipulation of
    Reality." In *Resurgent Antisemitism: Global Perspectives*. Edited by Alvin
    Rosenfeld. Bloomington: Indiana University Press, 2013.
Hayes, Saul. "Report on Anti-Semitism in Canada." Canadian Jewish Congress
    Charities Committee National Archives ZA 1949/3/26.
Herman, Dana. "'An Affair To Remember': The Outremont Dispute of 1988."
    Canadian Jewish Studies 16–17 (2008–9): 139–66.
Hertzberg, Arthur. *The French Enlightenment and the Jews*. New York: Colum-
    bia University Press, 1968.
Heschel, Susannah. *The Aryan Jesus: Christian Theologians and the Bible in
    Nazi Germany*. Princeton, NJ: Princeton University Press, 2008.
Himmelfarb, Gertrude. *The People of the Book: Philosemitism in England from
    Cromwell to Churchill*. New York: Encounter, 2011.
Hsia, R. Po-chia. *The Myth of Ritual Murder: Jews and Magic in Reformation
    Germany*. New Haven, CT: Yale University Press, 1988.
Hughes, Everett C. *French Canada in Transition*. Chicago: University of Chi-
    cago Press, 1963.
Israel, Jonathan. *European Jewry in the Age of Mercantilism, 1550–1750*.
    Oxford: Clarendon Press, 1985.
Jedwab, Jack. "The Politics of Dialogue: Rapprochement Efforts between Jews
    and French Canadians: 1939–1960." In *Renewing Our Days: Montreal Jews
    in the Twentieth Century*. Edited by Ira Robinson and Mervin Butovsky.
    Montreal: Véhicule, 1995.
Johnson, Martin P. *The Dreyfus Affair: Honour and Politics in the Belle Époque*.
    New York: St. Martin's Press, 1999.
Jones, Richard. *L'idéologie de L'Action Catholique (1917–1939)*. Quebec: Pres-
    ses de l'Université Laval, 1974.
Jordan, William. *The French Monarchy and the Jews*. Philadelphia: University
    of Pennsylvania Press, 1989.
Julius, Anthony. *Trials of the Diaspora: A History of Anti-Semitism in England*.
    Oxford: Oxford University Press, 2010.
Kallen, Evelyn. *Spanning the Generations: A Study in Jewish Identity*. Don
    Mills, ON: Longman Canada, 1977.
Kaplan, Yosef, Henry Méchoulan, and Richard H. Popkin, eds. *Menasseh Ben
    Israel and His World*. Leiden, New York: E.J. Brill, 1989.
Katz, Jacob. *From Prejudice to Destruction: Anti-Semitism, 1700–1933*. Cam-
    bridge, MA: Harvard University Press, 1980.
Katz, Steven. *The Holocaust in Historical Context*, vol. 1: *The Holocaust and Mass
    Death before the Modern Age*. New York: Oxford University Press, 1994.

Kayfetz, Benjamin, and Stephen Speisman. *Only Yesterday: Collected Pieces on the Jews of Toronto*. Toronto: Now and Then, 2013.

Keefer, Michael. *Antisemitism, Real and Imagined: Responses to the Canadian Parliamentary Coalition to Combat Antisemitism*. Waterloo, ON: Canadian Charger, 2010.

Keogh, Dermot, and Andrew McCarthy. *Limerick Boycott 1904: Anti-Semitism in Ireland*. Cork, Ireland: Mercier Press, 2005.

Kernaghan, William. "Freedom of Religion in the Province of Quebec with Particular Reference to the Jews, Jehovah's Witnesses, and Church–State Relations, 1930–1960." Doctoral dissertation, Duke University, 1966.

King, Joe. *From the Ghetto to the Main: The Story of the Jews of Montreal*. Montreal: Montreal Jewish Publication Company, 2001.

Kinsella, Warren. *Web of Hate: Inside Canada's Far Right Network*. Toronto: HarperCollins, 1994.

Koffman, David. "Canadian Jewish Studies since 1999: The State of the Field." In *Canada's Jews in Time, Space, and Spirit*. Edited by Ira Robinson, 451–67. Boston: Academic Studies Press, 2013.

Klein, A.M. *The Collected Poems of A.M. Klein*. Toronto: McGraw-Hill Ryerson, 1974.

———. *Beyond Sambatyon: Selected Essays and Editorials, 1928–1955*. Edited by M.W. Steinberg and Usher Caplan. Toronto: University of Toronto Press, 1982.

Korn, Eugene. "Rethinking Christianity: Rabbinic Positions and Possibilities." In *Jewish Theology and World Religions*. Edited by Alon Goshen-Gottstein and Eugene Korn. Oxford: Littman Library of Jewish Civilization, 2012.

Langlais, Jacques and David Rome. *Jews and French Quebecers: Two Hundred Years of Shared History*. Waterloo, ON: Wilfrid Laurier University Press, 1991.

Langmuir, Gavin I. *History, Religion, and Antisemitism*. Berkeley: University of California Press, 1990.

———. *Toward a Definition of Antisemitism*. Berkeley: University of California Press, 1990.

Laurendeau, André. *Witness for Quebec*. Toronto: Macmillan of Canada, 1973.

League for Human Rights of B'nai Brith Canada. *Review of Anti-Semitism in Canada 1982*. Downsview, ON, 1983.

———. *Review of Anti-Semitism in Canada 1985*. Downsview, ON, 1986.

———. *Audit of Anti-Semitic Incidents 1988*.

———. *Audit of Anti-Semitic Incidents 1990*.

———. *The Heritage Front Report: 1994*. Toronto, 1994.

————. *1995 Audit of Anti-Semitic Incidents.* Downsview, ON, 1996.

————. *1997 Audit of Anti-Semitic Incidents.* Downsview, ON, 1998.

————. *1998 Audit of Anti-Semitic Incidents.* Downsview, ON, 1999.

————. *2000 Audit of Anti-Semitic Incidents.* Downsview, ON, 2001.

————. *2001 Audit of Anti-Semitic Incidents.* Downsview, ON, 2002.

————. *2002 Audit of Anti-Semitic Incidents.* Downsview, ON, 2003.

————. *2003 Audit of Anti-Semitic Incidents.* Downsview, ON, 2004.

————. *2004 Audit of Anti-Semitic Incidents.* Downsview, ON, 2005.

————. *2009 Audit of Anti-Semitic Incidents.* Downsview, ON, 2010.

————. *2012 Audit of Anti-Semitic Incidents.* Downsview, ON, 2013.

————. *2013 Audit of Anti-Semitic Incidents.* http://bnaibrith.ca/wp-content/
uploads/2014/04/Audit-2013-English.pdf.

Leonoff, Cyril Edel. *The Jewish Farmers of Western Canada.* Vancouver: Jewish Historical Society of British Columbia, 1984.

Leverdure, Paul. *Sunday in Canada: The Rise and Fall of the Lord's Day.* Yorkton, SK: Gravelbooks, 2004.

Levine, Allan. *Coming of Age: A History of the Jewish People of Manitoba.* Winnipeg: Heartland, 2009.

Levitt, Cyril H., and William Shaffir, *The Riot at Christie Pits.* Toronto: Lester
and Orpen Dennys, 1987.

Liebman, Charles, and Stephen Cohen. *Two Worlds of Judaism: The Israeli and
American Experience.* New Haven, CT: Yale University Press, 1990.

Linteau, Paul-André, René Durocher, and Jean-Claude Robert. *Quebec: A History, 1867–1929.* Toronto: James Lorimer, 1983.

Linteau, Paul-André, René Durocher, Jean-Claude Robert, and François
Ricard. *Quebec since 1930.* Toronto: James Lorimer, 1991.

Lipinsky, Jack. *Imposing Their Will: An Organizationsal History of Jewish
Toronto, 1933–1948.* Montreal and Kingston: McGill-Queen's University
Press, 2011.

Lipset, Seymour Martin, and David Riesman. *Education and Politics at Harvard.* New York: McGraw-Hill, 1975.

Lipstadt, Deborah E. "The Iranian President, the Canadian Professor, the
Literary Journal, and the Holocaust Denial Conference That Never Was:
The Strange Reality of Shiraz Dossa." In *Global Antisemitism: A Crisis
of Modernity,* vol. 5: *Reflections.* Edited by Charles Asher Small, 71–82.
http://isgap.org/wp-content/uploads/2013/12/05_ISGAP_Vol.
-V_120114_Web.pdf. Accessed March 13, 2104.

Littman, Sol. *War Criminal on Trial: The Rauca Case.* Toronto: Lester and
Orpen Dennys, 1983.

———. *Quebec's Jews: Vital Citizens or Eternal Strangers: Analysis of Key Newspaper Coverage of Three Pertinent Incidents*. Los Angeles: Simon Wiesenthal Center, 1991.

———. *Holocaust Denial: Bigotry in the Guise of Scholarship*. Toronto: Simon Wiesenthal Center, 1994.

MacFayden, Joshua D. "Nip the Noxious Growth in the Bud: Ortenberg v. Plamondon and the Roots of Canadian Anti-Hate Activism." *Canadian Jewish Studies* 12 (2004).

MacLeod, Roderick, and Mary Anne Poutanen. "Little Fists for Social Justice: Anti-Semitism, Community, and Montreal's Aberdeen School Strike, 1913." *Labour/le Travail* 70 (Fall 2012).

Marcotte, Gilles. "Le romancier canadien-français et son Juif." In Naïm Kattan, ed., *Juifs et canadiens, deuxième cahier du Cercle juif de langue française*. Montreal: Éditions du Jour, 1967.

Marcus, Jacob R. *Early American Jewry*. 2 vols. Philadelphia: Jewish Publication Society, 1951–55.

Martire, Gregory and Ruth Clark, *Anti-Semitism in the United States: A Study of Prejudice in the 1980s*. New York: Praeger, 1982.

Marrus, Michael. "Is There a New Antisemitism?" In *Antisemitism in the Contemporary World*. Edited by Michael Curtis. Boulder, CO: Westview, 1986.

———. "Is Anti-Semitism Sweeping Canada?" http://www.jewishtoronto.com/page.aspx?id=37867. Accessed July 29, 2014.

Marttila, John. "Highlights from an Anti-Defamation League Survey on Anti-Semitism and Prejudice in America. New York: Anti-Defamation League, 1992.

Matas, David. *Nazi War Criminals in Canada: Five Years After*. Toronto: Institute for International Affairs of B'nai Brith Canada, 1992.

Matas, David, with Susan Charendoff. *Justice Delayed: Nazi War Criminals in Canada*. Toronto: Summerhill Press, 1987.

McRoberts, Kenneth. *Quebec: Social Change and Political Crisis*, 3rd ed. Oxford: Oxford University Press, 1993.

Medjuck, Sheva, and Morty M. Lazar. "Existence on the Fringe: the Jews in Atlantic Canada." In *The Canadian Jewish Mosaic*. Edited by M. Weinfeld, William Shaffir, and Irwin Cotler. Toronto: John Wiley, 1981.

Medres, Israel. *Montreal of Yesterday: Jewish Life in Montreal 1900–1920*. Translated by Vivian Felsen. Montreal: Véhicule Press, 2000.

———. *Between the Wars: Canadian Jews in Transition*. Translated by Vivian Felsen. Montreal: Véhicule Press, 2003.

Mendelson, Alan. *Exiles from Nowhere: The Jews and the Canadian Elite.* Montreal: Robin Brass Studio, 2008.

Mendes-Flohr, Paul, and Jehuda Reinharz. *The Jew in the Modern World: A Documentary History*, 3rd ed. New York: Oxford University Press, 2011.

Menkis, Richard. "Historiography, Myth and Group Relations: Jewish and Non-Jewish Québécois on Jews and New France." *Canadian Ethnic Studies* 23, no. 2 (1991): 24–38.

———. "Antisemitism in the New Nation: From New France to 1950." In *From Immigration to Integration: The Canadian Jewish Experience, a Millennium Edition.* Edited by Ruth Klein and Frank Dimant, 31–51. Toronto: Institute for International Affairs, B'nai Brith Canada, 2001.

Mertl, Steve, and John Ward. *Keegstra: The Trial, the Issues, the Consequences.* Saskatoon, SK: Western Producer Prairie Books, 1985.

Mosse, George L. *Toward the Final Solution: A History of European Racism.* London: J.M. Dent and Sons, 1978.

Muller, Jerry Z. *Capitalism and the Jews.* Princeton: Princeton University Press, 2010.

Mundill, Robin R. *England's Jewish Solution: Experiment and Expulsion, 1262–1290.* New York: Cambridge University Press, 1998.

Nadeau, Jean-François. *Adrien Arcand: Führer canadien.* Montreal: Lux, 2010.

Netanyahu, Benzion. *Toward the Inquisition.* Ithaca, NY: Cornell University Press, 1997.

Neusner, Jacob. *The Way of Torah: An Introduction to Judaism*, 7th ed. Belmont, CA: Wadsworth/Thomson, 2004.

Newman, Peter C. *Izzy: The Passionate Life and Turbulent Times of Izzy Asper, Canada's Media Mogul.* Toronto: HarperCollins, 2008.

Nigro, Mario, and Clare Mauro, "The Jewish Immigrant Experience and the Practice of Law in Montreal, 1830 to 1990." *McGill Law Journal* 44, no. 4 (1999).

Nirenberg, David. *Communities of Violence: Persecution of Minorities in the Middle Ages.* Princeton, NJ: Princeton University Press, 1996.

———. *Anti-Judaism: The Western Tradition.* New York: W.W. Norton, 2013.

Normand, Sylvio. "L'affaire Plamondon: Un cas d'antisémitisme à Québec au début du XXᵉ siècle." *Les Cahiers de Droit* 48, no. 3 (September 2007): 477–504.

Oliver, Michael. *The Passionate Debate: The Social and Political Ideas of Quebec Nationalism, 1920–1945.* Montreal: Véhicule, 1991.

Osterhamel, Jürgen. *The Transformation of the World: A Global History of the Nineteenth Century.* Princeton, NJ: Princeton University Press, 2014.

Ottolenghi, Emanuele. "Present Day Antisemitism and the Centrality of the Jewish Alibi." In *Resurgent Antisemitism: Global Perspectives*. Edited by Alvin Rosenfeld. Bloomington: Indiana University Press, 2013.

Palmer, Howard. "Politics, Religion, and Antisemitism in Alberta, 1880–1950." In *Antisemitism in Canada: History and Interpretation*. Edited by Alan Davies. Waterloo, ON: Wilfrid Laurier University Press, 1992.

Penslar, Derek J. "Antisemitism and Anti-Zionism: A Historical Approach." In *Contemporary Antisemitism: Canada and the World*. Edited by Derek J. Penslar, Michael R. Marrus, and Janice Gross Stein. Toronto: University of Toronto Press, 2005.

Penslar, Derek J., Michael R. Marrus, and Janice Gross Stein, eds., *Contemporary Antisemitism: Canada and the World*. Toronto: University of Toronto Press, 2005.

Perry, Thomas Whipple. *Public Opinion, Propaganda, and Politics in Eighteenth-Century England: A Study of the Jew Bill of 1753*. Cambridge, MA: Harvard University Press, 1962.

Pollack, Eunice G., ed. *Antisemitism on the Campus: Past and Present*. Boston: Academic Studies Press, 2011.

Pontbriand, Mathieu. "L'affaire Delisle: Champ universitaire et scoop médiatique." In *Faute et réparation au Canada et au Québec contemporains*. Edited by Amélie Bolduc and Martin Paquet. Quebec: Éditions Nota Bene, 2006.

Prutschi, Manuel. "The Zundel Affair." In *Antisemitism in Canada: History and Interpretation*. Edited by Alan Davies. Waterloo, ON: Wilfrid Laurier University Press, 1992.

Report of the Inquiry Panel Canadian Parliamentary Coalition to Combat Antisemitism. https://www.jewishvirtuallibrary.org/jsource/anti-semitism/can adareport2011.pdf. Accessed July 31, 2014.

Rexford, Irving Elson. *Our Educational Problem: The Jewish Population and the Protestant Schools*. Montreal: Renouf, 1924.

Richler, Mordecai. *Oh Canada! Oh Québec! Requiem for a Divided Country*. New York: Knopf, 1992.

Rivkin, Ellis. *What Crucified Jesus? Messianism, Pharasaism, and the Development of Christianity*. New York: UAHC Press, 1997.

Robin, Martin. *Shades of Right: Nativist and Fascist Politics in Canada, 1920–1940*. Toronto: University of Toronto Press, 1992.

Robinson, Ira. "Vers des échanges plus fructueux dans le domaine des sciences humaines." In *Juifs et Canadiens français dans la société québécoise*. Edited by Pierre Anctil, Ira Robinson, and Gérard Bouchard. Sillery: Septentrion, 2000.

————. *Rabbis and Their Community: Studies in the Eastern European Ortho-dox Rabbinate in Montreal, 1896–1930*. Calgary: University of Calgary Press, 2007.

————. "The Field of Canadian Jewish Studies and Its Importance for the Jewish Community of Canada." *Jewish Political Studies Review* 21, nos. 3–4 (Fall 2009): 75–86.

————. "Reflections on Antisemitism in French Canada." *Canadian Jewish Studies* 21 (2013): 90–122.

————. "David Ahenakew and His Antisemitism." In *Zionism, An Indigenous Struggle: Aboriginal Americans and the Jewish State, Israzine* 48, no. 4 (November 21, 2014). http://www.isranet.org/israzine/zionism-indigenous -struggle-aboriginal-americans-and-jewish-state/editorial/#ira.

————. "Who Is a Marrano? Reflections on Modern Jewish Identity." In *History, Memory, and Jewish Identity*, forthcoming.

Rome, David. "On the Early Harts, Part 3." *Canadian Jewish Archives*, n.s., 17. Montreal: Canadian Jewish Congress, 1980.

Rome, David, Judith Nefsky, and Paule Obermeir. *Les Juifs du Québec: Biblio-graphie rétrospective annotée*. Quebec: Institut Québécois de Recherche sur la Culture, 1981.

Rosen, Philip. "Hate Propaganda." Library of Parliament 85–6E. http://www .parl.gc.ca/Content/LOP/researchpublications/856-e.htm. Accessed July 9, 2014.

Rosenberg, Louis. *Canada's Jews: A Social and Economic Study of the Jews of Canada*. Montreal: Canadian Jewish Congress, 1939.

Rosenberg, Stuart. *The Jewish Community in Canada*. Vol. 1. Toronto: McClel-land and Stewart, 1970.

Roth, Cecil. *A Life of Menasseh Ben Israel: Rabbi, Printer, and Diplomat*. Phila-delphia: Jewish Publication Society, 1934.

Rozenblit, Marsha. "Note on Galician Jewish Immigration to Vienna." *Aus-trian History Yearbook* 19 (1983): 143–52.

Rubin, Miri. *Gentile Tales: The Narrative Assault on Late-Medieval Jews*. New Haven, CT: Yale University Press, 1999.

Rürup, Reinhard. "Anti-Jewish Prejudices, Antisemitic Ideologies, Open Vio-lence: Antisemitism in European Comparison from the 1870s to the First World War. A Commentary." In *Quest. Issues in Contemporary Jewish History. Journal of Fondazione CDEC* no. 3, July 2012. www.quest-cdec journal.it/focus.php?id=305.

Ryan, Claude. "A French Canadian Looks at the Jews," *Viewpoints* 4 (1969): 5–14.

Ryerson, Stanley B. *Unequal Union: Confederation and the Roots of Conflict in the Canadas, 1815–1873*. New York: International, 1968.

Sable, Martin. "George Drew and the Rabbis: Religious Education in Ontario's Public Schools," *Canadian Jewish Studies* 6 (1998).

Sack, B.G. *History of the Jews of Canada*. Montreal: Harvest House, 1965.

Sacks, Jonathan. "Europe's New Anti-Semitism." http://www.huffingtonpost .com/chief-rabbi-lord-sacks/europe-new-anti-semitism_b_1663157.html. Accessed July 15, 2012.

Said, Edward. *Orientalism*. London: Penguin, 1987.

Salvatore, Filippo. *Fascism and the Italians of Montreal: An Oral History, 1922–1945*. Toronto: Guernica, 1998.

Sarna, Jonathan. "The Pork on the Fork: A Nineteenth Century Anti-Jewish Ditty." http://www.brandeis.edu/hornstein/sarna/antisemitism/ theporkonthefork.pdf. Accessed December 25, 2014.

Sasley, Brent. "Who Calls the Shots? An Inquiry into the Effect of Jewish and Arab Lobbies on Canadian Middle East Policy." *Literary Review of Canada*. http://reviewcanada.ca/magazine/2011/05/who-calls-the-shots/. Accessed July 30, 2014.

Schechter, Ronald. *Obstinate Hebrews: Representations of Jews in France, 1715–1815*. Berkeley: University of California Press, 2003.

Scheinberg, Stephen. "From Self-Help to National Advocacy: The Emergence of Community Activism." In *Nazi Germany, Canadian Responses: Confronting Antisemitism in the Shadow of War*. Edited by L. Ruth Klein. Montreal and Kingston: McGill-Queen's University Press, 2012.

Scott, W. *The History of Canada*, 2nd ed. Toronto: Grey House, 2010.

Seeley, John R., R. Alexander Sim, and Elizabeth W. Loosley. *Crestwood Heights*. Toronto: University of Toronto Press, 1956.

Senese, Phyllis. "'La Croix de Montréal': A Link to the French Radical Right." *Canadian Catholic Historical Association, Historical Studies* 53 (1986): 81–95.

Shapiro, James. *Shakespeare and the Jews*. New York: Columbia University Press, 1997.

Shternshis, Anna. *Soviet and Kosher: Jewish Popular Culture in the Soviet Union, 1923–1939*. Bloomington: Indiana University Press, 2006.

Silver, M.M. *Louis Marshall and the Rise of Jewish Ethnicity in America*. Syracuse, NY: Syracuse University Press, 2013.

Slonim, Reuben. *Family Quarrel: The United Church and the Jews*. Toronto and Vancouver: Clarke, Irwin, 1977.

Smith, Tom W. *Anti-Semitism in Contemporary America*. New York: American Jewish Committee, 1994.

Sniderman, Paul M., David A. Northrup, Joseph F. Fletcher, Peter H. Russel, and Philip E. Tetlock. *Working Paper on Antisemitism in Quebec*. Toronto: Institute for Social Research, York University, 1992.

Speisman, Stephen. *The Jews of Toronto: A History to 1937*. Toronto: McClelland and Stewart, 1979.

————. "Antisemitism in Ontario: The Twentieth Century." In *Antisemitism in Canada: History and Interpretation*. Edited by Alan Davies. Waterloo, ON: Wilfrid Laurier University Press, 1992.

Srebrnik, Henry Felix. *Creating the Chupah: The Zionist Movement and the Drive for Jewish Communal Unity in Canada, 1898–1921*. Boston: Academic Studies Press, 2011.

Statistics Canada. *Immigration and Ethnocultural Diversity in Canada*. http://www12.statcan.gc.ca/nhs-enm/2011/as-sa/99-010-x/99-010-x2011001-eng.cfm. Accessed July 31, 2014.

Stedman, Mercedes. *Angels of the Workplace: Women and the Construction of Gender Relations in the Canadian Clothing Industry, 1890–1940*. Toronto: Oxford University Press, 1997.

Stingel, Janine. "From Father to Son: Canadian Jewry's Response to the Alberta Social Credit Party and the Reform Party of Canada," *Canadian Jewish Studies* 9 (2000).

————. *Social Discredit: Anti-Semitism, Social Credit, and the Jewish Response*. Montreal and Kingston: McGill-Queen's University Press, 2000.

Stoker, Valerie. "Drawing the Line: Hasidic Jews, Eruvim, and the Public Space of Outremont, Quebec." *History of Religions* 43 (2003): 18–49.

Swetschinski, Daniel. *Reluctant Cosmopolitans: The Portuguese Jews of Seventeenth Century Amsterdam*. London: Littman Library of Jewish Civilization, 2000.

Teboul, Victor. *Mythes et images du Juif au Québec: Essai d'analyse critique*. Montreal: Éditions de Lagrave, 1977.

Terwey, Susanne. "British Discourses on 'the Jew' and 'the Nation,' 1899–1919." In *Quest: Issues in Contemporary Jewish History. Journal of Fondazione CDEC*, no. 3 (July 2012). http://www.quest-cdecjournal.it/focus.php?id=298.

Thompson, John Herd and Allen Seager, *Canada 1922–1939: Decades of Discord*. Toronto: McClelland and Stewart, 1985.

Trachtenberg, Henry. "The Winnipeg Jewish Community in the Inter-War Period, 1919–1939: Anti-Semitism and Politics." *Canadian Jewish Historical Society Journal* 4, no. 1 (1980).

Troper, Harold B. *Only Farmers Need Apply: Official Canadian Govern-ment Encouragement of Immigration from the United States, 1896–1911*. Toronto: Griffin House, 1972.

———. "Ethnic Studies and the Classroom Discussion of Antisemitism: Per-sonal Observations." In *Approaches to Antisemitism: Context and Curricu-lum*. Edited by Michael Brown. New York: American Jewish Committee, 1994.

———. "New Horizons in a New Land: Jewish Immigration to Canada." In *From Immigration to Integration: The Canadian Jewish Experience, a Millennium Edition*. Edited by Ruth Klein and Frank Dimant. Toronto: Lester, 2001.

———. *The Defining Decade: Identity, Politics, and the Canadian Jewish Com-munity in the 1960s*. Toronto: University of Toronto Press, 2010.

Troper, Harold, and Morton Weinfeld. *Old Wounds: Jews, Ukrainians and the Hunt for Nazi War Criminals in Canada*. Markham, ON: Viking, 1988.

Tulchinsky, Gerald. "The Third Solitude: A.M. Klein's Jewish Montreal, 1900–1950." *Journal of Canadian Studies* 19, no. 2 (Fall 1984): 96–112.

———. "Goldwin Smith: Victorian Antisemite." In *Antisemitism in Canada: History and Interpretation*. Edited by Alan Davies, 67–91. Waterloo, ON: Wilfrid Laurier University Press, 1992.

———. *Canada's Jews: A People's Journey*. Toronto: University of Toronto Press, 2008.

Tulchinsky, Gerald. *Joe Salsberg: A Life of Commitment*. Toronto: University of Toronto Press, 2013.

Vaugeois, Denis. *The First Jews in North America: The Extraordinary Story of the Hart Family*. Montreal: Baraka, 2012.

Vigod, Bernard. *Quebec before Duplessis: The Political Career of Louis-Alexan-dre Taschereau*. Montreal and Kingston: McGill-Queen's University Press, 1986.

———. "When the System Fails: The Malcolm Ross Case in New Brunswick." In League for Human Rights of B'nai Brith Canada, *Review of Anti-Semi-tism in Canada, 1987*, 28–34. Downsview, ON, 1987.

Volkov, Shulamit. "Antisemitism as a Cultural Code: Reflections on the History and Historiography of Antisemitism in Imperial Germany." *Leo Baeck Institute Year Book* 23 (1978): 25–46.

Waldron, Jeremy. *The Harm in Hate Speech*. Cambridge, MA: Harvard Uni-versity Press, 2012.

Walker, James W. St.G. *"Race," Rights and the Law in the Supreme Court of*

Canada: Historical Case Studies. Waterloo, ON: Wilfrid Laurier University Press, 1997.

———. "Claiming Equality for Canadian Jewry: The Struggle for Inclusion 1930–1945." In *Nazi Germany, Canadian Responses: Confronting Anti-semitism in the Shadow of War.* Edited by L. Ruth Klein, 218–62. Montreal and Kingston: McGill-Queen's University Press, 2012.

Waller, Harold M., and Morton Weinfeld. "The Jews of Quebec and 'Le Fait Français.'" In *The Canadian Jewish Mosaic.* Edited by M. Weinfeld, William Shaffir, and Irwin Cotler. Toronto: John Wiley, 1981.

Ward, W. Peter. *White Canada Forever: Popular Attitudes and Public Policy Toward Orientals in British Columbia.* Montreal and Kingston: McGill-Queen's University Press, 2002.

Weinberg, Robert. *Blood Libel in Late Imperial Russia: The Ritual Murder Trial of Mendel Beilis.* Bloomington: Indiana University Press, 2014.

Weinfeld, Morton. "La question juive au Québec." *Midstream* 23 (1977): 20–29.

———. "The Jews of Quebec: An Overview." In *The Jews in Canada.* Edited by Robert J. Brym, William Shaffir, and Morton Weinfeld. Toronto: Oxford University Press, 1993.

———. *Like Everyone Else … But Different: The Paradoxical Success of Canadian Jews.* Toronto: McClelland and Stewart, 2001.

———. "The Changing Dimensions of Contemporary Canadian Antisemitism." In *Contemporary Antisemitism: Canada and the World.* Edited by Derek J. Penslar, Michael R. Marrus, and Janice Gross Stein. Toronto: University of Toronto Press, 2005.

———. "Quebec Anti-Semitism and Anti-Semitism in Quebec." Jerusalem Center for Public Affairs, January 1, 2008. http://jcpa.org/article/quebec-anti-semitism-and-anti-semitism-in-quebec/. Accessed August 24, 2014.

———. "Jewish Life in Montreal." In *Canada's Jews: In Time, Space and Spirit.* Edited by Ira Robinson, 152–67. Boston: Academic Studies Press, 2013.

———. "If Canada and Israel Are at War, Who Gets My Support? Challenges of Competing Diaspora Loyalties: Marshall Sklare Award Lecture." *Contemporary Jewry* 34 (2014): 167–87.

Weinrib, Lorraine E. "Ensuring Equality: The Role of the Community." In *From Immigration to Integration: The Canadian Jewish Experience, a Millenium Edition.* Edited by Ruth Klein and Frank Dimant. Toronto: Lester, 2001.

———. "'Do Justice to Us!': Jews and the Constitution of Canada." In *Not Written In Stone: Jews, Constitutions and Constitutionalism in Canada.* Edited by Daniel J. Elazar, Michael Brown, and Ira Robinson. Ottawa: University of Ottawa Press, 2003.

Weinryb, Avi. "The University of Toronto—The Institution Where Israel Apartheid Week Was Born." http://jcpa.org/article/the-university-of-toronto-the-institution-where-israel-apartheid-week-was-born/. Accessed July 31, 2014.

Weiman, Gabriel, and Conrad Winn. *Hate on Trial: The Zundel Affair, the Media, and Public Opinion in Canada.* Oakville, ON: Mosaic Press, 1986.

Weisbord, Merrily. *The Strangest Dream: Canadian Communists, the Spy Trials, and the Cold War.* Montreal: Véhicule Press, 1994.

Wilson, Stephen. *Ideology and Experience: Antisemitism in France at the Time of the Dreyfus Affair.* Rutherford, NJ: Fairleigh Dickinson University Press, 1982.

Wistrich, Robert S. *Antisemitism: The Longest Hatred.* London: Methuen, 1991.

———. *A Lethal Obsession: Anti-Semitism from Antiquity to the Global Jihad.* New York: Random House, 2009.

Woodsworth, James S. *Strangers within Our Gates, or Coming Canadians.* Toronto: University of Toronto Press, 1972.

Yovel, Yirmiyahu. *The Other Within: The Marranos, Split Identity and Emerging Modernity.* Princeton, NJ: Princeton University Press, 2009.

Index

www.ingramcontent.com/pod-product-compliance
Lightning Source LLC
Chambersburg PA
CBHW060028030426
42334CB00019B/2232